Culture and Conduct in the Novels of Henry James

CULTURE AND CONDUCT IN THE NOVELS OF HENRY JAMES

ALWYN BERLAND

*Professor of English
and Dean of Humanities
McMaster University*

CAMBRIDGE UNIVERSITY PRESS

Cambridge
London   New York   New Rochelle
Melbourne   Sydney

Published by the Press Syndicate of the University of Cambridge
The Pitt Building, Trumpington Street, Cambridge CB2 1RP
32 East 57th Street, New York, NY 10022, USA
296 Beaconsfield Parade, Middle Park, Melbourne 3206, Australia

First published 1981

Printed in Great Britain by The Anchor Press Ltd
and bound by Wm Brendon & Son Ltd
both of Tiptree, Essex

British Library Cataloguing in Publication Data
Berland, Alwyn
Culture and conduct in the novels of Henry James.
1. James, Henry – Criticism and interpretation
2. Civilization in literature
I. Title
813'.4 PS2124 80–40868
ISBN 0 521 23343 7

Contents

Preface

This is a study of Henry James's fiction in relationship to his particular view of civilization as culture. I believe this view was of great importance in determining his treatment of the novelist's material: human beings in their relations with each other, with their societies and institutions, and with themselves. His view of civilization affected a number of his characteristic fictional themes and concerns, and I think it important to demonstrate their connections.

The artist's vision of human experience affects not only his themes, of course, but with equal significance his forms and techniques, insofar as they serve to organize and to render meaningful the experience with which he deals. I shall not discuss in any comprehensive way the distinctive technical achievements of James's fiction; I think this omission justified not only on the grounds of the considerable body of formal criticism already in existence, but also because of the concentration of focus of my study. I have dealt with technical matters whenever I feel them to bear particularly on my central subject.

The ideas developed here stem from my reading of the novels themselves. Although more than one critic has observed before now that James cared intensely for civilization, no critic I have read has developed this idea adequately or, more important, demonstrated its permeating effects on James's fiction.

I am not particularly concerned with the bearings of James's biography on his novels, and the biography itself has already been well documented. I have thought it important to think afresh about the tradition, or traditions, in which James's work was founded; to that degree this study is concerned with literary and social history. My concern is not with James's specific debts and borrowings, which are comparatively few, but with his concerns and commitments, which are many.

I begin with a general discussion of James's concern with civilization, and with his tendency to see civilization primarily as culture, rather than as a wider social, historical, institutional (and cultural) construct. I am interested in demonstrating that James's dependence on a nineteenth-century aesthetic tradition is larger than has previously been recognized. This aesthetic movement, especially as it found expression in the writings of Matthew Arnold, seems to me most helpful in defining and in understanding James's own commitments and the framework of his fiction.

I go on to consider a number of representative themes and motifs in James's fiction in the light of his central vision of civilization as culture. Then I turn to a consideration of those novels which seem to me most interesting both in themselves and as illuminating James's most characteristic and important themes.

I begin with James's first novel, *Roderick Hudson*, which stakes out, if with some immaturity, James's central and recurring subjects. In it I find opportunity for considering some important questions about the literary traditions most significant in shaping James's own literary career.

I have given a large part of my argument to a close study of *The Portrait of a Lady*. The intrinsic merit of the novel justifies this attention, I believe; further, it provides the best single occasion for an examination of James's view of civilization as culture as it affected his art. Readers who agree with my treatment of this novel will find that it illuminates many others as well.

The Portrait of a Lady treats the idea of civilization directly, and richly, through the strategy of the international theme. A second, less central approach which James explored for dealing with his interests is the dramatic confrontation of different attitudes toward, or conceptions of, civilization. Views which are alternative or hostile to his own are given fictional voice through various characters whose attitudes and behaviour may be examined for their consequences. James's conception of civilization was a minority view, held in the face of stronger and more popular claims, the errors or inadequacies of which James wished to expose to fictional demonstration. *The Bostonians, The Princess Casamassima*, and *The Tragic Muse* are all novels in which James tests or defends his own special feelings about civilization in relation to other views. These novels are the major works which follow after *The Portrait of a Lady*, where James's own ideas and commitments to civilization as culture are most fully developed and explored.

James returned to the international theme and to his central concern in *The Ambassadors*, but with the added complexity of vision and of style that justifies the usual grouping of late novels. Furthermore, certain ideas always present in James became more important in the late novels: for example, the themes of acquisition, of appropriation, of the 'modern love of things'. For this reason, I have related my discussion of *The Ambassadors* to *The Golden Bowl* and *The Ivory Tower*. I have not included *The Wings of the Dove*, however much I might welcome an occasion for discussing both its marvels and its lapses. For while James deals with the theme of civilization in it, again on the international level, the novel adds nothing and changes nothing that is relevant to my concern in this study.

There remains a large group of novels which are peripheral to my subject, though they include in their number some very good works. I have not undertaken to discuss these except incidentally where there is some special relevance to my central argument. In some of these novels James is interested in describing and evaluating single elements of the civilization which he finds in moving between America and Europe and which in themselves are incomplete or fragmentary. *The Europeans*, a very good novel, and *The Reverberator*, a much slighter work altogether, are both examples of this more limited treatment. Other novels look at the manners and conventions of the society of his own time which, satirically or tragically, he examined for their effects on the lives of his characters. The early *Washington Square* and the later *The Awkward Age* and *What Maisie Knew* all look at the impact on culture and on conduct of the manners of his age.

I should not like to suggest that James was occupied in constructing a systematic study of civilization, working out definitions, noting exceptions, labelling attributes, and all the rest. There is no conscious organization of an over-all pattern in James's novels such as, for instance, one finds in Balzac's *La Comédie Humaine*, or even in the looser organization of William Faulkner's Yoknapatawpha novels and stories. James did have a central vision of the importance of civilization and its bearings on the human condition, a vision which informed his representative themes, actions, characters, techniques. This is quite a different matter, however, from a conscious plan or organization. Indeed, in approaching the creative impulse, which so often laughs at diagrams and which confounds the critic's schema, it is well to remember the words in which Lambert Strether pays his high tribute to Mme de Vionnet in *The Ambassadors*:

he felt the roughness of the formula, because, by one of the short-cuts of genius, she had taken all his categories by surprise.

I have used the New York edition of James's fiction, and the Macmillan edition of 1923, as my texts. The latter includes all the fiction published in James's lifetime which for one reason or another was omitted from the New York edition. I have not given page references in the body of this study for the innumerable quotations from the novels; to do so, I felt, would be too tedious and distracting for the reader. References are given for all material drawn from James's criticism, notebooks, letters, and autobiographical volumes, as well as for material derived from secondary sources.

Parts of this study have appeared, in somewhat modified versions, in *The University Review*, *The Cambridge Journal*, *The Journal of the History of Ideas*, and *The Wascana Review*. I acknowledge with thanks their permission to reproduce this material here.

I am grateful to the Arts Research Board of McMaster University for a research grant, and to the Canada Council (now the Social Science and Humanities Research Council of Canada) for a leave fellowship, both of which facilitated my work on James.

For their criticism and encouragement I am most grateful to Mrs Joan Bennett of Cambridge University, to Peter Burbidge, to the late Dr Oscar Cargill, to Dr David Daiches, to Dr Julian Markels, and to Allen Tate.

Finally, I wish to acknowledge the largest debt of all, in more ways than I can possibly say, to my wife Jayne Berland.

What are the conditions that produce a classical national author. He must, in the first place, be born in a great commonwealth . . . He must find his nation in a high state of civilization, so that he will have no difficulty in obtaining for himself a high degree of culture. He must find much material already collected and ready for his use, and a large number of more or less perfect attempts made by his predecessors. And finally, there must be such a happy conjuncture of outer and inner circumstances that he will not have to pay dearly for his mistakes, but that in the prime of his life he may be able to see the possibilities of a great theme and to develop it according to some uniform plan into a well-arranged and well-constructed literary work.

Goethe

I can't look at the English-American world, or feel about them, any more, save as a big Anglo-Saxon total, destined to such an amount of melting together that an insistence on their differences becomes more and more idle and pedantic; and that melting together will come the faster the more one takes it for granted and treats the life of the two countries as continuous and more or less convertible, or at any rate as simply different chapters of the same general subject. Literature, fiction in particular, affords a magnificent arm for such taking for granted, and one may so do an excellent work with it. I have not the least hesitation in saying that I aspire to write in such a way that it would be impossible to an outsider to say whether I am at a given moment an American writing about England or an Englishman writing about America (dealing as I do with both countries,) and so far from being ashamed of such an ambiguity I should be exceedingly proud of it, for it would be highly civilized.

Henry James

The major theme

THE PROGRESS OF CRITICISM

Even if Henry James were not as *present* in every consideration of modern fiction as he is, too much has been written about him during the last fifty or sixty years to justify another re-evaluation now. The writing about James in these years provides, with its divergent assumptions and conclusions, if not a consistent evaluation of James's fiction, at least some curious insights into contemporary cultural history.

What makes this history so interesting in relation to James is not so much its variety as its contradictions. Novelists manifestly second-rate have had their defenders; novelists clearly very good have been attacked. But no other novelist in English has had the ambiguous triumph of being called the very best and – in terms of really serious claims – the worst; the richest and the dullest, the most meaningful and the most devoid of substance. If the enterprising reader will but look for them he will find critics enough who write off Scott as too boring, Dickens as too vulgar, Sterne as too sentimental, or Jane Austen as – too much a lady. But these objections are rarely at the extreme, just as the praise given them, with a possible exception in Miss Austen's case, is rarely unqualified. But when one gets to Henry James, nothing is taken for granted; there is no peace in the land. He has been called a fraud and a genius. And while these terms are not necessarily mutually exclusive, they are meant to be so in James's case.

Certain aspects of James's fiction antagonize readers, whether they happen to be literary critics or not. And there are elements in the contemporary cultural tradition which are strong enough to make readers, even when they are not antagonized, feel that they should be. One consequence is that a good deal of James criticism is not merely discriminatory, weighing the good and the bad and striking a balance, but apologetic. It insists so strongly on the good that any mention of the bad is embarrassing. Or it deals so extravagantly with the bad that even the hostile critic feels compelled to buttress his attack with a machinery of apologetics, most frequently that of social and biographical explanation.

I want then to be unambiguous. I think it is worth insisting that the superior James novels rank with the very best of modern fiction, indeed, with the best of *all* fiction in English. At the same time, certain limitations emerge when one looks at James's collected fiction as a single created world, granting for the moment that this is really possible and not merely a critical cliché.

Excepting *The Princess Casamassima*, where the protagonist is a London artisan (though protected against mere plebeianism by an elaborate apologetic of being the bastard of an English lord), and several stories – 'Brooksmith', 'In the Cage', and 'The Bench of Desolation' most notably – the too exclusive concern in James's fiction is with characters from the upper middle class and aristocracy, a concentration which renders his world rather less full than one might wish.[1] True, his characters are sometimes without money, but they are apt to represent a fallen or embarrassed gentility; they think and act as aristocrats. As a consequence, there is not the richness of human reference, the completeness of lived experience, which the novel perhaps more than any other literary form is able to provide.

Further, his important characters tend too consistently to be extremely intelligent, subtle, and sensitive, remarkably conscious and articulate. James usually can manage a willing suspension of disbelief within each single novel, but when the reader comes to think of these people as a gallery of 'represen-

---

[1] Even in these stories there are usually special circumstances: Brooksmith is a butler spoiled by his civilized associations for his 'proper' station; his poverty seems simply accidental rather than essential.

tative' men and women, a certain amount of resistance, if not of revulsion, is almost inevitable. Given the dismal spectacle of the contemporary naturalistic novel, I should not wish to argue for the statistical average, nor even for the formula which William Dean Howells was defending in James's time: 'The simple, natural, and honest',[2] a formula which no doubt sounds better than its applications in fiction have, apart from Tolstoy, ever managed to be. What needs to be argued for is a sense of the variousness of the human condition. I wish that James did not so persistently see nobility of character in terms so indissolubly wedded to acute personal awareness and intelligence. When James insists that Hamlet and Lear are 'finely aware' and that this quality of articulate consciousness '*makes* absolutely the intensity of their adventure, gives the maximum of sense to what befalls them'[3] we can hardly disagree. Neither might we argue against a comparative indifference to what happens to the 'stupid, the coarse, and the blind', although it might be less chilling to say rather that we do not care in the same way. On the other hand, both Hamlet and Lear are capable of failures of intelligence which James's protagonists might blush to admit. But a more serious complication in this comparison is that in confronting life Shakespeare's two heroes are capable of a full vitality which James's characters might (one sometimes fears) also blush to admit.

Although James's protagonists have among them a certain range, they tend to be too much alike in their high controlled refinement. Although James does invent simpler characters for comic relief, his 'fools who minister' to the characters that 'count', they are usually too distinctly compartmentalized *as* comic relief, too manifestly props to the attention which rightly belongs to the happy few. A pantheon of intellectual and moral giants is doubtless more edifying than a world of grubs, as found in certain exponents of literary naturalism, but not necessarily more representative of human actuality.

James was aware that many readers were suspicious of, or hostile toward, his representative characters. His criticism, like

---

2 As in chapter 2 of Howells's *Criticism and Fiction* (New York, 1891).
3 Preface to *The Princess Casamassima*, p. ix.

that of T. S. Eliot, is primarily an exploration and defence of his own artistic intentions. His self-justification for his characters lies in the exercise of what he calls 'operative irony': his characters are not as men usually are, he admits, but they are as men might well be:

It's . . . a campaign, of a sort, on behalf of the something better . . . that blessedly, as it is assumed, *might* be . . . It implies and projects the possible other case, the case rich and edifying where the actuality is pretentious and vain.[4]

James disliked artistic campaigns in general, and his critical theories were all opposed to the didactic. Nevertheless, James's fiction is in its very essence a campaign on behalf of the 'something better', and his conception of character, though it may be thought to limit his range of human reference, is dictated by his central thematic concerns.

The very bulk of James criticism is prodigious. The amount of speculating, of theorizing, of false tracks laid down and then corrected, is staggering, especially when one remembers into what neglect James's fiction had fallen during his lifetime, or reads of his own battered awareness of that neglect. Still, a certain amount of the damage accomplished by some critics has been repaired by others. It may be useful here to remember Dr Johnson on Shakespeare:

The chief desire of him that comments an author is to show how much other commentators have corrupted and obscured him. The opinions prevalent in one age as truths above the reach of controversy are confuted and rejected in another, and rise again to reception in remoter times. Thus the human mind is kept in motion without progress.[5]

The much-advertised critical revolution of the twentieth century has meant mainly that Johnson's cycles of succeeding ages have been compressed into the arguments and tergiversations of succeeding issues of the quarterly reviews.

4 Preface to *The Lesson of the Master*, p. x.
5 Samuel Johnson, 'Preface to *The Plays of William Shakespeare*', in *Eighteenth Century Critical Essays*, ed. Scott Elledge (Ithaca, N.Y., 1961), vol. ii, p. 675.

Some progress may be claimed, nonetheless. The earlier and far-fetched charge that James was fundamentally anti-American in his sympathies has been disproved. Many critics have rallied to point out the frequent – indeed, sometimes embarrassing – moral triumphs of Americans in the conflicts of the famous international novels. Christopher Newman, Isabel Archer, Lambert Strether, Milly Theale, all emerge from their respective tales as better people than the Europeans with whom they deal. There is a hierarchy even among his Americans: those who remain loyal to their roots are better than the alienated, or deracinated, or superficially Europeanized, who actually are apt to be the most ominous characters in James's fiction. Christina Light, Madame Merle, Gilbert Osmond, Charlotte Stant – these are all Europeans by adoption, but by adoption only. Any claim that James categorically preferred the European aristocracy to his American characters can proceed only from naïveté or prejudice. It is necessary, in fact, to recognize the opposite prejudice as it functions in *The American*, for instance, or in *The Golden Bowl*.

On aesthetic and formalistic grounds, the economy and discipline, the tightening and deepening of fictional form, the self-consciousness of technique have been major factors contributing to the appreciation of James, and explain particularly the preference for the late novels as expressed directly or implicitly by such critics as Ezra Pound, Percy Lubbock, and F. O. Matthiessen. The last three novels, *The Ambassadors*, *The Wings of the Dove*, and *The Golden Bowl* – as well as the two unfinished novels, *The Ivory Tower* and *The Sense of the Past* – are claimed to represent James at his best. I consider *The Golden Bowl* essentially a failure, and *The Wings of the Dove* both very moving and very flawed. But I want to avoid the 'either–or' trap which too many critics have fallen into when arguing for a given Jamesian phase or period. It seems to me more useful here to be descriptive of important differences. The late works minimize 'story' in its traditional sense, substituting a deeper and deeper probing into 'character'. Character is not developed in a traditional focus on the individual so much as on a creation of character in terms of *others*. We are given not individuals so much as relationships, though the reader may ultimately remove from the tight context of their various relationships the rather fabulous individuals who make up the Jamesian world. The prose is difficult, convolute, analytical. It becomes more mannered and more personal than the early style. The demands of narration, exposition, or dialogue may vary, but the late voice is always the voice of the master.

The dialogue moves slowly, sometimes tortuously, through the steady intimations of what is never spoken at all. It progresses like agony in an echo-chamber, where each character, through interrogative repetitions of the other's phrases or sentences, forces still further revelations which seem impossible for direct statement. Or the characters leap across the chasms of the unspoken as on ice floes in the raging currents of the portentous.

The much-dressed symbolism and imagery of the late novels are not different from, but consonant with, the other developments of technique. The tendency toward intensive concentration within a limited frame is marked in plot, in situation, in characterization, *and* in the stylistic techniques employed for exploring all of these. The symbolism tends to be as sustained as the virtuoso passages of introspection, of investigated motive, of analysed response. While a good deal can be learned from a study of the later symbolism, it is a mistake, I think, to define the difference between early novels and late simply in terms of imagery.[6] James's use of symbolism and imagery, especially in the later novels, is one aspect of an increasingly complex and intensified concern with form, and this is related to the development of idea and of vision. What impresses me is not a qualitative change in James's use of symbolism, but the wonderful consonance expressed in almost every aspect of his art.

The increasing complexity and concentration of vision and form in the later novels of James is not necessarily all gain, however. Lambert Strether is a conception superior to Chris-

6 An eminent example of 'image analysis' of James's later fiction is M. Allott's 'Symbolism and image in the later work of Henry James', *Essays in Criticism*, III (1953), pp. 321–36.

topher Newman, certainly. But is Milly Theale really superior
to Isabel Archer? The cracked golden bowl in the later novel
is a richer and subtler symbol than Roderick Hudson's statue
of 'Thirst' in the earlier. But the imagery which evokes Prince
Amerigo in *The Golden Bowl* as a Palladian church, and the
much-extolled symbol of the Pagoda – Maggie Verver's vision
of the relationships of the four major characters – colourful as
these may be in their own terms, are really not convincing
vehicles for their human analogies. The overwrought inadequacy of the images is only one measure of the inadequacy of
the novel as a whole, and suggests that in James's fiction
symbolism and imagery are not determining causes – as they
often are in poetry – but elements of great but secondary value
for enriching, substantiating, and more closely defining other
fictional elements. If the Pagoda image is dazzling, it is also
contrived, over-extended, and finally false to the human value
it represents. Significantly, the reader can see the same dazzling
but false qualities working in the novel as a whole.

One other technical matter is worth mentioning in tracing
James's development. The burden that James places on the
ficelle – the friendly confidant who is involved only marginally
in the action – becomes heavier in the later fiction. Borrowed
from the drama, from the conventions of chorus and *confidante*,
these persons are messengers and expositors. They elicit information and feelings. As James tries to push his fiction ever
closer to the conditions of drama (and it is interesting that
James's 'drama' almost inevitably means French classical
drama), the *ficelle* becomes more and more important, and
sometimes irritatingly obtrusive. Susan Stringham in *The Wings
of the Dove*, and Fanny Assingham in *The Golden Bowl*, are
too vocal. On the other hand, Maria Gostrey in *The Ambassadors*
helps to mark the superiority of this novel by being worked
into the fabric of the action so well that it is no longer possible
to dismiss her as belonging to the manner and not the matter
of the novel, according to James's own definition of the *ficelle*.[7]

The style of the late novels, however mannered, is at its best
rich in meaning and highly evocative. It is constantly made

7 Preface to *The Portrait of a Lady*, p. xxi.

concrete by rich images and elaborate metaphors, presenting to the reader a simultaneous awareness of the feelings and intentions of several characters at any given moment. Remarkable too is the attempt to contain within narrative prose not only each possibility of motivation and reaction, each nuance of feeling, but also each consequent look and motion and gesture.[8] I speak of the style as analytical in the sense that it probes deeper and deeper into the elaborate and complex wholeness of feeling and thought which underlines each step of developing action, until finally the completely seen moral nature of the individual emerges as it is defined and experienced in its relationships with others. The result is a structure which is dramatic in form, but with an essentially poetic, and lyrical, density of effect.

What may well have marked a cyclical return to favour of the earlier works was begun with the argument of F. R. Leavis for *The Portrait of a Lady*. He considered it not only superior to the later novels, but, indeed, the greatest of all novels in English. He placed *The Bostonians* second.[9] His thesis was that the late novels suffer from *too* much technique and too little idea, an 'excess of doing' and a consequent weakening of content, although Leavis tended rather more to insist than to demonstrate. But the weighing of such alternative claims is not after all my immediate concern. In the end, the choice between early and late James may well be as false as an insistence that one must choose, absolutely, between Beethoven's 'Waldstein' and the Opus 111 piano sonatas. I prefer to rejoice in the existence of both.

THE IDEA OF CIVILIZATION

Because so much has been written about James, early and late, the task of investigating his fiction without preconceptions is a difficult one. What stands behind many attempts to do so, moreover, is James's own ambiguously intended fable, 'The

8 See P. N. Furbank, 'Henry James: the novelist as actor', *Essays in Criticism*, I (1951), pp. 404–20.
9 F. R. Leavis, *The Great Tradition* (London, 1948), p. 153.

Figure in the Carpet', which defies the critic to find the thread, or pattern, in a life's work which will explain *All*. The challenge may have been a good one to the degree that it has invited discussion and controversy, but it has certainly been a bad one in that it has suggested the availability of a single overriding formula. All writers can be reduced to a formula, no doubt; but no great writer can suffer the process without damage to his very greatness. Such formulas must be either so large and general ('Appearance and reality'; 'The redemptive role of work') as to prove useless, if not nonsensical; or so complex and conditioned as to challenge the very conception of formula.

Nevertheless, it is possible without resort to formula to identify James's created world and to define the frame of reference which gives it coherence and meaning. I do not speak of *theme* in the usual critical sense, but of the writer's significant personal vision of experience. I refer to that which sustains the creation of literary works and survives the conditions of their creation, whether those of the life of the writer or the circumstances of his age which gave rise to them. They survive because they continue to speak authentically about the human condition through their own distinctive fusions of intelligence, and fullness of feeling, and aesthetic mastery. Such works we come to call classics. They become so largely through their conceptions, though any conception is available only through technique. The technique realizes – makes real – the conception. Without the technical mastery there are simply the problematic claims for the mute inglorious Miltons.

James's eyes were fixed firmly on finite and mortal men living in a finite social world. His rare upward questionings were tentative and inconclusive. Moralist as he was, his vision was altogether secular and mundane. He was neither explorer nor anthropologist, and he cared little for the primitive or the unknown.[10] His concern with man was not cosmic, in the sense

---

10 See for instance his letter to R. L. Stevenson: 'Primitive man doesn't interest me, I confess, as much as civilized . . .' (*Robert Louis Stevenson and Henry James*, ed. Janet Adam Smith (London, 1948), pp. 228–9). The bland understatement is determined by the fact that James was writing to a friend who *was* devoting himself to the primitive, and should not disguise the very great distance between their commitments.

that, say, Hardy's or Conrad's was; his concern was local and social. Not man-in-the-universe but man-in-society was his consistent subject. The highly civilized eighteenth century was fond of looking to the East – or rather to its own imagination of the East – for formulas of Nature and of Wisdom. James stayed inside his own civilization and looked for them there. How he saw his own civilization is what I intend to demonstrate later on. Now it is enough to say that he loved Europe as the repository of Western civilization. He saw America as a recent and tentative addition. He saw no other. So enamoured of this civilization was he that he could not conceive of a better medium for man's existence, unless indeed it were that same civilization made better still, closer, that is, to the ideal which it suggested than to the actuality which so often disappointed expectation. His fiction constitutes a major attempt to think out such an ideal civilization and to ponder its effects on the men and women who might live in it. His investigation of its corruptions and compromises demonstrates his recognition of the negative elements in the actual; his continued commitment to the principle of civilization proves his loyalty to the ideal.

His fictional treatment of civilization is in part actual, in part ideal. His characters are made to match. Once given the desire to exalt a high civilization into a higher one still, it is more understandable that his characters should *begin* very high as well. Otherwise, the reaches to which they aspire would become impossible. The 'campaign . . . on behalf of the something better . . . that blessedly, as it is assumed, *might* be', by which he justifies his idealized human beings, is just the campaign for civilization, and for the civilized, which for James became the Highest Good.

The highest good for James is not, strictly speaking, a state of society so much as a condition of human development in which certain qualities can flower and thrive, in which culti-vated sensibility and moral integrity give men what he calls 'the power to be finely aware and richly responsible'.[11] These qualities are individual, of course, but they require the medium

11 Preface to *The Princess Casamassima*, p. ix.

of civilization both for their development and for their protection.

It will become evident that James uses the term 'civilization'
loosely, in ways that involve quite various connotations. But
most frequently he does not use the term to denote the domain
of the historian. His fiction yields extraordinarily little reflection
or comment on the political, social, economic processes of
history or of contemporary life, even if some of his implicit
attitudes do reveal themselves from time to time. James's term
is much closer to the earlier, non-sociological definition of
culture, as it is employed consistently in the writings of Matthew Arnold. The concern I speak of as so central to James's
fiction is for civilization-as-culture.

What needs to be demonstrated is the relevance of James's
commitment to civilization to almost every aspect of his fiction.
One possible technique for developing this subject, of relating
it to James's forms and themes, might be to analyse James's
ideas, to define his terms, to erect a system. But that *is* to work
by formula, and to violate the integrity not only of the novels
as works of art, but of the ideas themselves. I want to look
instead, from a far more interesting perspective, at the artistic
process itself. I want to examine the blending of conscious
views with technical discoveries, of preconceived ideas with
achieved vision, of particular theme with total sensibility –
which together make up the presented work of art. It will be
helpful to indicate in a general way what were James's responses
to civilization, and how these affected some of his most characteristic subjects and themes. But their particular significances
must of necessity be reserved for the discussions of particular
novels. The communicated vision which lies within the novels
is far more complex than any preconceptions which James
might consciously have held. Complication and enrichment of
form and style, as well as particular developments of 'story'
and 'character' all lead to (and are in part determined by)
complication and enrichment of vision. Any attempt to do
justice to the vision will succeed only when it is approached
through its various manifestations in the individual works.

In terms not of systematic philosophy, but of imaginative

literature, there are several basic ways of viewing the shaping
influences of civilization on the human condition. They have,
all of them, their exponents in modern literature, although
James is perhaps the last major novelist in English to see civilization as he does.[12] Recognizing man's vulnerability, his susceptibility to the impulses of his own worst, as well as best, self,
he welcomes civilization for the protection and enhancement
of human life. James, like Hawthorne and Melville before him,
rejected the nineteenth-century American transcendentalists'
optimism about man's essential goodness and his perfectibility.
In that tradition, when civilization is considered at all, it is
most likely to be seen as either bad or unnecessary, since man's
essential goodness blossoms from his natural state. Contrary to
this view, James saw man's nature to be fundamentally mixed,
capable of good and evil, of altruism and egotism, susceptible
both to high aspiration and to the pull of the abyss – the abyss
of the unprotected self; the self left without guard from its own
hungers and lusts and needs – the primitive imperatives of sex
and acquisition – without guard against its own assertively
egoistic being.[13] Outside civilization there is no guard against
that assertively egoistic being of *self*, nor against the egoism of
others: James is intensely aware of the dangers of both.

James's predecessor and his one American teacher, Hawthorne, makes much of an actual abyss in Rome, in *The Marble
Faun*, the abyss into which the barbarians are supposed to have
been driven and inundated in blood. Hawthorne suggests that it
is civilization here too – the crust of time, of Christianity, of
evolving society – which covers the abyss, which protects us
from what it represents. This crust does not always hold, as
the crime of Miriam and Donatello testifies, but it is strong
enough to render the barbaric act no longer the mode of human

12 One major twentieth-century novelist comes remarkably close to the
Jamesian view I am discussing here: Thomas Mann in *The Magic Mountain*,
especially in the chapter entitled 'Snow'.

13 If we look for an understanding of the working power of James's civilization, is it not first of all what protects us from the abyss? Not the economic
abyss, as it tends to be seen in E. M. Forster's *Howards End*, for instance.
Rather, it is the human, moral, personal abyss, of which the economic is
certainly one element.

intercourse,[14] but the special case. In the end, Hawthorne dodges the problems which he has posed: Miriam is an 'exotic' and so outside civilization; Donatello is a 'pagan' and so precedes it. James tries to stay inside his frame of reference.[15]

Civilization, as James sees it, cannot re-make human nature, but it can shape its development and expression. Civilization cannot guard against raw egoism by cancelling it, but it can direct and discipline it through forms and manners, through ritual, through a shared ethic, and through art.

The prizes for which James's figures struggle are almost invariably love or position, or both, and in this regard he is in the mainstream of the English novel. But the highly modulated and extremely subtle expression of these drives in his novels may be taken as James's index to the power of civilization to render them less stark, less direct, and therefore more susceptible to the check and measure of a postulated higher moral sense.

James's civilization sheathes the sharp edges and protects us from each other and from ourselves, since it is only through the created forms that we get at each other, or for that matter, see ourselves. 'Everything is terrible, *cara*, in the heart of man', says Prince Amerigo in *The Golden Bowl*. But there are possibilities of redemption as well as of damnation which reside within ourselves. The source of either dispensation is not supernatural, but lies within our experience of civilization. Civilization is not in itself morality, but it helps our moral sense to function at its highest possible level, even demonstrates that such a level exists and that it is admirable. I shall have more to say later about the obvious fact that traditional religious beliefs and sanctions have been transferred to the secular domain of civilization as culture.

James saw clearly enough that, while the great function of

14 That the crust does not always hold is the vivid lesson of the holocaust of our time, and it has undermined our optimism about civilization in ways that James did not foresee.

15 Interestingly enough, James's very early story, 'The last of the Valerii', was written under the strong influence of Hawthorne, and has one character, Count Valerius, who reverts to paganism, to a 'pre-civilized' conflict with modern life.

civilization is thus to shape and to improve, it does not always succeed. One theme which often informs his novels is the ways in which the 'forms' of civilization, in themselves good, are corrupted and used for base ends. But beyond that, one sometimes detects a certain ambivalence in James about the actual civilization of Europe in his time. How deep, how essential, was the corruption he so often saw? And were such corruptions to be seen as dishonouring the positive values of European culture, or as more fundamentally denying them?

The most explicit treatment of the last question is found in *The Princess Casamassima*. Insofar as the novel provides anything like an answer to this challenge, and to a revolutionary movement which is sworn to the total destruction of civilization, it is an affirmation of positive cultural values. But the affirmation is itself conditioned: Hyacinth Robinson, the protagonist of the novel, in groping between the conflicting claims of revolutionary ardour and of achieved culture, finds his answer only in the stoical act of suicide.

I do not believe that James found a clear or final answer to the question of how deep or essential were the corruptions of European civilization. Generally, he defended this civilization when the challenging force was either the crude moralism or the crude materialism which America so often represented. But he attacked it when it was seen through the eyes of a character who aspired to the ideal, whether this person was American, like Isabel Archer, or European, like Fleda Vetch.

But even this vision was not always steady. In *The Golden Bowl* James, in the manner of some of his most unsympathetic characters, confuses the means of civilization with its ends, its hard cash surface with its moral and spiritual essence. James seems to recognize the symptoms of the acquisitive society without really understanding its causes. Similar problems perplex the development of *The Ivory Tower*, and there is good reason for supposing that in the last part of his career he became progressively more uncertain of his ground. The reason James gave for not completing *The Ivory Tower* was that the First World War made it impossible to write of contemporary life. I shall have more to say on this subject in chapter 6; here it is enough to state that James's explanation simply reinforces the evidence of an unresolved and crippling conflict on the subject. Through most of his fiction he was shrewd enough to see that if the evil perpetrated through the forms of civilization is less frequent, less essential, it is only more ingenious, not less cruel, than the direct frontal attack. Still, my reading of the novels (at least those preceding *The Golden Bowl*) is that civilization's corruptions, terrible as they may be, are incidental rather than essential, important in the sense of damaging the good, but not of an importance capable of denying it.

As so often in James, what he says about the novel turns out to have direct bearings on what he thinks about life. A simple analogy for his feeling about civilization may be found in his frequent defence of the novel as a high art form, a defence all the more determined for his many attacks on the compromises and betrayals of many practising novelists. No Emersonian transcendentalist, he insisted on the reality of evil and doubted the social perfectibility of man. But neither was he in any real sense a fatalist. He believed religiously in the amelioration (as distinguished from perfectibility) possible through civilization-as-culture, despite his occasional doubts. It was with tremendous shock then that he responded to the advent of the First World War:

The plunge of civilization into this abyss of blood and darkness . . . is a thing that so gives away the whole long age during which we have supposed the world to be, with whatever abatement, gradually bettering, that to have to take it all now for what the treacherous years were all the while really making for and meaning is too tragic for any words.[16]

CULTURE AND THE AESTHETIC TRADITION

I do not believe that questions about an author's vision, and its sources, can be limited to issues of dramatic propriety or of artistic effectiveness. One is driven inevitably to questions about value and meaning, about the artist's philosophy and the reader's belief. The main object of the novel, James insisted

16 *The Letters of Henry James*, ed. P. Lubbock (London, 1920), II, p. 398.

on a number of occasions, is to represent life, wherein lies its morality. But as James was aware, this is a liberal definition, with all the advantages and disadvantages of a *largesse* too broad for discriminations. What authors best represent life? Is it a matter simply of taste? Do some authors reveal attitudes to life which enable them to represent it more tellingly? Since inevitably all authors have attitudes and beliefs, are some better than others? Or does greatness in art depend solely on execution? James himself did not think so.

It has often been assumed that T. S. Eliot's famous aphorism of 1918, that James 'had a mind so fine that no idea could violate it',[17] must mean that James suffered from an intellectual and philosophical virginity which could not be taken even by force. James's fiction, it follows, was conceived and written as *pure* art in the sense that George Moore, say, spoke of pure poetry. Such a view is of course nonsense. In his essay on Alphonse Daudet, Henry James wrote:

saying that Alphonse Daudet's insight fails him when he begins to take the soul into account – . . . amounts, after all, to saying that he has no high imagination, and as a consequence, no ideas. It is very true, I am afraid, that he has not a great number of ideas. There are certain things he does not conceive – certain forms that never appear to him. Imaginative writers of the first order always give us an impression that they have a kind of philosophy.[18]

This dictum, that great literature includes and must in part be evaluated for its ideas, is made even more explicit in an essay on Turgenev:

The great question as to a poet or novelist is, How does he feel about life? What, in the last analysis, is his philosophy? When vigorous writers have reached maturity we are at liberty to look in their works for some expression of a total view of the world they have been so actively observing. This is the most interesting thing their works offer us.[19]

17 T. S. Eliot, 'Henry James', *The Little Review*, v (1918), p. 32 (reprinted in Edmund Wilson, *The Shock of Recognition* (New York, 1943), p. 856).
18 *Partial Portraits* (1888), p. 238.
19 *French Poets and Novelists* (London, 1878), p. 97.

These are convictions not always associated, even now, with James's assumed 'aestheticism'. In his later development James did tend to be less explicit in his treatment of ideas, and the most interesting things his own work seems to offer for discussion when he considers it in the prefaces to the New York edition, for instance, are mainly the overcoming of formal and technical problems and the achievements of execution. But there is little reason for requiring a serious writer to explicate in prefaces the ideas which are contained within his own novels; Joseph Conrad's diffidence on such matters is no less than James's. However, even in James's prefaces there are some discussions of the writer's 'total view' or philosophy, as in the preface to *The Portrait of a Lady*, where he speaks of 'this enveloping air of the artist's humanity which gives the last touch to the worth of his work'.[20] It is this concern with ideas or, if you will, with the author's vision of experience, that justifies the attempt to define and to place James's attitudes and his manipulation of themes.

Consider, to begin with, James's related themes of culture and of stoicism. He developed one character, Basil Ransom of *The Bostonians*, whom he explicitly labelled as a 'stoic': 'He was by natural disposition a good deal of a stoic and . . . in social and political matters, a reactionary.' Ransom sees as the only solution to the evils of society the return to the 'masculine character' which enables one to 'look the world in the face and take it for what it is . . . a very queer and partly very base mixture'. His response to the reform movements satirized in the novel is this: 'What strikes me most is that the human race has got to bear its troubles.' When Hyacinth Robinson in *The Princess Casamassima* is led to believe that the evils of society and the positive values of culture are two sides of the same coin, his penultimate reaction is a close echo of Ransom's speech; his ultimate reaction is suicide. Lambert Strether in *The Ambassadors* rates very high the ability to 'take things as they come'.

James's stoicism lacks the high rhetoric of Senecan stoicism, and even more, the Senecan *sententiae*. But the intense self-

20 Preface to *The Portrait of a Lady*, p. xi.

B

consciousness and self-dramatization which the Elizabethans seem to have identified with the Senecan mode – these are to be found frequently in James. For the most part, renunciation takes the place of suicide or noble death; renunciation, that is, of possibilities for worldly happiness or for worldly prizes. Forms and manners have changed, as have conventions of rhetoric. What can be recognized still as in the literary tradition are James's long, intensely introspective 'soliloquies' in time of crisis: Isabel Archer's night-long vigil in which she reviews her marriage, or Lambert Strether's inner struggle with his responsibilities to Mrs Newsome and to his own moral sense after his discovery that Mme de Vionnet and Chad Newsome are lovers.

James's sympathy with the tradition of stoicism in sanctioning attitudes to life and in justifying moral decisions[21] suggests a familiar failure of any more active religious belief. It stems, at least in part, from a dilemma common to the literature and the criticism of James's time, just as James's alternatives suggest to a surprising degree a common resolution.

In the critique of Alphonse Daudet quoted earlier, James speaks of the author's 'lack of high imagination' and associates this with a lack of ideas or philosophy. It is an echo from Matthew Arnold's famous criteria for the greatest art: truth and high seriousness. I think the resemblance in itself is not terribly important, but it touches on a far deeper resemblance, one closer to the heart of James's work. If we want to know 'what, in the last analysis, is his philosophy', we must inquire into the nature of this resemblance to an intellectual tradition prominent in later nineteenth-century thought, especially in the work of Matthew Arnold.

T. S. Eliot has scolded Matthew Arnold and Walter Pater for

---

21 James's familiarity with the classical tradition of stoicism, especially as it affected his age, can be demonstrated. Long's translation of Marcus Aurelius was an important subject for Matthew Arnold in the volume which James reviewed in 1865; I shall refer to this again later. In April 1866, James reviewed T. W. Higginson's edition of *The Works of Epictetus* for the *North American Review*. The possible influence of Epictetus on James has been treated by C. B. Cox, 'Henry James and Stoicism', *Essays and Studies*, VIII (London, 1955), pp. 72–88. But even Cox's persuasive study points out important limits to James's agreement with Epictetus, and I think one must look elsewhere for James's primary source.

confusing the province of art with that of religion, and that of religion with morality. Both Arnold and Pater – and Ruskin before them – were concerned to find a structure of value and of belief to replace those religious certainties or sanctions which they felt to be no longer available. This is what Henry James was to do in his consecration of culture, and the parallels are worth some investigation, particularly because James's place in this tradition seems heretofore to have been largely overlooked.

Ruskin's aesthetic was based on the conviction that the human sensibility, or spirit, is single and unified, irreducible to specialized compartments or categories, a conviction that is identical with James's conception of sensibility.[22] Ruskin's argument is opposed to any theory of specialized components or discrete faculties. He urges instead the conception of a singleness of psyche in which aesthetic sensibility and religious sensibility, intellectual awareness and spiritual perception, are all parts. Perhaps it is not quite accurate to say even that they are each a part of the whole, for that too much implies the possibility of separation or specialization:

each form of human activity springs not from a special faculty – an organ of the mind, so to speak, – but from the whole nature of the person concerned: so that art is not the product of a special part of the mind called the 'aesthetic faculty', nor morality the product of a special 'moral faculty', but each alike is an expression of the whole self.[23]

22 For evidence of James's early familiarity with Ruskin, see T. S. Perry's reminiscences of James in 1858, in *Letters of Henry James*, I, pp. 5–9. For a discussion of references to Ruskin in James's early essays, as well as for an interesting discussion of James's admiration for Ruskin's 'sensibility' and his reservations on Ruskin's narrow moralizing, see Roger B. Stein, *John Ruskin and Aesthetic Thought in America 1840–1900* (Cambridge, Mass., 1967), pp. 210 ff.

23 R. G. Collingwood, *Ruskin's Philosophy* (London, 1919), p. 16. I must here acknowledge a general debt to Graham Hough's *The Last Romantics* (London, 1949) for its excellent treatment of the aesthetic–moral thought underlying the work especially of Ruskin, Morris, and Pater. I have drawn freely on this study in my treatment of James's relations to this tradition, but have shifted emphasis a good deal with the addition of Arnold who, for Hough's purposes, had only a marginal interest, and of Henry James who had none.

Serious writers steeped in a religious tradition which they can no longer accept as the centre of authority for moral values must inevitably find new sanctions apart from religion, or else insist on a morality with no sanctions at all. George Eliot, whom James admired so consistently throughout his career, was faced with the same dilemma. Her solution – her commitment to the imperative of 'Duty' even in default of 'God' and 'Immortality'[24] – while superficially resembling James's attitude, differs in its basis. George Eliot developed a morality stemming mainly from rationalistic ideas of altruism and the common welfare, whereas James identified his morality with ideas of civilization, or culture, or art. To the degree that James's morality became identified with an ideal centred in culture, he moved away from George Eliot's commitment, and his values are sufficiently different to qualify seriously the totality of debt which F. R. Leavis, for one, argued that James owed to George Eliot. If the feeling in James for the necessity of moral commitment resembles that of George Eliot, the base for such commitment James derived from another source: from the aesthetic tradition that began with Ruskin, from the movement which came to identify morality with art, religion with poetry, and 'life' with both.

Very early in his career James seems to have felt the need for a more positive or vital commitment than any he found in George Eliot, whose work he otherwise admired. One sees this in an early criticism of George Eliot's novels first published in October 1866 in *The Atlantic Monthly*:

Of all the impressions – and they are numerous – which a reperusal of George Eliot's writings has given me, I find the strongest to be this: that (with all deference to *Felix Holt, the Radical*) the author is in morals and aesthetics essentially a conservative. In morals her problems are still the old, passive problems. I use the word 'old' with all respect. What moves her most is the idea of a conscience harassed by the memory of slighted obligations. Unless in the case of Savonarola, she has made no attempt to depict a conscience taking upon itself great and novel responsibilities . . . Of a corresponding tendency in the second department of her literary character, – or perhaps I should say in a certain middle field where morals and aesthetics move in concert . . . [a] tolerably good [example] is furnished by her inclination to compromise with the old tradition – and here I use the word 'old' *without* respect – which exacts that a serious story of manners shall close with the factitious happiness of a fairy-tale.[25]

James, it should be particularly noted, makes a significant connection between the 'old' passive morality and the 'old' happy ending. Let no reader confuse James's great renunciations with mere artifices of plot.

James's earlier stories, in which the ideal of civilization as culture is still absent or only minor, often represent a close analogy to the 'idea of a conscience harassed by the memory of slighted obligations'. Here a chief difference is that frequently James is too concerned with the picturesque, with the sights and sensations sought out by an enthusiastic and intelligent American tourist, and rarely with the author's own community, with its shared life and common assumptions, which is the fictional world of George Eliot. One consequence is that James himself – to say nothing of his fictional innocents abroad – was more easily taken in by appearances, by façade. But the fiction beginning roughly with *Roderick Hudson* moves into the more characteristic commitment to culture. The pursuit of this ideal demands of his characters that they take upon themselves 'great and novel responsibilities'. Thereafter, the relationship between the theme of culture and the theme of stoicism or renunciation becomes obvious, most particularly in such novels as *The Portrait of a Lady* and *The Ambassadors*, and James breaks sharply with the 'old' tradition that 'a serious story of manners shall close with the factitious happiness of a fairy-tale'.

Daniel Deronda, written after James had published the article on George Eliot I have quoted from, does present in the title

25 'The Novels of George Eliot', *Atlantic Monthly* (Oct. 1866); reprinted in *Views and Reviews* (Boston, 1908), pp. 36–7. Lord David Cecil in *Early Victorian Novelists* (London, 1934) says more explicitly of George Eliot what James only suggests: '. . . her standards of right and wrong were the Puritan standards. She admired truthfulness and chastity and industry and self-restraint, she disapproved of loose living and recklessness and deceit and self-indulgence.' James's morality in no way contradicts this code, as *Roderick Hudson* (for instance) demonstrates. But he adds to it the 'great and novel responsibilities' he had found wanting in George Eliot.

character a figure pledged to an ideal which transcends that of the welfare of his own immediate community or of the family. Gwendolen Harleth is a study of egotism, in George Eliot's more traditional manner, meant to contrast with the noble selflessness of Deronda's Zionism. But a Jamesian figure like Isabel Archer must be seen to combine the idealism of Deronda with the frailty of Gwendolen Harleth. That James *does* invest Isabel with an ideal as intense as Deronda's, if less programmatic, and as opposed to Gwendolen's selfishness, I intend to show in a later chapter. My concern now is the illustration of the ideal for which James leaves the company of George Eliot for that of Arnold, Ruskin, and Pater.

Ruskin, I have suggested, begins the involved nineteenth-century movement that was to elevate art to the level of a religious concern. One implication of Ruskin's theory of the single sensibility is that it required him to place morality *in* art, and allowed him to exalt art as a religion without destroying ethical sanctions. Further, his conviction that good art is pro-duced only by good men (a thesis adopted by James, as I intend to show), leads to a replacement of religious orders with a new priesthood of art.

T. S. Eliot was strongly opposed to the attempt of Arnold and Pater to 'do away' with religion and to place culture in its stead. Yet his own doctrine that religion and culture are the same – or different aspects of the same – 'total way of life' contains the essential Ruskinian thesis, and underlines in another way James's debt to this tradition. Eliot wrote:

Aesthetic sensibility must be extended into spiritual perception, and spiritual perception must be extended into aesthetic sensibility and disciplined taste before we are qualified to pass judgement upon decadence or diabolism or nihilism in art. To judge a work of art by artistic or religious standards, to judge a religion by religious or artistic standards should come in the end to the same thing; though it is an end at which no individual can arrive.[26]

26 T. S. Eliot, *Notes Toward a Definition of Culture* (London, 1948), p. 30. Eliot's 'culture' is different from, and larger than, Arnold's or James's. He sees it as a total expression of group behaviour as would a contemporary sociologist or anthropologist. It includes the expressions of *all* elements and strata of the group – from dog-racing and Wensleydale cheese to Gothic

But surely this is the end that Ruskin and his followers had in mind. Eliot's argument becomes narrowed down to his objection to the displacement of religion, in its ordinary sense, by something else, like art or culture. Although on the level of categorical *ought* his objection might be reasonable, or arguable, it is naïve and unhistorical in its suggestion that certain perverse individuals such as Arnold and Pater must accept the willed responsibility for the alternative: for the loss of religious conviction common to the late nineteenth and to the twentieth centuries. Granting this loss, however unfortunate it may have been, one must credit at least the attempt to replace as much of its moral and spiritual content as possible. The very attempt to do so is a confirmation of moral and spiritual needs. The alternative is obscurantism. Ruskin's own attempt is rooted in his theory of spiritual oneness, and developed in his insistence that the perception and appreciation of beauty are identical with moral perception.

The precise historical development of this line of thought in Arnold and Pater is not my primary concern, but rather, its reflection in the work of Henry James. I should like, however, to quote a passage on Ruskin's position once more, because it is singularly Jamesian in its implications:

[Ruskin] means . . . that the perception of beauty is not isolated from the rest of human life . . . that it is not the affair of the intellect or purely of the senses, but of the emotions. The extent to which we are capable of receiving impressions of beauty depends on the quality of our emotional life in general; and the quality of our emotional life is to Ruskin . . . a moral concern. There is, in fact, a relationship between the kind and amount of beauty that we perceive, and the moral quality of our lives.[27]

To deny this relationship by isolating beauty is the 'art for art's

---

churches and the music of Elgar. James's 'culture' includes the fine arts, and country houses, and manners, but no football pools, and certainly no 'boiled cabbage cut into sections'.

27 Hough, *The Last Romantics*, p. 18. Compare this with James's famous 'house of life' passage in the preface to *The Portrait of a Lady*, cited later in this chapter (see p. 25).

sake' or aesthetic fallacy; to deny it by isolating the moral is the Puritan fallacy. James's conception of civilization-as-culture was opposed to both.

T. S. Eliot cites two 'errors' which can be avoided by seeing religion and culture both as aspects of the same 'total way of life': the first, that 'culture can be preserved and extended and developed' in the absence of religion, is the error which we must hold James, as well as Arnold and Pater, guilty of, so long as we agree to the ordinary definition of religion. The second is the Puritan fallacy I referred to above: 'That the preservation and maintenance of religion need not reckon with the preservation and the maintenance of culture; a belief which may well lead to the rejection of the products of culture as frivolous obstructions to the spiritual life.'[28]

The crux of Eliot's argument, of course, is in his insistence that religion *is* religion, and not something else. But if, in the tradition of the late nineteenth century (and despite Eliot's example, of the twentieth) we take only its moral content, an interesting parallel results. By substituting *morality* for *religion* we can read Eliot's two 'heresies' as central concerns of Ruskin and his contemporaries, and of Henry James as well. They become the recognizable framework for James's most frequent treatment of his two terms, European culture and American-Puritan morality. Like Eliot, James argued the limitations of these terms separated one from the other. He insisted that culture must include morality; his argument with actual European civilization is that it often does not. Similarly, he insisted that while Puritan morality may be one aspect of a 'culture', it must be a culture which apart from its morality scarcely exists. The sensibility of his prototypic American lacks aesthetic imagination; of his European, moral imagination. Neither alone is, in Ruskin's terms, a unified sensibility.

James believed, like Ruskin, that good art comes from good men; consequently the problem of moral judgement in dealing with the work of art is the same as that of aesthetic judgement. The preface to *The Portrait of a Lady* illustrates this point very well. 'Recognizing so promptly the one measure of the worth

28 Eliot, *Notes Toward a Definition of Culture*, p. 25.

of a given subject ... is it valid, in a word, is it genuine, is it sincere, the result of some direct impression or perception of life?' Therein, he goes on to say, lies its beauty, which is at the same time its morality. Both stem from the nature of the sensibility which produces it:

There is ... no more nutritive or suggestive truth in this connection than that of the perfect dependence of the 'moral' sense of a work of art on the amount of felt life concerned in producing it. The question comes back thus, obviously, to the kind and the degree of the artist's prime sensibility, which is the soil out of which his subject springs. The quality and capacity of that soil, its ability to 'grow' with due freshness and straightness any vision of life, represents, strongly or weakly, the projected morality.

He goes on to speak of the 'enveloping air of the artist's humanity – which gives the last touch to the worth of the work', which in turn leads to the famous description of the 'house of fiction', of which I quote only the conclusion:

The spreading field, the human scene, is the 'choice of subject', the pierced aperture, either broad or balconied or slit-like and low-browed, is the 'literary form', but they are, singly or together, as nothing without the posted presence of the watcher – without, in other words the consciousness of the artist. Tell me what the artist is, and I will tell you of what he has *been* conscious. Thereby I shall express to you at once his boundless freedom and his 'moral' reference.[29]

The influence of Walter Pater on James, while obvious, is the least interesting, the least individually significant, within the tradition I have been describing. Pater did contribute to the programme begun by Ruskin, particularly in his advocacy of a quality of life which might compensate for the loss of supernaturally governed purpose and of the idea of immortality. Burning with a hard, gem-like flame is putting the best of two worlds into one. The same passion for experience found in the Conclusion of *The Renaissance* is one of the great themes of Henry James, whose characters are so often cultural pilgrims

29 Preface to *The Portrait of a Lady*, pp. x–xii.

eagerly seeking to follow the gospel of Lambert Strether: 'Live all you can.'[30] Isabel Archer, for whom the portals of experience are opened as with the magic key of a fairy-tale, is given this most Pateresque characterization: 'a combination of the delicate, desultory, flame-like spirit and the eager and personal creature of conditions'.

The affinity to stoicism in James – the predilection for renunciations – has its affirmations also in *Marius the Epicurean*, notably in the figure of Cornelius Fronto, the Stoic philosopher-professor. The epicurean, he claims, feels the absence of a central principle of conduct, a sanction for his behaviour which, if it has been conventionally moral, has been so without conscious motive. The doctrine of stoicism, Fronto argues – speaking for the Pater who was troubled by the materialism of his time (as was James) – results in a fineness of conduct in sharp contrast to the expediencies of contemporary life:

Pitched to a really high and serious key, the precept – *Be perfect in regard to what is here and now* – the precept of 'culture', as it is called – that is, of a complete education – might at least save him from the heaviness and vulgarity of a generation, certainly of no general fineness of temper, but with much material well-being.[31]

No sensitive reader of James can fail to see in this statement a clear reflection of a theme running through much of his fiction, especially *The American, The Princess Casamassima, The Tragic Muse, The Spoils of Poynton, The Ambassadors,* and *The Ivory Tower,* as well as a number of the short stories.

Studies in the History of the Renaissance was published in 1873. James's 'The Madonna of the Future' (1875) was written under its influence, especially the elaborate impressionistic description of the Raphael Madonna. The facts of chronology suggest that much of Pater's development, stemming largely from Matthew Arnold's influence (as in the passage from *Marius* quoted above) took place concurrently with James's. Similarly,

---

30 It is precisely this passion for experience, for ever-widening areas of consciousness, that distinguishes James's stoicism so sharply from that of Epictetus, as Cox also points out in the article referred to above.

31 Walter Pater, *Marius the Epicurean* (London, 1885), I, pp. 156–7.

the stoicism of *Marius* was not unique to this work, but the reflection of an important intellectual current of the time:

Matthew Arnold's notebook, Long's translation, Renan's lectures, Symonds's peculiar synthesis of Aurelius and Whitman, Edward Caird's comments on the popularity of Stoicism, and such articles as F. Pollock's on Aurelius, in *Mind*, January 1879 – 'This doctrine . . . comes nearer to our own ways of thinking, and has more lessons for us than appear at first sight . . .' – suggest the extent of the attention then given to stoicism as an assimilable religious philosophy.[32]

The conjunction of the exaltation of an ideal of culture with a leaning toward stoicism is in any case clearly present, and important, in the writings of Arnold and Pater. It is this tradition, rather than the more negative and stringent stoicism of Epictetus, which exerted a strong and direct influence on James's fiction, in which the same ideal of culture is joined so frequently to the theme of stoic renunciation.

It is worth noting, in this connection, that James reviewed Arnold's collection, *Essays in Criticism*, with great enthusiasm in 1865, virtually at the beginning of his own career. It was in this collection that James would have found Arnold's essay 'Marcus Aurelius', written on the occasion of Long's translation. Matthew Arnold, whose influence on Pater is manifest in the *Marius* quotation above, brought to his treatment of culture a more explicit concern with conduct and character which particularly appealed to James. Although one can find a number of passages especially in the early fiction of James that echo the impressionism, even the purple writing, of Pater, James wanted to stress the *criticism* of life as a sanction for art. He was troubled by the occasional moral earnestness of Ruskin and the intellectual flabbiness of Pater. But these reservations do not cancel out James's susceptibility to some of their basic doctrines; rather it implies a less reserved sympathy with Matthew Arnold. James could respond warmly to Arnold's affirmation that 'conduct is three-fourths of life' and respond at the same time to Arnold's criticism of art as that of a highly trained

32 R. V. Osbourn, 'Marius the Epicurean', *Essays in Criticism*, I (1951), p. 402.

literary sensibility. His influence on James is the most interesting and significant of all that we will find in tracing this tradition.

Henry James met Arnold for the first time in March 1873, while visiting William Wetmore Story in Rome. There is evidence of some later friendship. Writing to Charles Eliot Norton on 6 December 1886, James referred familiarly to Arnold thus: 'I saw Matt Arnold the other night, and he spoke very genially of you . . .'[33] Interestingly enough, in the same year that James met Arnold, 1873, Henry James Senior wrote to his son these touching words: 'Goodbye, my lovely Harry. Words can't tell how dear you are to my heart; how proud I am of your goodness and truth, and of what Mr. Arnold calls your "sweet reasonableness".'[34]

James's first autobiographical volume, *A Small Boy and Others* (1913) recounts a childhood memory of seeing the stage version of *Uncle Tom's Cabin*, followed later by another and fuller version which gave him an early opportunity for critical comparisons. In this way, he recalls, he 'got his first glimpse of that possibility of a "free play of mind" over a subject which was to throw him with force at a later stage of culture, when subjects had considerably multiplied, into the critical arms of Matthew Arnold'.[35] And the second autobiographical volume, *Notes of a Son and Brother* (1914), will recall an idyllic summer in Massachusetts (in 1865) when his group talked, discussed, read 'Matthew Arnold and Browning', and dealt with 'a hundred human and personal things'.[36]

From the same season most likely stems the later reminiscence in an article on 'Mr. and Mrs. James T. Fields' in *The*

33 *Letters*, I, p. 125, Arnold later visited the Jameses during his American lecture tour in 1883. F. M. Hueffer, writing of the European visitors in the James household, says – with some confusion of chronology – 'nothing of their personalities "rubbed off" . . . on to the by then adolescent James – or, if anything came at all, it was only from the restrained muse of Matthew Arnold, whose temperament, in its rarefied way, was as "New England" as was ever that of Emerson or James Russell Lowell' (*Henry James* (London, 1913), pp. 100–1).

34 Letter quoted by F. O. Matthiessen, *The James Family* (New York, 1947), p. 219.

35 *A Small Boy and Others* (London, 1913), p. 171.

36 *Notes of a Son and Brother* (London, 1914), p. 426.

Atlantic Monthly (July 1915), where James recalls the pub-
lisher's allowing him to read Arnold in proof :

I even invest with the color of romance, or I did at the time, the
bestowal on me, for temporary use, of the precursory pages of
Matthew Arnold's *Essays in Criticism*, honourably smirched by the
American compositor's fingers, from which the Boston edition of
that volume, with the classicism of its future awaiting it, had just
been set up. I can still recover the rapture with which, then suffering under the effects of a bad accident, I lay all day on a sofa in
Ashburton Place and was somehow transported, as in a shining
silvery dream, to London, to Oxford, to the French Academy . . .
to ancient Greece; all under the fingered spell of the little loose
smutty London sheets.

James had also read *Culture and Anarchy*, as is demonstrated
in *The Middle Years* (1917), where he speaks of having met
Frederick Harrison, 'eminent to me at the moment as one of
the subjects of Matthew Arnold's early fine banter'. And
Arnold's *Discourses in America* is referred to in James's essay
on 'Emerson', collected in *Partial Portraits* (1888).

There are a number of ways in which James's familiarity
with Arnold is explicitly revealed in the fiction. James is fond
of the label 'Philistine' which he had commended to his readers
in his early review;[37] while Arnold's 'Barbarians' show up in
the story 'The Solution' (1889), whose central character is
named Mrs Goldie and whom James calls 'Barbarian', and in
the title character of 'Lady Barberina' (1884).[38] Arnold's conception of poetry as a 'criticism of life' finds frequent echoes
in the fiction, and James often uses the tag 'critic of life' for his
characters.

More important, Arnold's well-known opposition of culture
to the mere machinery of social reform, the occasion for *Culture
and Anarchy*, finds its strong and extended re-affirmations in
James, implicitly in *The Bostonians*, explicitly in *The Princess*

37 'Matthew Arnold's Essays', *North American Review* (1865); reprinted in
Views and Reviews (Boston, 1908). James also wrote a very sympathetic
general article, 'Matthew Arnold', for the *English Illustrated Magazine* (January 1884).
38 James changed the spelling to Barbarina for the New York edition, as
though to emphasize this intention.

Casamassima, and somewhat obliquely in *The Tragic Muse*, fuller discussions of which I reserve for a later chapter.

But most interesting of all, in terms of the uses to which James puts them, are Arnold's famous symbolic terms, Hebraism and Hellenism, the call to duty and the call to beauty. These become in James – without the labels – his most typical treatment of American and European as they tend respectively to represent 'strictness of conscience' and 'spontaneity of consciousness'. Arnold of course had in mind primarily historical phases of national temper; but James adapted the Hebraism–Hellenism configuration to the conflict between individuals or national tempers at any given time.

Perhaps a particular passage from *Culture and Anarchy* will demonstrate the connection with James. If we substitute for 'Hebraism' a particular Jamesian character – Mr Wentworth of *The Europeans*, or Waymarsh of *The Ambassadors*, for instance – and oppose to these the 'Hellenism' of Felix Young in the first novel or, in the second, of Lambert Strether under the spell of Paris and Mme de Vionnet – we have the very essence of James's central conflict and his favourite theme:

But while Hebraism seizes upon certain plain, capital intimations of the universal order, and rivets itself, one may say, with unequalled grandeur of earnestness and intensity on the study and observance of them, the bent of Hellenism is to follow, with flexible activity, the whole play of the universal order, to be apprehensive of missing any part of it, of sacrificing one part to another, to slip away from resting in this or that intimation of it, however capital. An unclouded clearness of mind, an unimpeded play of thought, is what this bent drives at. The governing idea of Hellenism is *spontaneity of consciousness*; that of Hebraism, *strictness of conscience*.[39]

It is no accident that Waymarsh is described as a 'Hebrew Prophet', or that Felix Young should want to do a portrait of Mr Wentworth as 'an old prelate, an old cardinal, or the prior of an order'. Later, when Felix wishes to assure Mr Wentworth that he is not himself given to the wilder implications of 'Bohemianism', he will say, ironically enough: 'at bottom, I am a terrible Philistine'.

39 M. Arnold, *Culture and Anarchy* (Cambridge, 1935), pp. 131–2.

The opposition of Hebraism and Hellenism may be seen, in varying dramatic forms, over and over in James, not only in the characters already mentioned, but in very many others. I cite here only such contrasted figures as Mark Ambient and his wife in 'The Author of Beltraffio'; the Unitarian minister Babcock and the progressively 'Hellenized' Christopher Newman; and Mrs Newsome and Mme de Vionnet in *The Ambassadors*. The list could be extended. Brought to Rome to develop his art, the young American sculptor Roderick Hudson defensively exclaims : 'I'm a Hellenist; I'm not a Hebraist.'

Like Arnold, James rejected each of these two terms alone, each without some interfusion of the other, as fragmentary. He welcomed both together as comprising man's wholeness. If each alone is fragmentary, it can still be admirable within its limits, so that the 'grandeur' of Hebraism finds its frequent echo in James and helps to explain our qualified admiration for such characters as Mr Wentworth and Waymarsh. When Waymarsh, enraged and baffled by the 'civilized' talk of Strether and Maria Gostrey, and barred by his own Hebraic bent from their visible enjoyment of Europe, stalks off to 'buy things' at a nearby jeweller's, Strether's explanation is that he has done it 'for freedom'. The particular freedom Strether means is 'To be as good as you and me. But different.' Given the values of Hebraism and of Hellenism, and short of an ideal marriage of the two, a *genuine* Hebraism is better than a lightly-taken Hellenism – and infinitely more so than a spurious one. We may smile a little at James's Waymarsh or Mr Wentworth – as we do at elements of his characterization of Emerson – but it is a smile complicated by ungrudging admiration, even awe. In writing of Emerson's conscience, James says, 'It must have been a kind of luxury to be – that is to feel – so homogenous.'[40] We shall not find the same kind of sympathy for the American who has abdicated from any genuine Hebraism, but who has not become truly Hellenized either. Such figures are sometimes comic in James, but they also may be his most striking villains, as Madame Merle and Gilbert Osmond must remind us.

James's frequent use of artists and writers as subjects for his

40 *Partial Portraits*, p. 5.

fiction is yet another demonstration of his absorption in this nineteenth-century movement. The life of the artist becomes a central symbol of positive values. Defections from or distortion of these values – the heresies in the priesthood of art – become in turn subjects for a number of stories, such as 'The Author of Beltraffio' or 'The Aspern Papers'.

If the new concept of culture has become a religion it has not only its heretics but its saints and martyrs. The dedication proper to the artist may be seen to have its ironic lapses, as in 'The Lesson of the Master'. But 'The Death of the Lion', 'The Middle Years', and 'The Next Time' are each in their own ways stories of the martyrdom and sainthood of the dedicated artist. James's artists, like the narrator of Arnold's 'The Scholar Gypsy', must

waive all claim to bliss, and try to bear.

The brave and total disinterestedness of the artist, the way he practises art not only as a profession but as a way of life: are these not the qualities that attract Isabel Archer to Gilbert Osmond, or rather, to the *appearance* of Osmond? That make Nick Dormer, the man of public affairs in *The Tragic Muse*, so admire Gabriel Nash, the artist? Culture may become, like a religious vocation, the one true way, and the emblems of culture the outward signs of an inward state. Always implied is the unity of art and conduct. 'The Author of Beltraffio' deals shrewdly with the conflicts and ambiguities of aestheticism, in conduct as much as in literature, and James is perhaps *too* harsh in his suggestion that the demand for explicit morality in art – a Philistine morality – can accompany a cruel immorality in life.[41] 'The Aspern Papers', with its evocations of the Romantic movement, treats devastatingly the disastrous separations of art and life in standards of conduct, and underlines besides the terrible contrast between the symbol of Shelley, that most passionate of idealists, and the *idée fixe* of his former mistress,

41 There is an interesting resemblance between James's description of William Morris's wife – a 'grand synthesis of all the Pre-Raphaelite pictures ever made', etc. (*Letters*, I, pp. 17–18) – and his characterization of Miss Ambient, Mark's sister.

whose eye is inalterably fixed, behind its mask, on the dollar.

The dominant spiritual movement in nineteenth-century America had been Emersonian transcendentalism, and James commemorated it in the fine study of Emerson already cited. His attitude toward American culture is detached and ambiguous. He praises it for its dedicated loyalty, matched in no other place, for its devotion to the moral imagination – to the lecture hall and the podium. His awareness of all the omitted possibilities is suggested very gently :

It would require some ingenuity, the reader may say too much, to trace closely this correspondence between his genius and the frugal, dutiful, happy but decidedly lean Boston of the past, where there was a great deal of will but very little fulcrum – like a ministry without an opposition.[42]

The last phrase indeed may remind one of Arnold's observations about Hebraism without an opposing Hellenism. James calls Emerson a 'moral' genius; nowhere in his essay does he seem conscious of the fact that Emerson was dealing with religion a good deal of the time, and not just with morals. In James's secularized world it is a distinction easily overlooked. James questions Arnold's propriety in contesting 'Emerson's complete right to the title of a man of letters' in *Discourses in America*; but later in his own essay James comments on the 'completeness' of Emerson's claim :

The confession of an insensibility ranging from Shelley to Dickens and from Dante to Miss Austen and taking Don Quixote and Aristophanes on the way, is a large allowance to have to make for a man of letters, and may appear to confirm but slightly any claim of intellectual hospitality and general curiosity put forth for him. The truth was that, sparely constructed as he was and formed not wastefully, not with material left over, as it were, for a special function, there were certain chords in Emerson that did not vibrate at all.[43]

James wishes to keep before his readers that Emerson was not simply a special case, but a product of the 'social conditions in which [he] moved, the company he lived in, the moral air he

42 *Partial Portraits*, p. 8.
43 *Ibid.*, pp. 29–30.

breathed'.[44] From those conditions come James's fictional New Englanders. They have, like Emerson, the 'rare singleness that was in his nature (so that he was *all* the warning moral voice, without distraction or counter-solicitation).'[45] The reader may place this beside Arnold's description of Hebraism and find a congruence that should convince him that James was closer in sympathy to Arnold than perhaps he himself realized. Further, the impression made on him by Arnold was not, as Hueffer thought, a mere duplication of the 'New England temperament' of Emerson and Lowell. Rather, it was the impression made by a man of European culture whose critique of the New England temperament New England was unable to make for itself. It was an impression peculiarly available to James because of his own early distancing from his roots. Much criticism of James has attributed his basic moral attitudes to a Puritan New England source, either directly or with the assistance of Hawthorne. But it seems to me obvious that James's relationship to this background was fundamentally affected by a strong infusion of Matthew Arnold's wider cultural sense.

The 'rare singleness' that James found in Emerson had its own undeniable beauty, as well as its severe limitations, and James tried to do justice to both. In any case, Emersonian transcendentalism was not James's point of view; it was simply his occasional subject matter. His fiction could find a place for the excesses and fringe movements of the transcendentalist tradition. Of the countless novels on nineteenth-century American agitation and reform, *The Bostonians* is undeniably the best.

But it was something else that engaged James's sustained interest in this background. Occasionally, this America of the lecture hall and podium produced some singular soul, whose passion would go beyond the Hebraic genius. Inevitably he (and frequently *she*) must come to Europe for fuller initiations. Most often they have acquired a thirst from an early visit to Europe, and augmented it (or even discovered it) with ambitious tastes in reading or in art. Beneath these experiences – what

44 *Ibid.*, p. 3.
45 *Ibid.*, p. 4.

makes them important – is some innate predilection for culture, some special fine sensitivity, a sympathy for the full life, an appreciation of the 'finer appearances'. These gifts are roused to life by their early experiences, direct or vicarious. The touching Miss Caroline Spencer in 'Four Meetings', one of the best of James's earlier stories, has never seen Europe, but to do so is the passion of her life.

The great dream of the Jamesian pilgrim is the Arnoldian ideal: the marriage of Hebraism and Hellenism. It is what the 'braver imagination' desires, what most appealed to James 'as a "critic of life" in any sense worthy of the name', what he hoped for as 'the dauntless fusions to come'.[46] James's heroes never achieve this perfect marriage, although Lambert Strether almost does. But it is their striving toward such a synthesis which very often gives them their special appeal.

The lunatic fringe of transcendentalism in *The Bostonians* is not central to James's fictionally reconstructed America, any more than is the excessive aestheticism of the pre-Raphaelites and the 'Nineties' to his Europe. What is central to James is this dichotomy of American–Hebraic and European–Hellenic. In the ideal civilization which James projects, both are present as elements of a single high culture. In searching for it he left America not only because of the narrow cultural life which he felt it offered, but because of the growing disparity between its older moral professions and its newer consuming acquisitiveness. He sought it in Europe because there he found his desired richness of cultural reference. This richness often enough lacked the completeness of the ideal, requiring a stronger measure of moral awareness to accompany its richness of tradition, of sensual beauty, of forms.

Culture, in the 'accumulated monuments and treasures of art', was Europe, and Europe was the altar of a culture newly dedicated by Ruskin and Arnold and Pater, before which the American must come to worship. But culture meant more – not so much an achieved condition as a state of becoming, of striving. Arnold had said that the 'study of perfection' is *not* perfection, but the movement toward it. It is this movement, this

46 Preface to *Lady Barbarina*, pp. ix–x.

striving, which is at the heart of much of the fiction of Henry James.

It was the essence of his belief that so rich a culture as Europe represented must, as index of so fine a sensibility, imply at least the potential of a fine moral element. If, as Ruskin said, only good men produce good art, must not the same thing be true of those who receive and live with it? If, as Arnold claimed, culture is the study of perfection, where art is the best testimony of character as well as of beauty – or, to be more precise, of the beauty which properly belongs to man's character as well as to his artefacts – then life must burn at its brightest where the ambient sense of beauty has proved itself most.[47]

Yeats, whose feeling was that life should be lived as ritual, and who admired the ceremony of civilized life represented for him by Lady Gregory's Coole Park, came to the fullest statement of its appeal only after the First World War, the advent of which had so shattered James's hopes. The old civilization was manifestly crumbling, and its representative great houses were in danger of being lost not only as tokens of any future renascence, but even as symbols of a present glory. In Yeats's poems such as 'Ancestral Houses', 'Coole Park, 1929', or 'Coole and Ballylee, 1931', the vision has become backward-looking and to that degree resigned:

> O what if levelled lawns and gravelled ways
> Where slippered Contemplation finds his ease
> And Childhood a delight for every sense,
> But take our greatness with our violence?
> What if the glory of escutcheoned doors,
> And buildings that a haughtier age designed,
> The pacing to and fro on polished floors
> Amid great chambers and long galleries, lined
> With famous portraits of our ancestors;
> What if those things the greatest of mankind
> Consider most to magnify, or to bless,
> But take our greatness with our bitterness?[48]

47 Arnold almost certainly led James to Goethe, where he would have found certain confirmations, as in 'Truth and Poetry': 'moral culture [is] so intimately allied to, nay incorporated with aesthetic culture . . . that to their mutual perfection the one cannot be conceived without the other'.

48 From W. B. Yeats, 'Ancestral Houses', *Collected Poems* (New York, 1934), pp. 232–3.

To replace a fallen structure of belief, Yeats committed himself to a private mythology which was to include a grotesquely romanticized authoritarianism, as earlier he had taken to Celtic life and folklore. James began and ended with his single dedication, to the delights and pleasures, the refinements and consolations, and even the redemption which he hoped for in civilization-as-culture.

To conclude, then, James sees his characters through the mediation of a civilization which can redeem them, or at least show the way to redemption, from their own and from others' worst possibilities: their naked drives and passions. Civilization imposes a set of measurements and conventions by means of which we arrive at moral value. Manners point to morals; conduct in its everyday social sense points to Conduct in its Arnoldian, ethical sense. The signposts of civilization, of culture, become the signposts of morality as well as of personal awareness, of intellectual fineness, of aesthetic perception and appreciation. James's civilization is less quantity than quality, a quality the appearance of which – the show of which – is ideally the same as the ethical essence which lies behind it. The civilized man reveals the outward signs of an inward state. James's civilization – 'those things the greatest of mankind/ Consider most to magnify, or to bless' – is exalted not as an expedient social body, but as the vessel of man's highest achievements in thought, in beauty, in conduct. Civilisation as culture both invites and expands curiosity, ministers to our need for beauty, heightens our conception of character. Civilization, in brief, develops and protects, expands and harbours, the potential of human sensibility. And sensibility for James means the wholeness of the moral, the aesthetic, and the intellectual qualities which together constitute man's essential humanity.

2

The related ideas

Once given James's central concern, his search for and defence
of civilization as culture, a number of the familiar ingredients
of his fiction take on new significance. The relationships of
these subsidiary themes and motifs to the major concern
will best be studied in their particularity in the discussions of
the individual novels. However, I think that it will prove useful
first to identify and define them.

INNOCENCE AND BETRAYAL

The frequently recurring motif of innocence-and-experience in
James's fiction can be seen over and over again to represent
individuals in their various relations to civilization. The representative thirst for knowledge, for experience, for life itself,
proves to be the constant yearning after civilization or for the
way of life it represents: for the power to be finely aware and
richly responsible. The difficulty of this quest is never more
clearly seen than when the innocence-and-experience configuration gives rise, as it so often does, to the theme of betrayal.

Betrayal, in James's novels, is usually related to the disparity
between the actual experience of civilization and the idealization of it to which his characters cling. In their innocence they
mistake the spurious for the genuine, frequently with the assistance of people who encourage such mistakes for their own
gain. James's villains – who have just been defined – are all
'explained'. They are none of them motivated by malignancy
or natural depravity. Absent are those intimations of evil
beyond the represented case so familiar in Hawthorne. James's
villains are seen to want something, to be after something,

which their victims can help them to get; their villainy is a pragmatic means to a pragmatic end. Themselves intelligent and sensitive and subtle, they are civilized enough to know how to appeal to their aspiring victims. Like Madame Merle and Gilbert Osmond in *The Portrait of a Lady*, they seem veritable messengers of civilization, ready to welcome the passionate, and innocent, pilgrims. That they happen to be false messengers escapes their victims' innocence, but becomes the central fact of their experience. The prince of darkness, we have been told, is a gentleman; he has never appeared more like one than in the novels of Henry James.

We all know the Aristotelian concept of the tragic hero whose fall inspires us with fear lest we might suffer in the same way and with pity at the spectacle of undeserved misfortune. Such misfortune is, however, earned insofar as the tragic character is presumed to have shared in the responsibility for his fall. It can still seem undeserved in that the tragic fate seems in excess of the cause, the punishment greater not only than the character deserves, but than we (the 'same kind of men') expect or think adequate.

In the tragic fiction of James (which includes – a point worth noting for many reasons – almost all of the important novels) the tragic fate is terrible not because it is necessarily incommensurate with moral justice, but rather with the character's sense of it, and therefore with our own while we are identified with his (or her) life. The whole course of action evolves and only at the end, after the fact, do the characters see the long way they have moved, the steep distance of the downward plunge. The disproportion between this vision and their earlier sense of moving only a little, or falling hardly at all, carries with it tremendous dramatic impact. The apotheosis of the action, and the particular source of its emotional release, can seem almost unbearably freighted with the sense of *nemesis*, precisely because the weight of the whole, scarcely-realized process of corruption or of betrayal is embedded in some final expression. Kate Croy cries out, at the end of *The Wings of the Dove*: 'We shall never be again as we were!' That cry takes on the same dramatically packed quality of similar outcries in poetic drama, when so much that has happened is suddenly compressed and hurled at us as a single missile: *'She should have died here-after;/There would have been a time for such a word.'*

The victims and agents alike reach only gradually a threshold of consciousness of the cumulative process of evil. Then the whole impact of what has been happening to them strikes them all at once like a physical blow. The counterpart of Kate Croy's cry are the words spoken about Milly Theale by Susan Stringham at just such a threshold: 'She has turned her face to the wall.' There is no great distinction in these words removed from their context, but in the novel they become appallingly alive because the weight of the whole action is embedded in them. Or we have the all-night vigil in *The Portrait of a Lady*, Isabel Archer's terrible scene of recognition and dismay, when she sees in the dark room, as imaged within a single point of time, the loss of youth and the thwarting of hope over the preceding four years. The scene is as vivid and as pivotal as a dramatic soliloquy, adapted to the novel in form, but in function the same as a direct address over the footlights.

Or we are given Maggie Verver in possession of the golden bowl, through which she has learned of the whole incredible relationship of her husband and her father's wife. The innocence of Maggie Verver is perhaps more conditional than the innocence of Milly Theale or Isabel Archer, but the tremendous disproportion between her sense of innocence and her real situation – particularly at that crucial moment when Fanny Assingham crashes the golden bowl to the floor just as Prince Amerigo enters the room – makes her discovery of betrayal violent indeed.

What these characters have in common, not only with each other but with the whole tradition of tragedy, is the combination of consciousness and conscience. The tragic muse should be portrayed as Janus-faced, with an awareness of right and an involvement in wrong; an ideal sense of good, a human commitment to evil. The heroism of James's characters (even of Kate Croy and Merton Densher, James's most sympathetic villains) is in the nobility with which they suffer the consequences of the double mask. They are all gifted or, as it sometimes seems, damned with the combined burden of consciousness and of conscience. And this is the measure of their appeal to us. Paradoxically, the appeal seems even stronger because the stern justice which these characters administer to themselves lacks the justification of a fixed or traditional system. There is no reference to God or to a religious code of ethics, or to ethical rationalism, or even to a naturalistic fatalism.

INVOLVEMENT

James sometimes portrays another kind of character, of far less appeal. I speak elsewhere (see pp. 67–8) of the resemblance of Rowland Mallett, in *Roderick Hudson*, to Myles Coverdale in Hawthorne's *The Blithedale Romance*. Both stand on the far edges of the arenas of conflict in their respective tales; both are committed not to an action but to a sensibility. The sensibility is so finely charged that all involvement turns finally inward. This type of character is not exhausted for James in Rowland Mallett. He will reappear, with whatever changes or minor transfigurations, again and again. He is the observer who keeps free of the dust and hazards of the race. He will be Oliver Lyon, the painter-narrator of 'The Liar', and Littlemore of 'The Siege of London', and Bernard Longmore of 'Madame de Mauves', Winterbourne of 'Daisy Miller', the unnamed, possessed narrator of *The Sacred Fount*, Vanderbank of *The Awkward Age*. His apotheosis perhaps is John Marcher in the magnificent story, 'The Beast in the Jungle'. There, the magnificence is just that James recognizes Marcher so clearly for what he signifies.

If the first characters may be described, with some oversimplification, as the men and women who know what they should not do and yet are driven to do it, the second are those who know, with some righteousness, what they should or should not do, and do nothing. The double mask of Janus gives way to the single; the persona is all awareness, but lacks involvement. John Marcher is the exception in that he finally recognizes his own nemesis: his involvement is so completely with himself that this is his tragedy. The outside world, the emotions and needs of others, life itself, never penetrate. There *is* a beast in the jungle; but the beast is his own egoism.

These characters originate frequently as technical devices, as centres of consciousness for the telling of a tale. They are given parts within the action which often bring James to grief. James does recognize Winterbourne (in 'Daisy Miller') and Marcher; their characterizations include his awareness and judgement of their non-involvement. The others appear to have his sympathy without either his condemnation or even his stronger irony. At first glance it might seem that James's passion for form and for narrative technique has played him false and that the invention of a technical device, the centre of consciousness, results in a wrenching of idea. But in the successful works we are conscious only of a rightness and a singleness which exists between techniques and matter, form and vision. The failure in these instances of non-involvement is rather a failure of vision, the consequence of a peculiar flaw of sensibility to which James was particularly prone.

It is worth noting, in passing, that James's *ficelles* are rarely allowed to possess the centre of interest as do these others, the observing but scarcely-involved centres of consciousness. The *ficelles* are usually peripheral, comic, 'flat' characters. They do not pretend to an actual involvement in the action, and so do not present problems of interpretation. The centres of consciousness are almost always men; the *ficelles*, women.

The narrator of 'The Liar', Oliver Lyon, gets 'on the track' of a woman whom he has loved, but who is now married to Colonel Lapadose, an inveterate liar (they are so often on the track of something; their passion, when we feel the word justified at all, is usually the passion of a fierce but unenlightened curiosity). The woman has always seemed unexceptionable in her integrity, yet now she either supports her husband in his lying or remains ignorant of it, and the narrator relentlessly proceeds to determine which. It becomes a game. Like the narrator of *The Sacred Fount*, Lyon follows stringent rules which he defines as honourable, and will consult or involve no other person. It is all intensely, if superficially, civilized. The honour of the game is taken to be a demonstration of the honour of the player; manners point to morals. Oliver Lyon makes his discovery; the woman *does* support her husband's mythomania, even so far as to second his accusation of an innocent inconsequential artist's model of a crime which she knows that he has himself committed. And the narrator is finished with both of them. He is himself in an ambiguous position, having deliberately deceived both husband and wife with displays of friendship so that he might paint the Colonel's portrait in order to expose the man's real character to the public. The woman's motivation for lying – her love for her husband – is made to seem less extenuating than Oliver Lyon's motives for false friendship. He is jealous, but his stronger, 'honourable' motivation presumably is a dedication to his art which sacrifices human loyalties. His allegiance to the 'truth' of art proves to oversimplify vastly the problem of truth in life. It has been suggested that the portrait of Oliver Lyon is an ironic one. I can see the theoretical possibility that this is so, but the story does not sufficiently register such irony. The position of the dedicated artist seems at the end far more admirable than that of the loyal wife. My argument is not so much that James should have seen one position as more defensible than the other, as that he should have done justice to the moral complexity implicit in both.

In *The Sacred Fount*, the narrator makes himself actually obnoxious in his pursuit of clues to a suspected illicit relationship between fellow guests at a country house. *His* passionate curiosity revolves around a theory he has devised to explain the ebb and flow of energy, of vitality, of intelligence and wit, between variously coupled specimens of unengaging humanity who share with him the pleasures of the house. He is given at least the suggestion of a personal involvement in that he sympathizes with the woman whose part in her particular mating he feels to be tragic. He tries to cover up for her, but it is largely because of his zeal in prying that she most needs protection. The chief effect of the novel is an intense irritation with the narrator whose hypertrophied civilization creates a world made up mainly of his own peculiarly sterile and avid curiosity. His obsession is so intense that he fails, even as a centre of con-

sciousness, to give the reader a coherent account of the action.
Despite James's love of verisimilitude, and the famous 'solidity
of specification', he fails to invoke the people who are responsible for this absurd week-end even by name.

At the end of the novel the narrator admits that he no longer
hangs together as once he did. He has lost some principle of
wit, of coherence, of social intelligence. The grounds for this
disintegration are never made explicit, but it seems to me that
the simple (if dreary) truth is that he too has become part of the
pattern of exchange. The woman he so sympathizes with had
lost her wit to her partner, but now the narrator is in love with
her. She seems to revive, and it is now *his* vital power that has
been drained, as from the sacred fount of love. James seems
committed to the vain notion that this excess of subtlety will
make up for the deficiency of significant meaning.

As in the case of 'The Liar', the narrator's involvement is
seen primarily as a matter of curiosity, and it is this stronger,
more evident passion which we believe in finally, at the expense
of the other. The springs of action seem somehow sterile, despite the alleged honour of the procedures whereby curiosity is
pursued.[1] What both characters fail to recognize is that the
subtle subversion of human relationships which is disguised by
their falsely decorous manners turns the essential meaning of
civilization upside down. If they are finely aware, even by their
own account, they have ceased to be richly responsible for any
genuine human value.

Rowland Mallett is supposed to be in love with Mary Garland, Vanderbank with Nanda (in *The Awkward Age*), Winterbourne with Daisy Miller. But they all suffer – with a suffering
singularly unconvincing – in silence. Vanderbank and Winterbourne are immobilized because they cannot quite approve of
their respective maidens who may know too much to be proper

---

1 Curiosity, the free play of intelligence and consciousness, the desire to
see the object as it is: these are important elements in James's civilization.
Although James is prone to ambiguities of conception or of execution that
seem occasionally to elevate the 'game' of curiosity to a unique prominence
at the expense of everything else, I am sure he would not assent to a philosophy of life that so displaced such other emotions as loyalty or love. For a
study of James that mistakes his lapses for high principle and exhibits it as
for admiration, see O. Andreas, *Henry James and the Expanding Horizon*
(Washington, 1949).

and marriageable *jeunes filles*. In *The Europeans*, Robert Acton becomes infatuated with a woman who is both older and conspicuously more experienced than these other young ladies, and he gives her up as altogether too dangerous a gamble. But at least Robert Acton is more objectively seen. He is *not* a narrator and almost never a centre of consciousness for *The Europeans*. James's ironic characterization makes us wonder why the detachment which he achieves with Acton is so lacking when he deals with many of Acton's counterparts.

Rowland Mallett and Bernard Longmore are made to suffer because of unrequited love. In each case the portrayal is marred either by an unrealized ambiguity or by an unintended prudishness. Their love is apt to be stated, rather than rendered – made convincingly dramatic – and their other commitments loom so much larger that we come to suspect not a delicacy of feeling so much as an absence of feeling. Whatever involvement is attributed to them seems unconvincing, and so whatever suffering they are held to be victims of is unconvincing as well. They are vessels of awareness insufficiently encumbered with its hazards or penalties, and for just that reason we reject the tragic in their own dilemmas, and themselves as judges of the dilemmas of others.

What they do have is a high moral tone, a positive sententiousness of moral feeling. A certain primness of effect results from the ways in which their civilized scruples ornament, rather than elevate, their relationships. If sentimentality in literature is recognized as an excess of feeling beyond the represented case, so too there is a similar failing in the moral sphere when the proposed scruples, the displayed moral agitations, stand in excess of *their* represented case. And a high moral tone is the source of nothing but of high irony, when it is not that of simple embarrassment.

INTELLIGENCE AND EXPERIENCE

To minimize the acute significance of intelligence in the fiction of James is to miss his essential quality as an artist. Almost every aspect of his work as a novelist – his justly praised rendering, his characterization, even his subjects or *données* – reflect the felt value of intelligence as a guiding principle of art and of life.

Henry James was a better pragmatist than his brother William seems to have suspected. Perhaps any good novelist is a pragmatist in that he investigates the actual and concrete consequences of human ideas and values and actions. The pragmatist, according to William James, 'turns away from abstraction and insufficiency, from verbal solutions, from bad *a priori* reasons, from fixed principles, closed systems, and pretended absolutes and origins. He turns towards concreteness and adequacy, towards action and towards power.' Henry James did not, of course, adopt the philosophical system of pragmatism; but he demonstrated over and over again his recognition of the value of experience, and of the free use of intelligence, as well as his aversion to fixed principles and closed systems.[2]

Therefore a not uncommon pattern in James's fiction is the testing, through experience, of an initial position which seems to define a protagonist and his probable actions. There follows a working away from an initial, fixed moral or philosophical position, whether political (as in *The Princess Casamassima*) or moral (as in *The Ambassadors*) when this position is found through experience to be limited, and at variance with the true nature of things. The stories are largely about the victory of intelligence over the circumstances that serve to limit or to blind it. And the methods which he uses in the telling of these stories constitute great technical achievements at the same time that they embody James's pervading faith in intelligence.

Whether or not the high intelligence of James's figures is prohibitive to the widest kind of audience is not now my concern. He was himself acutely conscious of the ill-repute of intelligence in English and American fiction :

The picture of an intelligence appears for the most part, it is true,

2 Some critics go much further in arguing for a more literal affinity of Henry James with his brother's philosophy. See Joseph Firebaugh, 'The pragmatism of Henry James', *The Virginia Quarterly Review*, XXVII (1951), pp. 419–35, and Richard Hock, *Henry James and Pragmatic Thought* (North Carolina, 1979).

a dead weight for the reader of the English novel to carry, this reader having so often the wondrous property of caring for the displayed tangle of human relations without caring for its intelligibility.[3]

Nevertheless, James claimed for the teller of stories the attribution of intelligence as the 'very essence of his affair'. In his own writing, this became particularly important since not only the story but the all-important *telling* of the story depended on it. Indeed, so central to the whole intent of James's fiction is this aspect of his material that the very process of telling can become, in a very real sense, the story itself. The technical manipulation of point of view becomes in large measure the thematic substance.

James disliked the separation of the various aspects of fiction into disparate blocks of a whole. For him, the overlapping and interdepending parts which make up the organic unity called *art* were subject to recognition and discussion, but care had to be taken against too strictly defining and categorizing them. In treating 'experience', one cannot completely distinguish between doing and feeling, between history and personality, between 'story' and 'character'. Telling a story involves the unfolding of character as both active and receptive. It may either be reported by an omniscient author or rendered from within the consciousness of the character in the very act of experiencing. James preferred the latter method for several reasons. First, because the beauty and intensity of a situation rested for him on the subjective *act* of experience. And second, because the strictly enforced point of view, solidly imposed between the objective situation and the reader – 'the particular attaching case *plus* some near individual view of it' – commits the author in a way that the 'mere muffled majesty of irresponsible authorship' rarely does. The omniscient author reports on his characters and their reactions, and can thus demand of his audience only that they take his word for it, providing that his word is reasonably convincing. The author who devises a particular and consistent point of view places the relevant data

3 Preface to *The Princess Casamassima*, p. x.

in the reader's view, but his own authority is relatively unseen and unfelt. In its place he establishes the illusion of a direct relationship between character and reader. He has, in the words which James admiringly quoted Taine as saying about Turgenev, 'perfectly cut the umbilical cord that bound the story to himself'. And thus the apparent indirection of an imposed centre of consciousness becomes not an indirection at all, but a device bringing the reader directly to the heart of the matter. The author separates himself from the scene by the use of a centre of consciousness who is actively involved in the unfolding story at the same time that he is acutely aware of the manifold aspects of his involvement.

What finally is important in considering an author's technique is what he does to give his material the greatest possible realization. Whatever it is that he knows of his subject must be disciplined with the greatest possible economy. For on the realization of his material depends the realization of intensity. 'I might produce illusion if I should be able to achieve intensity', James writes.[4] And later, 'Without intensity where is vividness, and without vividness where is presentability?'[5] He is saying something not only about art, but, as the novels themselves prove, about life. The intensity of experience, its richness and fulness, is not merely an aesthetic principle, it is the thing in life to strive for.

The realization of intensity in fiction requires not a literal relationship of art to life, but the imposition of an economy and an ordered discipline of the materials taken from life. This is what art demands; in large measure it is what art *is*:

Life being all inclusion and confusion, and art being all discrimination and selection, the latter, in search of the hard latent *value* with which it alone is concerned, sniffs around the mass as instinctively and unerringly as a dog suspicious of some buried bone . . . life persistently blunders and deviates, loses herself in the sand. The reason is of course that life has no direct sense whatever for the subject and is capable, luckily for us, of nothing but splendid waste. Hence the opportunity for the sublime economy of art, which

4 Preface to *Roderick Hudson*, p. xvi.
5 Preface to *The Princess Casamassima*, p. xiv.

rescues, which saves, and hoards and 'banks', investing and rein-
vesting these fruits of toil in wondrous useful 'works' . . .[6]

To discipline, to limit the treatment, no less than the subject,
is to enrich it. The focussed vision of a centre of consciousness
can convey more verisimilitude to the canopy of life, and with
greater intensity, than the 'inclusion and confusion' of the
panoramic vision of the all-seeing. The author of a so-disciplined
novel may indeed know more than he seems to tell, but his
omniscience is not flung at the reader indiscriminately:

I never see the *leading* interest of any human hazard but in a consciousness (on the part of the moved and moving creature) subject
to fine intensification and wide enlargement . . . the person capable
of feeling in the given case more than another of what is to be felt
for it, and so serving in the highest degree to *record* it dramatically
and objectively, is the only sort of person on whom we can count
not to betray, to cheapen, or, as we say, give away, the beauty of
the thing.[7]

This evaluation of the admirable individual in fiction tells us a
good deal about James's evaluation of individuals in life. The
interest of such a character depends on the degree to which
he feels his situation:

the power to be finely aware and richly responsible . . . *makes*
absolutely the intensity of their adventure, gives the maximum of
sense to what befalls them.[8]

The 'fine central intelligence' in the novel must not only
interest us completely in his active relationship to the case at
hand, but must manage, through his awareness of this relationship, to convey to the reader the full sense of the case itself.
His intelligence must serve to see for the reader the subject
which he should see, as well as to provide in itself the rich
material to be seen. If the kind of intelligence which James

6 Preface to *The Spoils of Poynton*, p. vi.
7 Preface to *The Princess Casamassima*, p. xv.
8 *Ibid.*, p. ix. To anticipate a later discussion, it is interesting that James
singles out the fictional example of George Eliot as lying behind his theory
and practice in this matter.

C

attributes to his characters sometimes makes them overwhelm-ing individuals, we must learn to accept this in much the same way that we accept the magnificence of language which Shakes-peare assigns to *his* characters.

Once granted his conception, which can be seen as artistic convention if nothing else, James *is* sensitive to the need for verisimilitude. Intelligence of a high order must exist, he pro-poses, but not with too uncanny an acuteness, for this would make it superhuman, exempt from human uncertainties or conflicts. It must minister to interest and to vividness, but also to some sense of reality. Given a superior consciousness, such as that of Rowland Mallett,

the beautiful little problem was to keep it connected . . . with the general human exposure, and thereby bedimmed and befooled and bewildered, anxious, restless, fallible, and yet to endow it with such intelligence that the appearances reflected in it, and constituting together there the situation and the 'story', should become by that fact intelligible. Discernible from the first the joy of such a 'job' as this making of his relation to everything involved a sufficiently limited, a sufficiently pathetic, tragic, comic, ironic, personal state to be thoroughly natural, and yet at the same time a sufficiently clear medium to represent a whole.[9]

This concatenation of 'pathetic, tragic, comic, ironic, personal' is the area of human life defined simply as 'bewilderment'. Its manifested presence is essential not only because of the de-mands of verisimilitude, to the need to remain 'natural and typical' as well as 'remarkable', but also for another crucial reason as well. James points out that

If we were never bewildered there would never be a story to tell about us; we should partake of the superior nature of the all-know-ing immortals whose annals are dreadfully dull so long as flurried humans are not . . . mixed up with them.[10]

Immediately after this statement, he warns the novelist against making his characters 'too *interpretative* of the muddle of fate, or in other words, too divinely, too priggishly clever'.

9 Preface to *Roderick Hudson*, pp. xxiii–xxiv.
10 Preface to *The Princess Casamassima*, p. xi.

Each character presents, in terms of his function in a novel, a new problem in proportion. Once determined, the balance – or rather the tension – of intelligence and bewilderment is not given to the reader as a solved or static equation, but is spun out as, gradually, it shows itself to exist. 'A character', James insists, 'is interesting as it comes out, and by the process and duration of that emergence.'

The Preface to *The Princess Casamassima* contains the richest single discussion of these problems and of James's reactions to them. It is here that James establishes a frame of reference for the application of these issues to the *donnée* of a particular work. It is here, also, that in discussing the development of the projected tale James amplifies his twofold concept of intelligence.

Intelligence is equated first with *awareness*: 'the agents in any drama are interesting only in proportion as they feel their respective situations'. There are degrees of such feeling, ranging from the 'barely intelligent' to the 'acute, the intense, the complete . . . the power to be finely aware'. In describing bewilderment, he establishes an inverse hierarchy, 'ranging from vague and crepuscular to sharpest and most critical'. It is the character's conveyed awareness of his situation that qualifies him as reporter, as well as worthy of report.

But awareness must respond to people and to situations; to be acutely aware in a vacuum is hardly to be 'richly responsible' for anything. Awareness, then, must feed on experience, and the nature and degree of experience itself constitutes a second aspect of intelligence.

Experience . . . is our apprehension and our measure of what happens to us as social creatures – an intelligent report of which has to be based on that apprehension.[11]

To amplify this point, there is the fine statement from James's early essay 'The Art of Fiction':

Experience is never limited, and it is never complete; it is an immense sensibility, a kind of huge spider-web of the finest silken threads

11 Preface to *The Princess Casamassima*, p. xii.

suspended in the chamber of consciousness, and catching every airborne particle in its tissue. It is the very atmosphere of the mind, and when the mind is imaginative – much more when it happens to be that of a man of genius – it takes to itself the faintest hints of life, it converts the very pulses of the air into revelations.[12]

Experience and awareness, story and treatment, overlap too densely in the measure of intelligence for precise definition. Hyacinth Robinson is acute enough to reflect his history in *The Princess Casamassima*, while his history consists of a measure of experience ample enough, rich enough, for reflection. His acuteness or awareness in the face of his experience is in large measure responsible for the interest and intensity of his adventure; this, in turn, qualifies him to tell his story, as a centre of consciousness, to the reader. The dialectic is self-enclosed, each aspect mutually contributing to the other.

Since the preface to *The Princess Casamassima* provides us with much of our theoretical groundwork, the novel itself can be used to illustrate James's typical dependence upon the intelligence of a centre of consciousness. The novel is from James's middle period; his practice is fairly typical of the techniques of the early and middle novels, although less so of the late novels.

James employs Hyacinth Robinson as a centre of consciousness only intermittently. The point of view shifts from Robinson to other characters around him, to various agents affecting his career in scenes where he himself is not present, to the view of a postulated observer, and to the author himself. Yet, while Hyacinth is not the exclusive source, he is still the dominating centre, of consciousness. In scenes where he does not appear, the author imposes Hyacinth's felt presence. Wherever it is that for the moment the centre of narrative resides, it is never far from, nor long in returning to, Hyacinth's own.

It is hardly possible here to trace throughout the novel the shifting point of view. It is enough to know that it becomes difficult to equate Hyacinth's awareness of his situation at every point with that of the reader. We know of conversations and decisions of which he is unaware. If later Hyacinth arrives at

12 *Partial Portraits* (London, 1888), p. 388.

some degree of awareness it is often through his sensitive manipulation of hints and guesses and intuitions. There are times when we have only the author's word to testify to Hyacinth's implicit knowledge of what we have learned so explicitly, and James is not above the occasional exercise of the 'mere muffled majesty' of the omniscient author.

Hyacinth is as acutely aware as any 'young man in a book' can be asked to be.[13] In a rush of impatience with Schinkel – one of the 'fools who minister' to those who really count – he exclaims, 'I make out things, I guess things quickly. That's my nature at all times, and I do it much more now.' Still, there *are* major realities which he fails to make out, and these failures minister both to the development of the plot and to his credibility as a character possessed of high acuteness and sensitivity, yet not 'too divinely, too priggishly clever'.

As for Hyacinth's role as reporter of his case, as distinct from that of actor in the unfolding action, the ground is considerably more uneven. All through the novel, the author interpolates his own comments on the characters and on the story. He points out that certain episodes are particularly important or significant for later developments. He addresses the reader directly :

The reader may judge if [Hyacinth] had held his breath and felt his heart-beats after placing himself on his new footing of utility in the world ...

He conducts us around corners where Hyacinth cannot see what the author is offering the reader. These are all practices common to nineteenth-century fiction, of course. There is actually more continuity with the tradition in James's techniques – at least up to the late novels – than many critics have taken account of, perhaps because they have drawn too heavily on the critical theory of the Prefaces (written in 1907–8) and on the single model of *The Ambassadors*.

These caveats are directed mainly against rigid notions of

13 James's extended and passionate defence of Hyacinth's awareness, in the Preface, suggests that James's readers had in fact asked for a great deal less.

'purity' of point of view, and consistency of technique in employing centres of consciousness. They should not obscure an awareness that James does place greater emphasis than his predecessors on the drama of the inner life as central both to 'story' and to narrative technique. And this greater emphasis is the inevitable consequence of the fact that James is so sure of intelligence as a moral force.

Hyacinth Robinson's initial view of the world is direct, unilateral, limited. He is pledged to a system of political values dedicated to the destruction of a different world of values, the entire Western cultural tradition. Not the least of the points made in the working out of Hyacinth's history is that the limited intelligence (the incomplete man) must choose between two worlds seen as mutually exclusive. It is both Hyacinth's tragedy and his victory that he cannot do this. He is unable to consent either to the political juggernaut or to an aesthetic ivory tower. A person less aware than Hyacinth would cling to his initial position. Or he might go one step further, to find the polarity of politics and culture a perfect equilibrium, allowing retreat from the entire dilemma. But his intelligence is one not only of acuteness, but of integrity – not as distinct from acuteness but implicit in it – and the morality of his resolution is inseparable from, and justified by, the experience from which it springs.

RENUNCIATION

Renunciation is one of the Jamesian motifs by which we come to recognize the author's hand. It is so frequent a resolution of stories and novels as to have inspired critical rapture, scorn, or silence, but never real explanation. I want to relate the significance of Jamesian renunciations to the author's central preoccupation, his search for and defence of civilization as culture.

James's career as a novelist developed in a period that has come to be known as the era of robber barons. It was a time of developing acquisitiveness in America and of a crumbling aristocracy in Europe. The lived reality of western civilization was reduced often to a mere avariciousness for its 'Things' and an empty (and therefore snobbish), pleasure-loving observance of its forms. Even that most problematic of American million-aires, Adam Verver in *The Golden Bowl*, worries, however ineffectually, about his life as 'A kind of wicked selfish pros-perity perhaps, as if we had grabbed everything, fixed every-thing, down to the last lovely object for the last glass case of the last corner . . . lying like gods together, all careless of mankind'. The power of acquisitiveness to undermine the significant effects of civilization, however well its surface might be main-tained, is amply portrayed in James's novels early and late, from *Washington Square* and *The Portrait of a Lady* to *The Spoils of Poynton* and *The Ambassadors* and *The Wings of the Dove*.

It is therefore no surprise that James should have come to admire such alternatives to acquisitiveness as asceticism, stoi-cism, and self-denial. He admired strong moral commitments made in the light of the ideal and believed that such commit-ments should not be undone by the pressures of expedience or of possible gain. Once his typical characters have made moral commitments they will not abandon them, at whatever cost to personal ease or pleasure. Isabel Archer, to cite a central example, refuses to leave Gilbert Osmond because she feels morally committed to her marriage – to the mistake of her marriage, if you will – even though she knows Osmond has married her in bad faith. Lambert Strether in *The Ambassadors* will not remain in Paris, much less marry Maria Gostrey, because he is determined that no personal gain shall come to him from his mission in Europe.

Fleda Vetch, in *The Spoils of Poynton*, renounces everything, as it turns out, because the man she loves is betrothed to a woman whom he does not love, a woman who will not break her engagement not because *she* loves Owen Gereth, but because she loves the spoils – his house and its treasures. James's inten-tion is that we should see how the spoils – the 'modern love of *things*' – create havoc in all personal relationships. To a large degree he succeeds. But his vision in *The Spoils of Poynton* is weakened by the insufficiently convincing 'fineness' of Fleda

Vetch's actions. Her renunciation, far from asserting the primacy of human values over 'things', ends by bringing misery to every single major character in the novel. Her renunciation seems never to have to surmount the imperatives of passion or of strong emotional commitment, and so seems boringly exquisite. We feel that she has admitted the principle of love mainly for the sake of renouncing it – and this is true for a number of James's other characters. How then does one discriminate between James's authentic renunciations and those that appear to be mere conventions?

Apart from direct religious sanctions, the traditional motive for self-sacrifice – at least in fiction, where motives attain to a moral firmness often wanting in life – is surely the recognition that self-sacrifice will contribute something to the happiness of other people, or to the general welfare of society.[14] Such motives are not wanting in James's fiction, but what is striking is the frequency with which the idea of self-sacrifice is invoked from motives not social or altruistic, but personal. The individual renounces happiness not because it will harm others, but because it will harm himself, will do damage to private, not public, moral sanctions. For the same reasons, we do not find in James that final reassuring movement that we expect of traditional tragedy: there are no final speeches that show the welfare of the state, if not the happiness of the protagonists, restored.

There is obvious drama, of course, in Jamesian renunciations. If it is not the kind that suits the popular taste for happy endings, neither is that the taste which James wished to recognize.[15] There are other popular tastes, and I wonder if James was not catering to them in his lesser things. The noble exaltation of foiled happiness can be as thrillingly romantic as the most gratifying of marriages, and contributes a tear or two as

14 George Eliot, whose moral passion no one would question, least of all James, held that self-sacrifice has meaning only in its relationship to the happiness of other people. See J. Bennett, *George Eliot* (Cambridge, 1948), pp. 84–5.

15 James's consciousness of the taste for happy endings is all too evident in some of the plays, which he claimed were written for money and for popularity. The stage versions of 'Daisy Miller' and *The American* were given happy endings contrary to the fictional resolutions.

well, to salt the pleasure. But there are reasons for James's renunciations more fundamentally serious than the appeals of daytime television drama.

Is it not, the appeal of this motif, the same classical appeal which the Elizabethans interpreted as the Senecan mode – the suffering hero triumphant in defeat, victorious in the personal moral ethos despite failure in the market-places of the world? And has James not absorbed it as a literary tradition particularly consonant with his own vision?[16]

Shakespeare's heroes generally have been committed from the beginning to the public world, even to what James in his later years was to call the 'world of grab'. Any moral victory won by renunciation is the more telling in Shakespeare because of this embroilment. But the Jamesian protagonists seem frequently, in contrast, to lack the emotional energies of embroilment, or are mainly unconcerned with the prizes of worldliness; or else their days in the market-place have ended (successfully) before the novel begins (as with Christopher Newman in *The American* and Adam Verver in *The Golden Bowl*). Beyond that distinction there is another. The Shakespearian hero typically acknowledges, at the end, *his* error, as it is recognized within a generally acknowledged public morality. The Jamesian hero typically retreats, at the end, to his private moral sanctions from a world that has little patience with them. At the best, the world approves the Jamesian renunciations without being able to lend them any public justification, which says more about modern history than about James. At the worst, the world is likely to view some of James's renouncing heroes with resentful bewilderment, or with a not unrelated contempt.

American Puritanism does not in itself provide the source for James's renunciations. Its asceticisms are of the senses primarily, and have little to do with material striving. Prosperity and success are acceptable rewards of Providence for virtue. With the somewhat stern moral dictum that virtue is its own reward the American Puritan tradition was not ever in real

---

16 I do not want to suggest by this that James's 'sources and influences' stem directly from Elizabethan theatre. James's stoicism has mainly nineteenth-century roots, as I have indicated.

sympathy, or not past that point where reward is manifested in terms that lend themselves to numerical calculation. But if Puritan self-denial or asceticism is not the source, there are ways in which the famous Puritan sense of duty is intimately related.

It is part of the Puritan ethos to set high goals and to be willing to make great personal sacrifices for their achievement. This is related obviously to the Puritan sense of mission and of vocation. James can be very self-conscious in flouting the rigorous American convention that young men should have some occupation, some 'use' in life. A number of his characters are in revolt against this demand for careers or professions: they think it less important to be *something* than simply to be.[17] One is tempted to wonder how much James himself was plagued by such questions when as a young man he wandered about the world. He would not have been persecuted by his own immediate family, whose eccentricity on the subject was one cause of James's early nomadism, but the New England community must have offered any number of counsellors and advisors who felt that James ought to be up to something respectable and useful.

What his young men (and women) are apt to be up to is the expansion and refinement of their own experiences and sensibilities in the light of their intense care for civilization as culture. However alien to nineteenth-century American expectation, this pursuit does become a vocation to which, in James, many are called. I am struck by the sobriety and the intensity of the Jamesian hero in search of civilization; the hero whom James with perhaps more aptness than he realized named the 'passionate pilgrim'. He prowls through museums and leaves cards at the right places, he courts salons and haunts the English country house. There is not the least suggestion of bohemianism in his make-up, nor of mere cosmopolitanism. He is prodigiously conscientious, the Jamesian pilgrim. As part of the civilizing process, he wants earnestly to learn to enjoy, to 'take things as

17 In a recurring cycle of cultural history the 1960s saw a resurgence of the desire not to be something, but to *be*, although with differences in both means and ends that would have baffled James.

they come'. But he does not enjoy lightly, and he takes things with painful scrupulosity. He reminds one frequently (and rightly) of his religious forebears, seeking the state of grace.

The zeal for mission and for vocation may stem from the Puritan background, but the *cause* – the pursuit of culture – for which this zeal is exercised and vocation tried, remains essentially private. What makes the resulting moral drama often difficult, as I have suggested, is that the *public* sanction for renunciations is absent. If the dedication to the vocation of culture resembles the dedication of Puritanism, there is still a crucial difference: the passionate pilgrims lack the shared God of Puritanism, are Puritans *manqués*. Nor do their renunciations take on resonance within other recognized world-views: James's characters do not see themselves as playing out their personal dramas within a rationally ordered universe with tacit but available laws. Nor do they invoke Hardy's 'crass casualty', against which the naturalist tradition has measured its verities.

Their resignation in the face of evil, their renunciation in the face of any possible suspicion of a lack of disinterestedness or of exalted moral vision, is much closer to a conception of stoicism with its affinities to the Senecan mode of which I spoke earlier. Such a conception involves the belief that no ill can befall the good man, since this is a contradiction of terms. Apparent ills are merely tests of character, to fail in which can lead only to self-reproach and to a loss of moral integrity. Traditionally, it was usually service to the gods, while for James it is service to the cause of an ideal civilization, which saves the individual from great evil – evil deeds, evil thought, the evil will.

The result of these combining elements is to make of James's world very often a place of extremely dedicated *individuals*, rigidly contained within their own moral frames, desperately seeking an honourable commerce with the world. They are more highly civilized than the often illusory civilization with which they must deal. The irony is that *their* ideal is real for them, while the actuality which they see about them proves to be a sham. They are pushed into a world where only ends matter, and not means. And of course it is the means for which James's good people live.

It is very well to speak of the dread race which leads to victory, but what if one does not care for the victory enough to assent to the race? This is the pattern of James's lesser tales. But granting the obvious fact that this state of affairs is in no time of the world's history a unique predicament, what if one is presented also with the spectacle of characters who seem to care intensely for the prize – whether it be love, happiness, or even 'Things' – and who nonetheless renounce? Then you have, in modern fiction its most eloquent exponent, the Henry James of the major novels. At his best, he gives us this thoroughly credible, completely human predicament. When he is not at his best he gives us the spectacle of a renunciation so glib that we must fail to believe in the value of the sacrifice and in the validity of the renunciation itself.

In George Eliot's *Middlemarch* the heroine commits herself, against all counsel, to marriage with an impossible man, and she suffers. He dies after a while, and Dorothea Brooke marries Will Ladislaw, despite her late husband's will, which deprives her of his fortune should she marry Ladislaw, of whom he was morbidly jealous. Her only sacrifice in marrying again is her first husband's fortune. We know well enough that this does not matter half so much as her happiness in marriage. Besides, she is still left with her own £700 a year, a handsome guarantee against starvation. Even George Eliot saw no need for a complete sacrifice.

James admired George Eliot beyond any other author for her moral intelligence and he frequently invoked her example in his criticism. It is for this reason that the contrast I am making here seems particularly justified. There is no direct parallel in James, but I have a strong suspicion that in his hands Dorothea Brooke would never re-marry. Once committed to her first husband, and to her own mistake, she would forever feel bound by him, and even more by her own moral commitment, and she would renounce Ladislaw as surely as ever a Jamesian hero or heroine renounced anything. As surely, indeed, as Isabel Archer renounced the alternative to her miserable life with Gilbert Osmond. A Jamesian Dorothea would end with the happiness of self-justification; with a private conception of moral integrity left intact; with the sense, all else failing, of having been *right*.

It is as though, for James, the civilized person must watch unarmed and alone the corruption or misappropriation of particular forms of civilization, a corruption which is not of his doing, but which inevitably must lead to his undoing. His characters suffer the evil done to civilization – done most likely in its name – because they cannot suffer in their own moral nature any wrenching from the strait and right. They fear irreparable damage to their moral natures as the consequence of action, of intervention, even, it sometimes appears, of contagion. The dilemma is that all breathlessly the Jamesian hero wants to undergo experience, wants to follow the famous apostrophe of Lambert Strether to 'Live all you can.' But when the challenge of experience knocks hard against the holy door of moral identity, he hears the knock, but will not, cannot, open the door.

Vanderbank, in *The Awkward Age*, watches in silence the process of 'corruption' which appears to make Nanda Brookenham unsuitable for marriage. Despite his fondness for her, he finally renounces her because of this very corruption which is conventional rather than real or essential. Lambert Strether, a more substantial figure by far, discovers that he cannot by acting according to Mrs Newsome's moral lights preserve his own, and is thus by dint of honest conscience freed of her injunctions. He discovers nevertheless that he cannot in conscience act positively for his own happiness.

These people are separated from the dense world of society which figures so strongly in the novels, and are condemned to an intense moral loneliness. Other characters may admire their cleverness and intelligence, may admire even their self-sacrifice, but only from the distance of a different moral world. They cannot attain to that high, isolated atmosphere of despairing judgement, of painful discrimination, in which lives – as monad, as ultimate unit of moral being – the Jamesian hero.

This self-sacrifice is inspired by the need for personal salvation, a salvation which resides in the preservation of an ideal civilization. Their moral inspiration is exalted before an ideal of civilization far above the standard of the highest realization of the civilized in the actual world. It is no wonder that they appear to us, and that their renunciations appear to us, as legendary. One thinks again of Yeats, who had so admired the ceremony of civilized life, of ritual, of the great houses:

> Now days are dragon-ridden, the nightmare
> Rides upon sleep; a drunken soldiery
> Can leave the mother, murdered at her door,
> To crawl in her own blood, and go scot-free;
> The night can sweat with terror as before
> We pieced out thoughts into philosophy,
> And planned to bring the world under a rule,
> Who are but weasels fighting in a hole.[18]

In his biography of James, F. W. Dupee wrote, 'Among the inalienable rights of man never quite recognized by the James family is the right to be unhappy.'[19] The case for Henry James is almost the reverse of this obtuse charge. James understood happiness, and he admired it, but he did not trust it. What he understood best was the individual made monstrous to the world, as if by physical deformity, by that peculiar complex of moral self-preservation and material self-immolation by which despite the risks of unhappiness, misunderstanding, loneliness, he maintained his sacred moral identity. Instead of the theme (so common in twentieth-century fiction) of the incommunicability of experience and of personality, and partially as prelude to it, James presents us with the essential incommunicability of moral identity.

The best of European civilization (or more strictly, of a European-American amalgam) poses a standard high enough in comparison with the world's average run of confusion and compromise. But James's dedicated characters pose a standard which is higher still, against which they must bear in essential silence their exaltation and their despair. James trusted to the

18 W. B. Yeats, 'Nineteen Hundred and Nineteen', *Collected Poems* (London, 1951), pp. 239–40.
19 F. W. Dupee, *Henry James* (New York, 1951), p. 92.

'braver imagination' to make out, in the more fully realized civilization of the future, new opportunities for communication. But his imagination was not brave enough (or perhaps not wild enough) to see them happily achieved in the present.

It is against such a framework, with its secularized Puritanism and its Arnoldism stoicism, both significantly related to James's central concern with the idea of a high civilization, that the theme of renunciation must be seen. At its worst, James gives us the spectacle of a happiness which we doubt his pale young men and astringent young women capable of surrendering, much less of enjoying. But at its best, as in *The Portrait of a Lady* and *The Ambassadors*, it is a spectacle of genuine human experience, of tragedy, of recognizable human pain and strength.

THE INTERNATIONAL THEME

The international theme was popular with James's readers for various secondary reasons : as comedy of manners, as analytical and often satirical portraiture of compatriots and foreigners, even as a source of a complex tension in which the reader might take sides – American v. European – in a duel between national virtues and vices. Whether or not James was especially interested in opposed nationalisms, there is evidence enough that he was encouraged to work so rich a vein by publishers and friends. He was not practising comparative anthropology, or did so only incidentally – and most thoroughly, it is worth noting, with his secondary or comic characters. James's deeper interest in the subject was in the measurement of those qualities and characteristics which might go into the making of an ideal civilization.

James's first novel, *Roderick Hudson*, deals with the advantages and disadvantages of American and European civilization in a number of ways. In an age that had seen several American writers dealing more or less self-consciously with Europe in relationship to America – Hawthorne, Melville, Mark Twain, and William Dean Howells, for instance – *Roderick Hudson* won some popularity for its treatment of the international theme. The novel is for these reasons a valuable text not only in its own right, but as an occasion for investigating the rough beginnings of James's major concern. It provides also the best single occasion for investigating some of the literary traditions and influences which helped to shape this theme.

The greatest novel of the early period, as well as the fullest and richest expression of James's concern, is *The Portrait of a Lady*. Because it is so important I shall discuss it at some length. It is significant to my purpose that two novels – this one and *The Ambassadors* – are generally acknowledged as his best, even by James himself. Both novels are international, but that this aspect is secondary to the larger preoccupation which is the main subject of this study is nowhere better affirmed than in the preface in the New York edition to *Lady Barbarina*. I think it worth quoting at some length, not only for what it tells us of James's attitude toward the international theme, but for what is suggests of James's conscious and deliberate conception of the theme of civilization as culture :

Nothing appeals to me more, I confess, as a 'critic of life' in any sense worthy of the name, than the finer – if indeed thereby the less easily formulated – group of the conquests of civilization, the multiplied symptoms among educated people, from wherever drawn, of a common intelligence and a social fusion tending to abridge old rigours of separation. This too, I must admit, in spite of the many-coloured sanctity of such rigours in general, which have hitherto made countries smaller but kept the globe larger, and by which immediate strangeness, immediate beauty, immediate curiosity were so much fostered . . . It is a question, however, of the tendency, perceptive as well as reflective too, of the braver imagination – which faculty, in our future, strikes me as likely to be appealed to much less by the fact, by the pity and the misery and the greater or less grotesqueness, of the courageous, or even of the timid, missing their lives beyond certain stiff barriers, than by the picture of their more and more steadily making out their opportunities and their possible communications. Behind all the small comedies and tragedies of the international, in a word, has exquisitely lurked for me the idea of some eventual sublime consensus of the educated; the exquisite conceivabilities of which, intellectual, moral, emotional, sensual, social, political – all, I mean, in the face of felt difficulty and danger – constitute stuff for such 'situations' as may easily make many of those of a more familiar type turn pale. *There*, if one will – in the dauntless fusions to come – is the personal drama of the future.[20]

'The eventual divine consensus of the educated' and the 'dauntless fusions to come' – this is the ideal civilization which dominates James's international theme.

It may be argued that this rather conscious programme came to James only late in his career, perhaps with the overview of his life's work that the preparation of the New York edition provided for him. But this is not true. What is in fact remarkable is how early James's central concern appeared to him, as is made clear in a letter written nine years before the publication of his first full-length novel :

We are Americans born – *il faut en prendre son parti*. I look upon it as a great blessing, and I think that to be an American is an excellent preparation for culture. We have exquisite qualities as a race, and it seems to me that we are ahead of the European races in the fact that, more than either of them, we can deal freely with forms of civilization not our own, can pick and choose and assimilate and in short (aesthetically, etc.) gain our property wherever we find it. To have no national stamp has hitherto been a regret and a drawback, but I think it not unlikely that American writers may yet indicate that a vast intellectual fusion and synthesis of the various national tendencies of the world is the condition of more important achievements than any we have yet seen. We must of course have something of our own – something distinctive and homogeneous – and I take it that we shall find it in our moral consciousness, in our unprecedented spiritual lightness and vigour.[21]

20 Preface to *Lady Barbarina*, pp. x–xi.
21 Letter to T. S. Perry, 20 September 1867 (*Selected Letters of Henry James*. ed. Leon Edel, (London, 1956)).

3

The beginnings: Roderick Hudson
and the tradition

HAWTHORNE TO GEORGE ELIOT

Early in *Roderick Hudson* a wealthy and well-travelled American, Rowland Mallett, meets a young American sculptor, Roderick Hudson, whose great talent has gone unrecognized in his parochial New England community. Rowland especially admires a handsome statue called 'Thirst', and asks what it is supposed to symbolize. Roderick answers: 'Why, he's youth, you know; he's innocence, he's health, he's strength, he's curiosity.' Rowland asks if the youth's cup is also a symbol: 'The cup is knowledge, pleasure, experience. Anything of that kind!' Rowland comments: 'Well, he's guzzling in earnest.' To which Hudson agrees: 'Aye, poor fellow, he's thirsty!'

This patent invitation to allegorical reading is followed by the story of Roderick's career, a development of just this theme. James is using a fictional strategy in his first novel (1876) which may well remind one, if with only a mild shock of recognition, of Nathaniel Hawthorne. Besides the common bond of allegory, it is the subject especially of *The Marble Faun* (1860) that comes to mind. Both novels import American sculptors to Rome; both deal with the life of art; both novels contain a good deal of art description, particularly of sculpture; and both exploit the Roman setting with a consciousness of introducing American readers – prospective tourists all – to that city's wonders.[1]

For each of these substantial resemblances, differences and distinctions also come to mind, and with them a note of caution on the subject of 'sources and influences'. Pursuing this subject,

1 In his study of Hawthorne (1879), James says of *The Marble Faun*: '[it] is part of the intellectual equipment of the Anglo-Saxon visitor to Rome, and is read by every English-speaking traveller who arrives there'.

66

the critic is too likely to play the part of the metaphysical poet who, once given his conceit, works every possible ingenuity to exhaust his material. Such a yoking together by violence of heterogeneous elements together may be found, for instance, in the series of articles first published in *Scrutiny* by Marius Bewley on 'The influence of Hawthorne on James',[2] a study which combines valid and original insight, in considering such matters, with a certain amount of over-ingenuity and special pleading.

Despite this warning, I should like to examine *Roderick Hudson* first in terms of Hawthorne, and then of others. A reader fresh from looking at both of the novels I have mentioned will be struck at once by a radical and characteristic difference of representational strategy and of tone. The similarities between characters, while present, are mostly superficial; the four central figures of *The Marble Faun* do not take us far in understanding the four of *Roderick Hudson*. Donatello is a romantic-allegoric metaphor no longer possible for James. Despite James's praise for her in his study of Hawthorne, Hilda is too vapidly sweet in a characteristic mid-nineteenth-century way, and too patent a Pharisee, to inspire imitation. Mary Garland has both greater complexity and greater individuality. In thinking of Mary Garland in relation to the contrasting figure of Christina Light, one may remember Hawthorne's contrasted women in both *The Marble Faun* and *The Blithedale Romance* and his thematic opposition of the innocent fair maiden (Hilda, Priscilla) with the worldly dark woman (Miriam, Zenobia). But a similar opposition will be found in Thackeray's *Vanity Fair* and in George Eliot's *Middlemarch*.[3] Even so, Mary Garland seems to me to have a stern strength of character that is in sharp contrast to Hawthorne's innocent young heroines.

Hawthorne's American sculptor, Kenyon, might at first glance suggest not Roderick Hudson, but Rowland Mallett, if only by virtue of a shared passivity. But I believe a more significant resemblance exists between Rowland Mallett and another

2 Collected in M. Bewley, *The Complex Fate* (London, 1952).
3 George Eliot, it is true, for once reverses complexions with Dorothea Brooke and Rosamund Vincy, but the basic contrast remains much the same.

Hawthorne hero, Myles Coverdale in *The Blithedale Romance*. The resemblance, I suspect, is not a result of literary influence, however, so much as of shared cultural roots. Like Rowland, Myles Coverdale is the recording voice of his story, the particular framing and refracting window through which the action is seen. One recognizes in both the delineation of a common type: the hero-as-passive-sensibility, the protagonist who serves passively in two roles – hero as observer and hero as sufferer. Coverdale is Hawthorne's one major invention in this mode; James's fiction offers a great many. Seeing them emerge in the stories and novels becomes in fact another of the particular notes by which one comes to recognize and characterize the hand of James.

In the case of Hawthorne, biographical speculation might prove tempting because of acknowledged resemblances to Hawthorne's own experiences at Brook Farm, as well as by unacknowledged resemblances in passivity as a dominant trait. By the end of *The Blithedale Romance*, in any case, Myles must strike the reader as a rather fatuous young man. His last-page confession of love for Priscilla makes of both his conduct and his sensibility a strange affair. His pronounced ambivalence of attitude toward Zenobia, his abashed unadmitted admiration for this dark lady of terrors, for her vitality, her force, her obvious sexual attraction, make of his last-minute profession of love for Priscilla a source of scepticism hardly intended by the author. The resemblance to Rowland Mallett is striking.

The dark lady of *Roderick Hudson*, Christina Light, is beautifully done; one of the best things in the novel. James was aware of her power, of a created vitality larger than the novel could find a use for, and later he took her up again as the title character of *The Princess Casamassima*. It marks the only major instance in James's fiction of such a transportation.[4] She is James's most brilliant study of the dark lady; beside her, even Madame Merle in *The Portrait of a Lady* may seem a little contrived. We see Christina Light at first as capable of other

4 Her retinue – the Prince and Mme Grandoni – reappear with Christina in *The Princess Casamassima*, and the sculptor Gloriani reappears briefly in *The Ambassadors*.

modes of conduct, but she evolves under the pressure of her actual experience to exert a singularly destructive influence. She is not, in terms of any worthwhile literary perception, a Hawthorne character at all. Hawthorne's dark women, his Zenobias and Miriams, come to us as *bad*; we do not discover this quality or its development for ourselves so much as we accept Hawthorne's word. The word may be his own, or it may be the label of other characters inside the novels, but it is not the word, or the recognition, that comes to us independently through the dramatic rendering of character. Indeed, Hawthorne's documentation of evil in directly rendered characterization is rare, despite his distinction as an allegorical commentator on evil. Even when in *The Marble Faun* we see – or rather, when Hilda sees *for* us – Miriam in the very act of willing the murder of her former lover, the indirectly registered effect is only melodramatic. Her villainy must be accepted as a given, stemming from an older tradition, the definition of which makes it sound, perhaps, terribly obvious. We accept as villain, to state it at its crudest, anyone we see in an evil act. A moral judgement is made obvious; but the psychological matrix, the texture of experience from which it springs and to which it leads, is not. The revelation, for instance, of the corrosively cynical mind of Shakespeare's Iago through his early speeches has no counterpart in Hawthorne, but it has in James. Hawthorne stays outside his dark women in his characterizations. The real psychological consequences of evil and the psychological sources of evil – the profound involvement, that is, of personality – is a subject which Hawthorne deals with allegorically, rather than analytically and realistically. Donatello loses the buoyancy and the faun's ears of his pre-Adamic Eden; Hester Prynne takes on her scarlet letter and Dimmesdale, in a rather more complex fashion, takes on his. In the better novel, *The Scarlet Letter*, the allegorical symbols work more closely in the direction of rendered character; but in *The Marble Faun* the allegorical representations of personal conditions take on an independent existence and they never altogether fuse with the psychic truths behind them.

In James the nature of villainy, of evil, has not necessarily changed, though there are differences even here. The nature of its portrayal, however, has changed considerably. The significant difference lies in the psychological depth and detail of characterization. We know Christina Light a good deal better than we know Hawthorne's women. If they have as much moral weight as Christina, she has infinitely more human substance, and we recognize every aspect of her characterization as morally relevant. The lived experience out of which rise temptation, wrong-doing, self-justification, is fictionally re-created. To the degree that it can be said that James derived this kind of portraiture from any other single author, it was not Hawthorne after all, but George Eliot.

For it was in the fiction of George Eliot that James found a close and acute psychological insight accompanying profound moral judgement. The springs of Christina Light's behaviour bear a remarkable resemblance to some of George Eliot's characters. Christina's badness is firmly placed for us, not as a Hawthornian innate depravity, nor as a native wrongness of moral fibre, nor yet as some ruling passion. She is bad because she is spoiled, hopelessly spoiled – as spoiled as Gwendolen Harleth (in *Daniel Deronda*) or as Rosamond Vincy (in *Middlemarch*). She is the idolized beautiful daughter of aspiring parents who understand well her commodity value. She has seen too much and known too much. She knows among other things that she has been bred to a given end – to marry as well as she can – which is to say, to marry as high above her station as her station is felt to be below her merits. Her cleverness, her charm, and especially her beauty, are the hallmarks of a precious object. Christina's reaction to this expectation of family and society (like that of Gwendolen Harleth) is the cultivation of a worldly cynicism which is addressed not to the denigration of her own value, sufficiently impressed upon her, but instead to the world's claims on her. Like Gwendolen, Christina is not merely wicked. She has some dignity of conscience and tries to escape the role she despises and to act in terms of principle. Gwendolen flies from Grandcourt, and Christina breaks her engagement to Prince Casamassima. To sustain them in these actions both women require external recognition and support, which in each case proves to be unavailable. Both are defeated, not by a hostile world crushing goodness, but by a world that is coolly practical, hard in its pragmatic tests, indifferently finding, and acting on, the internal weaknesses of the characters themselves. A particular weakness for both women is pride.

In the case of Christina, a final surprise is our discovery that her broken engagement, her attempt, however impulsive, at moral integrity, is *not* motivated by a rash love for the tempestuous Roderick Hudson. That affair is simply a flirtation, bred of some real attraction, but an even greater boredom, not too much unlike the affair in *Daniel Deronda* between Gwendolen and Rex Gascoigne. If we are to believe the testimony of Roderick in his last talk with Rowland Mallett, Christina's conduct is motivated by her unspoken and unrequited love for Rowland. When we add to Roderick's testimony all of the other evidence, as James intended us to do, it falls together like a previously known conviction. Christina's frankness with Rowland, her early blunt over-insistence on her dislike for him, as though her worldliness and pride were standing guard over her possible vulnerability (how like Gwendolen Harleth's first reactions to Daniel Deronda!) the recognition by her mother and the Cavaliere that only Rowland has influence with her – all these elements wait only for the connecting link supplied by Roderick's word to Rowland. It explains the last encounter between Rowland and Christina, in which James finds exactly the right note: Christina insists that she '*was* sincere' in breaking her engagement to the Prince, and then tells Rowland she wishes never to see him again. We understand this sharp break because now she is basely committed despite her ineffectual struggle. She has no such wish in the case of Roderick; determined to live as recklessly as she can, she is ready to use Roderick for that end, especially since his own readiness is obvious enough. She feels that her principles as well as her beauty have been sold to the highest bidder, and she can keep only the sincerity of her unspoken love for Rowland. This attempt at reformation – or at least this impulse toward scruple – which Rowland inspires in her, the result of admiration for a good man only indirectly concerned with her, is strongly reminiscent, again, of Gwendolen Harleth's history in her relations with Daniel Deronda. He, like Rowland Mallett, is a finer man than those in her customary circle. Both men share something of the same combination of admiration for noble beauty and disgust at the spectacle of its betrayal by ignoble uses, and of pity for what they sense to be the frustrated moral struggle which Christina and Gwendolen each represents. Deronda is a bigger man than Mallett, and his responses are more generous; Mallett would never have been portrayed quite so sympathetically by George Eliot as he is by James.

It should be obvious that the close resemblance between George Eliot's treatment of the Gwendolen Harleth–Daniel Deronda relationship and James's Christina Light–Rowland Mallett relationship is at least as close as some of the proven or demonstrated Jamesian sources and analogues. I cannot, even so, argue a case for a literal 'source' for *Roderick Hudson*. This novel, in fact, appeared serially at the very time that *Daniel Deronda* was being written; James could not have read it in time to make any difference in the writing of his own first novel. Besides this chronological argument against George Eliot's direct influence, there is also evidence to show that George Eliot was not influenced, after all, by Henry James.[5] Yet the resemblances between Christina Light and Gwendolen Harleth strike me as being as relevant and significant as the more frequently cited resemblances between Gwendolen Harleth and Isabel Archer. I am persuaded that George Eliot asserted a more general, more pervasive influence on James than is ordinarily acknowledged, or than is implied in the argument that one particular novel, *The Portrait of a Lady*, was directly inspired by a single work by George Eliot.[6]

5 Letter to J. Blackwood, 15 December 1875: 'when I am writing, or only thinking of writing, fiction of my own, I cannot risk the reading of other fiction. I was obliged to tell Anthony Trollope so' (J. W. Cross, *Life of George Eliot* (Edinburgh, 1885), III, pp. 239–41). James's novel appeared serially in the *Atlantic* through all of 1875, and was published in book form in 1876.

6 See F. R. Leavis, *The Great Tradition*, pp. 79–125. His argument for such an influence is anticipated in Cornelia P. Kelley's *The Early Development of Henry James* (University of Illinois, 1930).

GEORGE ELIOT AND OTHERS

James wrote a 'Life' of George Eliot, a 'Conversation' on *Daniel Deronda*, and a number of reviews of her novels and poems.[7] When in his first year in Paris he came to resent the indifference of the writers in the Flaubert circle to English and American literature, the ignored author he had most explicitly in mind was George Eliot.[8] Her name appears a number of times in the prefaces to the New York edition. One quotation in particular will indicate the nature, and the depth, of her influence:

I have for example a weakness of sympathy with that constant effort of George Eliot's which plays through Adam Bede and Felix Holt and Tito Melema, through Daniel Deronda and through Lydgate in 'Middlemarch', through Maggie Tulliver, through Romola, through Dorothea Brooke and Gwendolen Harleth; the effort to show their adventures and their history – the author's subject-matter all – as determined by their feelings and the nature of their minds.[9]

Again, in discussing the problems attendant on organizing an 'ado about Isabel Archer' – writing a novel, that is, with a 'mere young lady' as its centre – James argues his case through the example of George Eliot:

Challenge any such problem with any intelligence, and you immediately see how full it is of substance; the wonder being, all the while,

---

7 'Life of George Eliot', first published *Atlantic* (May 1885), reprinted in *Partial Portraits* (1888); '*Daniel Deronda*: A Conversation' in *Atlantic* (December 1876), reprinted in *Partial Portraits*; 'Felix Holt, the Radical', in *The Nation* (August 1866); 'The Legend of Jubal, and other Poems', in *North American Review* (October 1874); 'The Novels of George Eliot', in *Atlantic* (October 1866); 'George Eliot', in *The Nation* (October 1878).

8 *Letters*, I, p. 42. Percy Lubbock comments: 'He found the circle of literature tightly closed to outside influences; it seemed to exclude all culture but its own after a fashion that aroused his opposition; he speaks sarcastically on one occasion of having watched Turgenev and Flaubert seriously discussing Daudet's *Jack*, while he reflected that none of the three had read, or knew English enough to read, *Daniel Deronda*.'

9 Preface to *The Princess Casamassima*, p. xix. The passage is of particular importance because James is discussing a crucial concern of his fiction: a defence of intelligence for awareness, for the use of the centre of consciousness. In this connection, Joan Bennett has pointed out, as an 'embryonic Jamesian device', George Eliot's use of Dr Kenn in *The Mill on the Floss* as a disinterested spectator commenting on the action (*George Eliot*, pp. 127–8).

as we look at the world, how absolutely, how inordinately, the Isabel Archers, and even much smaller female fry, insist on mattering. George Eliot has admirably noted it – 'In these frail vessels is borne onward through the ages the treasure of human affection.' In 'Romeo and Juliet' Juliet has to be important, just as, in 'Adam Bede' and 'The Mill on the Floss' and 'Middlemarch' and 'Daniel Deronda', Hetty Sorrel and Maggie Tulliver and Rosamond Vincy and Gwendolen Harleth have to be; with that much of firm ground, that much of bracing air, at the disposal all the while of their feet and their lungs.[10]

It is worth remembering how frequently James came to use these 'frail vessels' (a phrase which James uses often, even without inverted commas) to carry the burden of his novels: *Washington Square, The Portrait of a Lady, The Bostonians, The Reverberator, The Tragic Muse* (in the Miriam Rooth sections), *The Spoils of Poynton, What Maisie Knew, The Awkward Age, The Wings of the Dove,* and *The Golden Bowl.*

The derivation of *The Portrait of a Lady* is not more important than the general impact of George Eliot on James's whole fictional career, and even this general impact is by no means simply 'derivative'. Despite great differences of method and of sensibility in the two authors, they were doing very similar things at almost exactly the same time, especially in their studies of egotism and pride, of its moral consequences, and of the relation of 'sin' to personality. The complex social and cultural history which gave rise to these common concerns is for a different study from this to determine. Should such a study come to be written, it would have to account for the fact that George Meredith's *The Egoist* (1879), presents still another closely related study. Sir Willoughby Patterne's intensely 'civilized' egoism and his attempt to ensnare Clara Middleton into a loveless marriage stand in interesting relation to George Eliot's Grandcourt and James's Gilbert Osmond.[11] Among these three,

10 Preface to *The Portrait of a Lady*, pp. xiv–xv.
11 Dr Leavis in *The Great Tradition* (p. 12) invites his readers to compare *The Portrait of a Lady* with *The Egoist* as a measure of the superiority of James's novel, without, however, discussing the particular connections between the two. These are primarily in the similarities between Sir Willoughby and Osmond, and in their relationships to the two heroines. Both novels have close affinities to the treatment in *Daniel Deronda* of the Grandcourt – Gwendolen Harleth relationship.

Osmond is unique in that he marries primarily for money; nevertheless, some of the parallels between Sir Willoughby and Osmond are striking. Here is Osmond's defence of his marriage to his unhappy wife:

'I think we should accept the consequences of our actions, and what I value most in life is the honour of a thing!' . . . He spoke in the name of something sacred and precious – the observance of a magnificent form.

Compare this with Sir Willoughby's appeal to Clara's father when she, like Isabel Archer, regrets her promises, though more wisely than Isabel, before rather than after her marriage:

'But I abhor a breach of faith. A broken pledge is hateful to me. I should regard it in myself as a form of suicide. There are principles which civilized men must contend for. Our social fabric is based on them. As my word stands for me, I hold others to theirs. If that is not done, the world is more or less a carnival of counterfeits.'[12]

The context of Osmond's fine little speech makes it resemble Sir Willoughby's more even than these bare quotations suggest, especially in the way a bald hypocrisy becomes manifest in each. Again, compare Osmond's assumed indifference to ambition, which conceals a restless and discontented egotism, with this profession of Sir Willoughby:

'People change, I find; as we increase in years we cease to be the heroes we were! I myself am insensible to change: I do not admit the charge. Except in this, we shall say: personal ambition. I have it no more. And what is it when we have it? Decidedly a confession of inferiority! That is, the desire to be distinguished is an acknowledgement of insufficiency.' (p. 315)

Osmond, we are told, has also changed in this way:

The desire to have something or other to show for his 'parts' – to show somehow or other – had been the dream of his youth; but as the years went on the conditions attached to any marked proof of rarity had affected him more and more as gross and detestable; like

12 G. Meredith, *The Egoist* (London, 1879), p. 419.

the swallowing of mugs of beer to advertise what one could 'stand'.

Or again, compare Isabel's early estimate of Osmond with Mrs Mountstuart's description of Sir Willoughby :

The secret of him is, that he is one of those excessively civilized creatures who aim at perfection . . . (p. 356)

In neither character does this perfection prove to be anything more lofty than the desire for the world's good opinion :

The breath of the world, the world's view of him, was partly his vital breath, his view of himself. The ancestry of the tortured man had bequeathed him this condition of high civilization among their other bequests. (p. 382)

This description of Sir Willoughby may be compared with Isabel's tardy recognition of the disparities between Osmond's professions and his realities :

he pointed out to her so much of the baseness and shabbiness of life, opened her eyes so wide to the stupidity, the depravity, the ignorance of mankind, that she had been properly impressed with the infinite vulgarity of things and of the virtue of keeping one's self unspotted by it. But this base, ignoble world, it appeared, was after all what one was to live for; one was to keep it for ever in one's eye, in order not to enlighten or convert or redeem it, but to extract from it some recognition of one's own superiority. On the one hand it was despicable, but on the other it afforded a standard. Osmond had talked to Isabel about his renunciation, his indifference, the ease with which he dispensed with the usual aids to success . . . She had thought it a grand indifference, an exquisite independence. But indifference was really the last of his qualities; she had never seen any one who thought so much of others.

James differs from Meredith in his avoidance of generalizing theories like 'The Comic Spirit', just as a primary difference from George Eliot is his freedom from philosophic machinery such as Spencerian rationalism. A further difference is that Meredith rather glibly associates the undesirable traits of a character like Willoughby with 'high civilization', whereas

James portrays the villainy of Osmond as compounded by his readiness to exploit decent forms of civilization for his own selfish purposes. This, with other differences, invites comparisons which are invidious for Meredith, who is too easy a target.[13]

'It is difficult to give the air of consistency to vanity and depravity', James wrote in his study of Alphonse Daudet, 'though the portraiture of the vicious side of life would seem, from the pictorial point of view, to offer such attractions.'[14] James was referring not so much to life that is not 'moral' as to life that is 'low' – a distinction consecrated in James's work by the frequent occurrence of the former and the complete absence of the latter. But the relevance is obvious: the Willoughbys, Grandcourts and Osmonds of the world have their pictorial attractions, clearly. Nevertheless, the similarities I have been documenting go beyond this appeal. The attraction of Meredith, George Eliot and James to the theme of egotism is striking; despite their individual differences they have in common a consistent critique of romantic individualism that is, I think, an important aspect of late-nineteenth-century literary history.

My concern is not with the question of sources, then, but with the question of significances. What elements of the literary climate of his time were important to James? I have already discussed one: the elevation of culture and art as moral agency and teacher, as a heightening of life as well as a 'criticism of life' – a structure of belief that in James's time had for many people superseded traditional religious sanctions. The second is the tradition of moral-psychological realism best exemplified in George Eliot (and with certain correspondences in Hawthorne). The intimate marriage of sensibility and morality so important in James is found in the studies of Esther Lyons,[15] of Rosamond Vincy, of Gwendolen Harleth – all those 'frail

13 James did not commit himself in print on *The Egoist*, but was explicit enough about *Lord Ormont and His Aminta* in a letter to Gosse: 'I doubt if any equal quantity of extravagant verbiage, of airs and graces, of phrases and attitudes, of obscurities and alembications, ever started less their subject . . .' (*Letters*, I, p. 224).
14 *Partial Portraits*, p. 197.
15 See also p. 113, below.

vessels' whom James praised in the quotation given earlier. Before George Eliot, the only author who exhibited something like it was Richardson in *Clarissa*. The devoted Austenite will at once object to this statement. I defend it on the ground that Jane Austen represents another tradition still (or the same one further back) which influenced George Eliot certainly and Henry James as well. There is in James a similar ironic sympathy of social observation, a stylized pattern of dialogue that 'places' the social conventions from which it springs. But the characteristic and remarkable lightness of Jane Austen which sees her through even the quasi-tragic episodes of her novels, where the lightness of touch is as of a wise but polite aloofness, is discarded for better or for worse by both George Eliot and James for a fuller register.[16]

If I have dispensed with Jane Austen in so cavalier a fashion, my concern with Richardson is even slighter. Intense as the study of the inner life is in *Clarissa*, its curious emotional voyeurism has no counterpart in James. Neither has the characteristic note of Richardson's morality: stolid, bourgeois, unleavened by any force stronger than the conviction that the rewards of virtue are the same as the ambitions of vice.

I have already discussed the Hawthorne tradition; the excursion from Hawthorne to George Eliot will indicate where, for James, the Hawthorne influence stops. The characteristic genius of Hawthorne – the mark left on him by the allegorizing bent of Spenser and Bunyan – does not find its echo in James. One must be struck by the absence in James of closely schematized symbolism, of surface allegory, or of the explicit moral diagrams which Hawthorne used as the 'iron rod' – as he himself called it – to hold his stories or novels together. Some years ago Quentin Anderson argued that the late novels in particular are allegories based on the philosophical system of Henry James Senior. If this were true it might mark an important parallel to Hawthorne's work. But I think the argument tenuous, and in terms of any recognizable change it makes in the reading of

16 I do not wish to deny that there is a certain darkening of tone in Jane Austen's *Mansfield Park* and in *Persuasion*.

the novels, irrelevant.[17] The particular resemblances sometimes adduced between Hawthorne and James seem to me to be almost always exaggerated, when they are not simply invented. What does resemble Hawthorne in James's work is an intense moral concern and, in the very early stories especially, a reminiscent style. However Hawthorne's scepticism of orthodoxies, of programmes and reforms as agencies of human perfection may have anticipated some of James's attitudes, so too did Matthew Arnold's *Culture and Anarchy* and George Eliot's *Felix Holt*. James and Hawthorne both reacted against the optimistic vision of Emerson seeing all around him virtue, and (what is perhaps less often emphasized) against the gratuitously sinister, morally inconsequent vision of Poe, seeing all around him horrors.

Finally, some of the French realists contemporary with James, notably Flaubert and (by adoption) Turgenev, influenced him in ways primarily technical and formal.[18] To deal with these matters fully would require a larger frame of reference than I am now concerned with. Two related aspects of these influences, however, are worth brief mention: the Flaubertian ideals of 'economy' and 'objectivity'. There are two kinds, if indeed there are not many, of economy which Flaubert represents: the economy of form in terms of the whole – the Aristotelian unity of the work; and second, the economy of the particular, of detail, of the famous *mot juste*. James was dedicated almost from the beginning to the first kind of unity. He insisted that his novels and tales be shaped and formed, that they have strict beginnings and consequent ends, that they comprise, much as a painting on a canvas, a recognizable composition within a limiting frame. The term 'economy'

17 See Quentin Anderson, 'Henry James and the New Jerusalem', *Kenyon Review*, III (1946). But James's sceptical view of his father's system is made clear in a letter to William James (*Letters*, I, p. 112), and there is no evidence of a change of heart. Indeed, *The Princess Casamassima* is diametrically opposed in theme to one large area of his father's thought.

18 *The Notebooks of Henry James*, ed. F. O. Matthiessen and Kenneth B. Murdock (New York, 1947), indicate the specific influence of Daudet on two occasions: of *Numa Roumestan* on 'The Liar', and of *L'Evangeliste* on *The Bostonians* – at least as starting points. The fullest case for Turgenev's influences will be found in O. Cargill's *The Novels of Henry James* (New York, 1961).

appears frequently in the prefaces to the New York edition, almost always in this first sense. He works, however, very far from Flaubert's model of *le mot juste*, especially in the later fiction. I do not mean that he is careless in diction, or indifferent to style, but that his style is expansive rather than lean. Three words, he often suggests, are richer than one, and these three might be helped by modification, by qualification. He moves in the direction of amplitude, of the additive, the incremental. He needs always to discriminate, to qualify, and each discrimination may call others to mind, each of which takes more words, more phrases and dependent clauses. 'Nothing for you will ever be the same as anything else', Maria Gostrey says to Lambert Strether in *The Ambassadors*. This is as cogent a description of the novelist as of his typical characters. The poetic imagination may synthesize, as Coleridge affirms, but the moral imagination differentiates. And the vocabulary of differentiation must be large.

The ideal of objectivity in the Flaubert–Turgenev school certainly influenced James. He quotes with obvious approval Taine's comment, 'that Turgenieff so perfectly cut the umbilical cord that bound the novel to himself';[19] and he attempted the same detachment in his own novels. The ideal of objectivity led him repeatedly to the use of a recording voice within the fictions, to a narrator or centre of consciousness, allowing the author a large degree of anonymity. The ideal of the independent work, separated completely from any voice outside its own artistic frame, is common to a large body of modern fiction, thanks largely to James, who took what he found in Flaubert and extended it remarkably. In contrast, he disapproved of such practises as Trollope's occasional intrusions to assure his readers that his fiction is heading for a happy ending or, worse, to suggest two different endings for the same novel. He thought such devices reduced the novel to a kind of mere entertainment, a game relating the reader to a disporting author instead of to the novel's represented world. The absence of the author's voice or of a control recognizably separate from the fiction itself – of the 'mere muffled majesty' of omniscient authorship

19 *Notebooks*, p. 101.

– is a vital element of James's technique. In practice it is something less absolute than the famous pronouncement of Joyce's Stephen Dedalus: 'The artist, like the God of the creation, remains within or behind or beyond or above his handiwork, invisible, refined out of existence, indifferent, paring his finger-nails',[20] which smacks more of Joyce's own arrogance than of James. But it is in the same tradition.

'RODERICK HUDSON' as 'first novel'

These considerations may appear to have taken us far from the occasion which gave rise to them, James's first novel, *Roderick Hudson*. But every aspect of James's background can be found working in this novel, as well as in the others, colouring and conditioning what we come to recognize as the Jamesian *world*. For a novelist presumed to be juggling influences from so diverse a group as Hawthorne, George Eliot, Arnold, and Turgenev, *Roderick Hudson* is a surprisingly good novel. It has been fashionable to write it off; Ford Madox Hueffer, whose own predilections convinced him that Flaubert alone launched James – as well as all that is most valuable in modern fiction – dismissed all the early works except 'A Passionate Pilgrim'. As recently as 1950, F. W. Dupee wrote:

Lively though it was for a first performance, *Roderick Hudson* is not much more than a museum-piece to the present-day reader, possessing some very good points but being dead in the center.

This somewhat harsh judgement stems perhaps from a misconception of what the novel is about:

an object lesson in the danger of converting an artistic genius into a mere flair for adventurous living.[21]

But isn't the case more exactly that the novel is a study of the impact of Europe on the culture and conduct of a young artist whose possibilities of development in both domains have

---

20 Joyce's career suggests that this tradition of 'objectivity' has more to do with the tendency to establish Art as a substitute for religion than has been recognized. Art must become as absolute and impersonal as godhead.

21 F. W. Dupee, *Henry James* (New York, 1951), p. 87.

D

hitherto been unrealized? When he becomes Roderick's patron, Rowland Mallett sees a scarcely realized promise growing into a major talent. At the same time, ironically, he must watch an equally latent irresponsibility develop into open recklessness and an abandonment of emotion which leads to tragedy. Both the genius and the recklessness are present as possibilities in Roderick from the first. There are ominous signs even before the characters plunge into the heady atmosphere of Rome: Roderick's impulsive destruction of the statue of his employer, his constant attendance on Rowland's widowed cousin Cecilia, his sudden betrothal to Mary Garland in the hope that it will 'keep him safe' from his acknowledged weakness for beautiful women. 'The mere flair for adventurous living' is no more a function of Europe alone than is the flowering, romantically brief and spectacular, of his genius. The chief objection to Dupee's formulation is to the implication that Roderick would have been better off had he stayed at home and developed his genius there – a conviction held in the novel mainly by Roderick's mother. But the very condition, the *donnée*, of the story, is that this is impossible. If Roderick stays at home he continues to work for Mr Striker, the benevolent Philistine who describes Roderick's sculpture as a talent for the 'light ornamental', and who worries about the practice of working with live models.[22] What will happen to his emerging but scarcely recognized talent if he stays in Northampton is at best problematic. So, for that matter, is the development of his irresponsibility, even in Northampton where (Roderick's mother argues) fewer opportunities for abandonment present themselves.

Europe holds two possibilities for Roderick which are essentially the same possibilities that European civilization will always provide for James's American protagonists. Europe at its best means culture and the liberated sensibility, sweetness and light. At its worst, Europe offers the corruption and licence which stems from the misappropriation of these ideals. James's Americans may succumb to these evils, or be victimized by them because of their own weaknesses mainly (like Roderick

22 Hawthorne writing in *The Marble Faun* of the art colony in Rome and its young American apprentices disapproved strongly of undraped statues.

Hudson), or because of the villainy of others (like Milly Theale) or, more convincingly, because of subtle combinations of both (like Isabel Archer). They may resist the evils altogether, of course, and emerge the finer for the experience, like Mary Garland and Rowland Mallett, or like Ralph Touchett and Lambert Strether. The Roderick Hudson of 1876 is first cousin to the Chad Newsome of 1903.[23] This basic pattern with its variations from novel to novel forms the mainstream of James's international stories. Two worlds force a moral choice which is determined by character and sensibility. Echoing George Eliot's pronouncement, 'Character is fate', Rowland Mallett tells Hudson that 'The power to choose *is* destiny.'

There is a romantic note in *Roderick Hudson* mainly absent in James's later studies of artists. The young Roderick, artistic genius that he is, is tempestuous, headstrong, dashing, impulsive. His temperament authenticates his claim to be an artist, even more than his being an artist 'explains' his volatility. Later, James finds such proof far less compelling, and in his more mature studies an artist is a man who paints, a writer a man who writes. The romantic note is heightened considerably in the portrayal of Roderick's development by a weakness which James himself recognized in his preface to the New York edition. He does not allow enough time for Roderick's disintegration. As a result, Roderick's decline is melodramatic – which

23 *Roderick Hudson* is filled with anticipations of James's later novels. Hudson's relations with Mallett, for instance, anticipate Chad Newsome's to Strether. Wanting to be free of Mary Garland, Hudson doesn't worry over terms and conditions, but allows Mallett to do so. 'Do what you can, my dear man, by all means', Roderick says. 'He stood there an instant limpidly, beautifully passive – the image of some noble and incurable young spendthrift winding up a slightly sordid interview with his disagreeably lucid but quite trusty man of business.' It is Mallett who feels desperate, not Hudson. Anticipating the symbolism of Mme de Vionnet's home and its 'true' culture, Mallett says of the beauties of Rome: 'they're the result of an immemorial, a complex, and accumulated civilization'. The contrasting symbolism of Maria Gostrey's home is similarly foreshadowed: 'Rome is the natural home of those spirits . . . with a deep relish for the element of accumulation in the human picture.' Ralph Touchett's moving statement to Isabel, that she has been 'ground in the mill of the conventional' has an earlier variation in Christina Light's 'Fancy feeling one's self ground in the mill of a third-rate talent!' Christina Light says of Mary Garland, 'She looks magnificent when she glares – like a Medusa crowned not with snakes but with a tremor of dove's wings.'

means, among other things, that it is unbelievable. Roderick's rise and fall take place in about two years. His rise is amply demonstrated by the two magnificent statues of Adam and Eve which he sculpts during his first year in Rome. It seems to me unlikely that a sculptor should despair so completely in the face of a beginning better even than the one facetiously promised by Rowland before he takes Roderick to Rome: 'A masterpiece a year . . . for the next quarter of a century.'

Even before Roderick's breakdown, his reckless impulses have shown themselves to be dangerous. His summer is spent in gambling and, presumably, flirting. Yet afterwards he manages to produce the statue called 'A Lady Listening' and, later, the bust of Christina Light. These do not meet altogether with his approval nor with that of his patron, and are followed by a 'dry' period of some months. But surely it is an exaggeration of the powers of genius to predicate imminent disaster on the basis of such a performance.

The skyrocket ascent, the meteoric drop: these are romantic and melodramatic. Roderick is both too good and too bad, and he is both much too fast. The poles are given early in the novel; we are quite prepared to accept his genius and his instability. Given a greater span of years both for his success and for his decline, the history of Roderick would not seem so strained. Even the dire fall from the Alps would be more acceptable did it not follow so soon after the rise from the pastoral innocence of Northampton.[24]

With a greater allowance of time, James might have avoided an irony which seems to me outside his intention. The contrast between the Northampton values and those of European culture is a double one, relating both to Roderick's art and to his character. Rowland, who has spent much time in Europe happily and usefully, begins by anticipating the beneficent effect on Roderick's art and (as he has every right to do) ignoring its

24 The pastoral associations of Northampton, the sheltered innocence of Roderick there, his great thirst for knowledge, and the statues of Adam and Eve, followed by the rapid disintegration of Roderick in the great world of Rome for which his innocence leaves him unprepared, and his fall – all these invite reading in terms of the general argument proposed by R. W. B. Lewis in *The American Adam* (Chicago, 1955).

possible effect on his conduct. Under the liberating influences of Europe, his art breaks from its old repressions and flourishes under new inspirations. But so too does his conduct, though with different effect. Unfortunately, there is from the first an excessively charged apprehension for Roderick's emotional welfare which his mother in particular makes apparent. Later, Rowland and Mary Garland fail to disguise a similar apprehension – one that builds up too strongly and too fast. This anticipation of catastrophe becomes itself a contributing cause for Roderick's disintegration. He has not only his own temptations and fears to contend with, but the dreadful, gasping, brooding fears of Mrs Hudson, the scrupulous hesitancies of Rowland, and the quiet but obvious sufferings of Mary Garland. All of these must contribute substantially to his own conviction that he is ruined. The irony in the spectacle of well-intentioned observers pushing to realization exactly what they are in agony to avoid might well have been turned to better thematic uses, but it remains a pathos outside the novel's manifest intentions. This element of complication, the result apparently of the writing process itself rather than of preconceived design, is not altogether without its own appeal. It makes the characterization of Mrs Hudson richer and more organic to the story's unfolding, and adds a useful tension to Roderick's relationships with his mother, with Mary Garland and with Rowland Mallett.

My final criticism of *Roderick Hudson* is with the figure of Rowland Mallett, James's centre of consciousness throughout the novel. Useful as he is for this purpose, and for advancing Roderick's career, his own progress through the story is illuminated by a light that is never very clear. T. S. Eliot wrote of James's portrayal of Rowland:

He too much identifies himself with Rowland, does not see through the solemnity he has created in that character, commits the cardinal sin of failing to 'detect' one of his own characters.[25]

25 T. S. Eliot, 'Henry James', *The Little Review* (August 1918), p. 37. Eliot's criticism would apply to a number of James's later centres of consciousness, especially of some of the short novels and tales. The criticism, incidentally, fits exactly Hawthorne's Myles Coverdale in *The Blithedale Romance*, for essentially similar reasons.

The best ground for accepting Eliot's criticism lies mainly, I think, on the measure of belief one is able to afford Rowland's falling in love with Mary Garland. It is for one thing terribly rapid – faster even than Roderick's parabolic rise and fall – and even more thinly represented. It seems less real in its own terms than useful in explaining Rowland's curious indifference (aside from 'connoisseurship') to Christina Light, and in accounting for his patient dedication to Roderick past a point otherwise credible. While his falling in love with Mary may be useful to the plot in these ways, the reader needs first to believe in the thing itself. The issue is not whether we believe in love-at-first-sight, but whether we can believe Rowland susceptible to it. Nothing in his characterization convinces me that he is at all vulnerable in this way. However romantic its beginning, James fails throughout the novel to make me feel enough the reality of this passion. Rowland's commitment seems all the more suspect in that it is prepared for too overtly; the tremendous appeal Mary is said to have for him even before they have spoken to each other is a false note. Once the appeal is made, however, James expects us to accept Rowland as a dedicated martyr to love for the rest of the book. A character's disposition to suffer for a cause only imperfectly felt by the reader recurs as a disturbing Jamesian failure. In later James, the cause may be as tenuous, but the suffering is usually more convincing because the mastery is firmer than it has yet become in *Roderick Hudson*. And while even the familiar Jamesian note of renunciation is touched on here, it is not insisted upon. In the end, Rowland is seen courting Mary Garland after Roderick's death, and while she seems rather sternly discouraging, there presumably is at least a hope for him in that future which follows the last pages of a novel.

Although *Roderick Hudson* is more interesting than as a work of apprenticeship, James is to a large degree still searching for his subject matter. The fact that the elements I have spoken of as important to James are not always perfectly obvious, or perfectly fused, in the novel is really less surprising than that they are present at all. This is not to suggest that James's formulations are static throughout his work, but it is worth mentioning now that neither do they suffer any radical change. That they do change, and do emerge more clearly in some works than in others, and with significant differences in impact, is the burden of this study.

On its own terms *Roderick Hudson* is still worth reading. It has a further interest because of its exploration of much that will remain significant throughout James's career. James's Northampton, despite his regret (in the preface to the New York edition) at having named it without rendering it more solidly, comes to us as a wonderfully done sketch. If it is not of a physically particular part of New England – as Sarah Orne Jewett or other 'local colourists' might have rendered it – it is a recognizable place in emotional and moral geography that continues, without major change, to have both real and symbolic importance in James's work.

Christina Light anticipates a long line of Jamesian characters: Madame Merle, Kate Croy, Charlotte Stant, all of whom appear in the major international novels. All but Kate Croy are deracinated Americans who have left behind them the moral imperatives of the American–Hebraic tradition and have assumed the elegant façade of European–Hellenic culture behind which they pursue their own self-serving goals. In contrast we are given the more salutary effects of Europe on Mary Garland. Her movement toward culture does *not* involve a loss of moral integrity, and her attempt at a higher integration forms (together with these same effects on Rowland Mallett) James's first major testimony to the positive values of Europe. As represented by Roderick alone, these values might seem altogether illusory.

One small scene in particular brings before us the peculiar Jamesian tension of the American coming to terms with Europe. Mary and Rowland have been speaking of the beauty of the Roman world during their last evening at the Villa Pandolfi:

'It seems to you very strange, I suppose,' Rowland presently said, 'that there should have to be anxiety and pain in such a world as this.'

'I used to think,' she answered, 'that if trouble came to me I should bear it like a stoic. But that was at home, where things don't speak to us of enjoyment as they do here . . . Beauty . . . penetrates to one's soul and lodges there and keeps saying that man wasn't made, as we think at home, to struggle so much and miss so much, but to ask of life . . . some beauty and some charm. This place has destroyed any scrap of consistency that I ever possessed, but even if I must say something sinful I love it!'

'If it's sinful, I absolve you – in so far as I have the power. We shouldn't be able to enjoy, I suppose, unless we could suffer . . . Yet we must take these things as much as possible in turn.'

This interplay of Hebraism and Hellenism, of the appeals of strictness of conscience and spontaneity of consciousness, the balancing of stoicism and the enjoyment of beauty,[26] is of course the very essence of James's international theme. How different characters make their way among these terms is just what the international novels are about, but the terms themselves remain fairly consistent.

There is a fine characterization in Mrs Hudson, a characterization rich in irony, and yet softened by both pity and admiration. She is, in her way, a preparation for the richer study of Miss Birdseye in *The Bostonians*, for despite her inanities of reform Miss Birdseye is much the same kind of person. Both are fine pictures of the New England matron who possesses a brimming charge of moral energy which is stronger than her physical or intellectual capacities, and larger than the occasions which call it into play. The progress of Mrs Hudson's tremulous, easily fluttered emotions from early doubt and concern, to pride in her son and gratitude to his benefactor, and then to alarm and dismay when Roderick seems really in danger, is all acutely seen and movingly rendered, even if one of its effects, as I have suggested, is to help push Roderick over the edge.

In comparison with *The Europeans*, written not long afterward, it seems fairly obvious that James had not yet seen all the possibilities in the international subject. *The Europeans*, a brilliant if small novel, is a significant signpost leading to still greater achievement in *The Portrait of a Lady*. In *Roderick Hudson*, the crucial contrast is between Americans in their responses to Europe. No major character in the novel is unequi-

26 Later in James it is most often the very commitment to culture that will justify stoicism.

vocally European. This is not surprising when we remember how recently James himself had come to live in Europe. The American contrasts effected in the novel have a greater richness than paraphrase has suggested. Roderick, weak in the moral fibre which ideally defines the New England character, meets Europe head on and is destroyed. Rowland and Mary Garland survive and flourish. She has the moral strength to resist the evil, and the imagination and intelligence to absorb the beauty, which Europe represents. Her sensibility is expanded and fulfilled by her experience, for she maintains her moral integrity at the same time that she gains an aesthetic one. The two together constitute what James believes to be true culture. And this is the general goal – however simplified in formulation – to which all of James's sympathetically seen Americans will aspire.

Mary Garland's development may be said to parallel Rowland's, while Christina Light's has close affinities with Roderick's. If it can be argued on Christina's behalf that she has not been given the chance to acquire the New England virtues – she is, after all, the deracinated daughter of an expatriate American lady who has managed to lose the better qualities of both countries – this does not cancel the argument that without them or their equivalent she is lost.

James smiles at his New England, but takes it even more seriously than he is apt to later on, for in *Roderick Hudson* he is still closer to it than he supposes. When later he achieves a more sufficient detachment, he will still never betray it, never depict it as without value or without its own special dry, fine integrity. But he will see it from further away, as from that point of vantage from which we may smile at the simplifications of childhood without ever sacrificing the memory of its essential truths.

4

The sacred quest: The Portrait of a Lady

THE STORY

The question inevitably asked about *The Portrait of a Lady* is this: why does Isabel Archer return to Italy at the end of the novel – to an unhappy marriage, an evil husband, an ambiguous, uncathartic resolution of her history? The question has its dangers, inviting as it does the pseudo-psychological extension of character outside the fiction which marks a large body of criticism. Nevertheless, the question can be a useful one, if only as a lever with which the weight of the entire novel can be raised for examination. Isabel Archer's return to Italy marks what, in the *Notebooks*, James calls the 'climax and termination of the story'.[1] The story, James tells us, developed from an initial *donnée* not of a plot or an action, but of a figure, 'the sense of a single character, the character and aspect of a particular engaging young woman, to which all the usual elements of a "subject", certainly of a setting, were to need to be superadded'.[2]

The story that James devised is, briefly, that this young woman should be rescued from a prosaic American setting, and from a forthright and impatient American suitor, and carried to England through the unexpected, miraculous, archetypally fairy-tale intervention of an unknown but fabled aunt of great wealth. Mrs Touchett brings Isabel Archer to Gardencourt, the beautiful country house where her expatriate but loyally American husband lives with their invalid son, Ralph. Mrs Touchett herself prefers, for magnificently eccentric reasons,

1 *Notebooks*, p. 18.
2 Preface to *The Portrait of a Lady*, p. vii.

90

her own palace in Florence for regular habitation. Two more strokes of the fairy wand assist Isabel's destiny here. She is proposed to by a personage, an authentic nobleman, Lord Warburton, and she is left a handsome fortune on the death of her uncle. She rejects Lord Warburton, is given another opportunity to put off her American suitor, Caspar Goodwood, and sets off to see Europe. At Gardencourt she has met Mrs Touchett's friend, Madame Merle, and this splendid woman brings Isabel into relation with Gilbert Osmond, an expatriate American living in Florence with his young daughter, Pansy. Isabel decides to marry Osmond, despite the objections of Ralph Touchett and of his mother. Osmond is an impoverished but highly cultivated gentleman who – to pursue the fairy-tale analogy one last time – represents for Isabel the handsome but impoverished Prince, the exquisite knight suffering the eclipse of fortune usual in such cases.

The marriage is a bad one. Osmond proves to be narrow and conventional, affecting an indifference to the world whose esteem he treasures above all else. Osmond's daughter Pansy is in love with Edward Rosier, a dilettantish expatriate American, fond of auctions, of enamels, of 'French things', and of Pansy, as perfect a *jeune fille* as any connoisseur might come upon. Osmond is unimpressed with Rosier, who is not rich or important enough, and prefers Lord Warburton, who has seen much of Pansy during a stay in Rome. Osmond asks Isabel to encourage this match. But she becomes convinced that Lord Warburton is still in love with her, and that his attentions to Pansy are – unconsciously but unmistakably – a pretext for his desire to remain close to Isabel. She discourages Lord Warburton, provoking Osmond's anger and, unexpectedly, Madame Merle's.

Ralph Touchett, feeling himself near death, determines to return to Gardencourt from his extended stay in Rome with Warburton. Isabel sends him off under the protection of Goodwood, who has come to Europe once again, and for the moment she is safe. She is free of Warburton, who leaves when he sees that he can gain nothing by staying on; of Goodwood, whose presence is embarrassing to her because she fears she has acted wrongly toward him; of Ralph Touchett, whom Osmond strongly dislikes, not so much for any reason as from an antipathy of natures. Her peace does not last long, however, for Ralph sends for her from Gardencourt, where he lies dying. She goes, but not before meeting the crisis of her marriage. Osmond forbids her to go on grounds of propriety. She learns, immediately afterward, that Madame Merle has been Osmond's mistress for many years and is Pansy's mother.

At Gardencourt Isabel confesses her unhappiness to Ralph, to whom earlier she had vowed silence should she be wrong about Osmond. He invokes her history with these words:

'You wanted to look at life for yourself – but you were not allowed; you were punished for your wish. You were ground in the very mill of the conventional!'

James's notes on the novel-in-progress confirm Ralph's role as auctorial commentator:

The idea of the whole thing is that the poor girl, who has dreamed of freedom and nobleness, who has done, as she believes, a generous, natural, clear-sighted thing, finds herself in reality ground in the very mill of the conventional.[3]

The repeated phrase 'the mill of the conventional' stresses also the nature of Isabel's nemesis, which is central to the novel's theme.

A further motive for Isabel's journey to Gardencourt, beyond her genuine love and concern for Ralph, is given her by Madame Merle's disclosure that it was really Ralph who made Isabel wealthy by persuading his father to give her a large portion of the inheritance intended for himself. Madame Merle's motivation for this disclosure is doubtless the desire to shift blame subtly from herself to Ralph as the instrument of Isabel's marriage, sensing as she does that Isabel now knows of her history with Osmond, and knowing too (as we know) that Osmond would never have married Isabel had she not been wealthy. It is with this tragic irony that Isabel takes leave of Ralph at

3 *Notebooks*, p. 15.

Gardencourt, that Ralph takes leave of the world. It is difficult to conceive a sense of culmination or of climax which this scene does not fulfil; what comes after it is anti-climactic, and to a certain degree false.

Warburton now appears at Gardencourt, still in love with Isabel. And then Goodwood also appears, with the sense of inevitability which these hovering presences, these lost alternatives, have assumed. Goodwood tries to persuade Isabel that she must leave Osmond and marry him. The distance between Osmond's courtship and the natural persuasion of Goodwood is registered all too well in this scene:

He glared at her a moment through the dusk, and the next instant she felt his arms about her and his lips on her own lips. His kiss was like white lightning, a flash that spread, and spread again, and stayed; and it was extraordinarily as if, while she took it, she felt each thing in his hard manhood that had least pleased her, each aggressive fact of his face, his figure, his presence, justified of its intense identity and made one with this act of possession. So had she heard of those wrecked and under water following a train of images before they sink. But when darkness returned she was free. She never looked about her; she only darted from the spot. There were lights in the windows of the house; they shone far across the lawn. In an extraordinarily short time – for the distance was considerable – she had moved through the darkness (for she saw nothing) and reached the door. Here only she paused. She looked all about her; she listened a little; then she put her hand on the latch. She had not known where to turn; but she knew now. There was a very straight path.[4]

4 Just a little earlier in this scene, Goodwood has said, 'The world's all before us – and the world's very big. I know something about that.' The Miltonic echo is even stronger in the first edition, where Goodwood says, 'The world is all before us – and the world is very large.' The speculative reader may brood about the last lines of *Paradise Lost*:

> They, looking back, all the eastern side beheld
> Of Paradise, so late their happy seat,
> Waved over by that flaming brand; the gate
> With dreadful faces thronged and fiery arms.
> Some natural tears they dropped, but wiped them soon;
> The world was all before them, where to choose
> Their place of rest, and Providence their guide.
> They, hand in hand, with wandering steps and slow,
> Through Eden took their solitary way.

Two days later Caspar Goodwood learns that Isabel has returned to Italy.

The scene is really astonishing. It is the first directly physical encounter in the novel and its terms seem wrenched from some other universe of discourse. Some of the images are unaccounted for and strange. Why, when Goodwood kisses her, should she think of catastrophe, of the experience of drowning? Why is her departure accomplished in 'an extraordinarily short time'? Why, for that matter, is the word 'extraordinarily' – a word not at all common in the novel – used twice in so short a passage?

The answers, I think, all suggest some loss of credibility in this scene. James wants us to feel Isabel's realization of Goodwood's power and feel it with some impact. This is difficult if for no other reason than that James has kept poor Goodwood hovering for some hundreds of pages. His appeal is physical only, limited in a way that will be made clear later in this chapter. But the intensity of Goodwood's passion is a value that James wants here very much, and he attempts it too much with rhetoric. There is a justification in theme for this final confrontation, but not enough in the surface, dramatic level of *story*. The thematic explanation, it seems to me, is that James is committed to dramatic renunciations in the grand stoical manner. Isabel must act at the end of the novel not only in the lurid light cast by Osmond's loathsomeness, but in the 'white lightning' of Goodwood's suddenly inspired appeal.

In the first edition, James had Isabel's friend, the comic American journalist Henrietta Stackpole, break the news of Isabel's departure for Rome to Goodwood. This was followed by these words, the last in the novel:

'Look here, Mr. Goodwood,' she said; 'just you wait!' On which he looked up at her.

As if to forestall any suggestion of a future stemming from these words, as a number of readers appear to have taken them, James added a new last paragraph to the New York edition:

On which he looked up at her – but only to guess, from her face, with a revulsion, that she simply meant he was young. She stood shining at him with that cheap comfort, and it added, on the spot, thirty years to his life. She walked him away with her, however, as if she had given him now the key to patience.

It is a distinguishing note, deeper than the present case, that Dickens should, under pressure, have changed his proposed ending for *Great Expectations* (a title, incidentally, that would suit James's novel perfectly) from the tragic to a promise of future happiness, while James should change his only to reinforce the tragic note.

It seems desirable to have this much of the novel's structure, however skeletal, in view before looking at it more closely. Seeing it first in this way makes more manifest the problem (the novel's theme) and the pattern (the novel's structure) of *choice*, which is largely the burden of *The Portrait of a Lady*. For never before in James, and rarely again, does the world present itself as on a tray for a person's seeing and judging, testing and *choosing*.[5] The initiating impulse of the story is the image of 'a young woman affronting her destiny'; the developing form provides a spectacle of alternatives so wide, of choices so handsome, as to make the reader fear for Isabel almost from the start. There is in fact a certain amount of foreshadowing almost from the beginning of the novel :

On the whole, reflectively, she was in no uncertainty about the things that were wrong. She had no love of their look, but when she fixed them hard she recognized them. It was wrong to be mean, to be jealous, to be false, to be cruel; she had seen very little of the evil of the world, but she had seen women who lied and who tried to hurt each other. Seeing such things had quickened her high spirit; it seemed indecent not to scorn them. Of course the danger of a high spirit was the danger of inconsistency – the danger of keeping up the flag after the place has surrendered; a sort of behaviour so crooked as to be almost a dishonour to the flag.

The qualities which Isabel, still a youthfully intrepid theorist

5 Choice is rather more limited even in *The Wings of the Dove* which, however different, has a good deal in common with this novel.

about life, recognizes so clearly to be wrong here – 'to be mean, to be jealous, to be false, to be cruel' – prove to be a fairly accurate description of the man she is all innocently to marry. There is a nice irony in her thinking she recognizes 'women who lied and who tried to hurt each other', while the last sentence of this quotation foreshadows a movement in the novel that will not be altogether illuminated except by the whole history of Isabel's relationships. The passage I have been quoting from the early pages of the novel continues:

But Isabel, who knew little of the sorts of artillery to which young women are exposed, flattered herself that such contradictions would never be noted in her own conduct.

That sentence, besides contributing to our sense of Isabel's engagingly conceited innocence, may be read as a reference, albeit an ambiguous one, to Isabel's decision at the end of the novel to uphold the honour of her marriage. Does the 'danger of keeping up the flag after the place has surrendered' take on additional resonance in anticipating Isabel's candid confession of her unhappiness to Ralph, despite her earlier, proud promise to keep silence?

There is still more in this early passage of special interest to us:

Her life should always be in harmony with the most pleasing impression she should produce; she would be what she appeared, and she would appear what she was. Sometimes she went so far as to wish that she might find herself some day in a difficult position, so that she should have the pleasure of being as heroic as the occasion demanded.

That may be taken as a direct foreshadowing of Isabel's return to Italy, and of an almost classically stated *hubris*, even though some have argued with the particular heroism and the particular occasion in which Isabel finds her 'pleasure'.

Even before this long passage, however, there has been some foreshadowing in a significant discussion with Ralph about the ghost at Gardencourt, which he tells her 'has never been seen by a young, happy, innocent person like you. You must have suffered first, have suffered greatly, have gained some miserable knowledge. In that way your eyes are opened to it.' . . .

'I told you just now I'm very fond of knowledge,' Isabel answered.

'Yes, of happy knowledge – of pleasant knowledge. But you haven't suffered, and you're not made to suffer. I hope you'll never see the ghost!'

. . . Charming as he found her, she had struck him as rather presumptuous – indeed it was a part of her charm; and he wondered what she would say. 'I'm not afraid, you know,' she said: which seemed quite presumptuous enough.

'You're not afraid of suffering?'

'Yes, I'm afraid of suffering. But I'm not afraid of ghosts. And I think people suffer too easily,' she said.

'I don't believe *you* do,' said Ralph, looking at her with his hands in his pockets.

'I don't think that's a fault,' she answered. 'It's not absolutely necessary to suffer; we were not made for that.'[6]

At the end of this early, and portentous, dialogue, Ralph tells her that 'The great point's to be as happy as possible.' She assures him, rather too smugly, that 'that's what I came to Europe for, to be as happy as possible'.

Despite her ready allowance for the possibility of suffering, despite her romantic desire to be in a 'difficult' position demanding heroism, she has the youthful, strong, blinkered self-assurance that is a private conviction of immunity to suffering, of just that *hubris* that must inevitably call down the fates. She has not the restless egotism of the hedonist, nor of the spoilt woman-child awaiting a career-marriage,[7] nor of the pseudo-intellectual (in contrast with the sublimely convinced Henrietta Stackpole), nor yet of the studied aristocrat (as opposed to Mrs Touchett, or to Gilbert Osmond). She *is* 'liable to the sin of self-

6 Ralph echoes this feeling at the end of the novel: 'I don't believe that such a generous mistake as yours can hurt you for more than a little.' This must be taken not as an augury of future happiness, but as an index of Isabel's growth. Ralph cannot bear to die without trying to find first some hope, some possibility of amelioration, for Isabel. She herself has put away such illusions.

7 Both are cardinal points of difference from George Eliot's Gwendolen Harleth (in *Daniel Deronda*), despite the often cogent arguments of F. R. Leavis. See also pp. 70–2.

esteem'; she 'often surveyed with complacency the field of her own nature, she was in the habit of taking for granted, on scanty evidence, that she was right; she treated herself to occasions of homage'. This young woman whose idea it was that 'people were right when they treated her as if she were rather superior' has undeniably attractive qualities, but they have been made to shine more brightly by the surrounding foil of her parochial background.

While she is 'no daughter of the Puritans', as James says with somewhat ambiguous consistency, she has a strong ethical bias. Like Olive Chancellor in *The Bostonians*, if with considerably less intensity, she is forever seeking out her 'duty'. Isabel desires happiness, but she must first be *right*; indeed, she cannot see the one as existing separately from the other. Her superiority is the consequence of intelligence ministering to morals, of the quality which at its best we call moral exaltation and, at its worst, self-righteousness, the quality which stems from the desire always to be *right* – less intellectually than morally right. Those things she so likes to be praised for – her intelligence, her grace, her wit, her perception – are for her finally all instruments of judgement, as judgement is of duty. So that early in the novel there is a rather satirical scene in which we see Isabel, still but newly arrived, compelled to 'judge' England and to contrast it judiciously with America. To discriminate is a duty imposed by her new experience. She has something like a sense of vocation, and her sudden unexpected fortune only increases this sense. Her wealth is a call, not to pleasure, but to duty – or, more precisely, to both, since her highest pleasure lies in seeing her highest duty. She has by nature of her character and of her milieu been called; she can only wait, and hope, to be chosen.

It is in this light that we must see the working out of Isabel's destiny, for it is the light that will determine her *choice*.[8]

8 An ostensibly innocent passage early in the novel is worth calling attention to as one of many which stresses this motif of choice at the same time that it subtly foreshadows subsequent action. 'You're too fond of your own ways,' says Mrs Touchett in consequence of Isabel's having ignored, innocently, a European convention of propriety. Isabel answers, 'Yes, I think I'm very fond of them. But I always want to know the things one shouldn't do.' 'So as to do them?' asks Mrs Touchett. 'So as to choose,' says Isabel.

THE NATURE OF CHOICE

Ralph Touchett tells his father that he wants to make Isabel Archer wealthy in order to see what she will do with herself. She wants, we know, to *see*. But Ralph knows that she must do more than that; even when he first asks his mother about his as yet unseen cousin he presses her for her ideas:

'All this time,' he said, 'you've not told me what you intend to do with her.'

To which his mother answers:

'Do with her? You talk as if she were a yard of calico. I shall do absolutely nothing with her, and she herself will do everything she chooses. She gave me notice of that.'

Ralph admires Isabel's independence of spirit; he wants her to have another kind of independence as well, so that her spirit might realize itself. Beyond the seeing, she must do something. Fairly early in the novel it becomes obvious enough that she will marry, despite (or perhaps because of) all her protestations, and we feel that her marriage will be a choice of central significance. Her rejection of both Goodwood and Warburton only emphasizes this feeling, and makes us wonder what exactly she is looking for.

What she is looking for, I suggest, is some fulfilment of her desire for, her search for, a high civilization. Her demands for its realization are somewhat romantic, and certainly hard, as hard as James's own must have been in 1880–1 when he wrote this novel in those still early years of his discovery of Europe. We may hesitate to read as self-portraiture Isabel's 'combination of the delicate, desultory, flame-like spirit and the eager and personal creature of conditions', even of an author who was still under the spell of Walter Pater. But she shares, with many of James's characters, the Pater-like hunger for experience, and the description just quoted is surely James's version of burning with a hard, gem-like flame. So too, Isabel's 'vocation', her search for an ideal civilization or culture, exemplifies the Ruskin–Pater–Arnold sanctification of Culture as – depending on individual emphasis – the vessel of the higher truth, the great exalter of the human spirit, the study of perfection in art and in conduct.[9] In any case, she will fall short of her vague, beautiful ideal, and take what is left.

She chooses, first of all, Europe – as James did. He will suggest with every resource but direct statement the degree to which Isabel feels the 'offices' of the old house at Albany, New York, where her story begins, an impossible ground for the free play of intelligence and imagination. The implied contrast between Albany and Gardencourt, to go no further than that, is a bold enough statement in its own right:

Her uncle's house seemed a picture made real; no refinement of the agreeable was lost upon Isabel; the rich perfection of Gardencourt at once revealed a world and gratified a need. The large, low rooms . . . the deep embrasures and curious casements, the quiet light on dark, polished panels, the deep greenness outside, that seemed always peeping in, the sense of well-ordered privacy in the centre of a 'property' – a place where . . . the tread was muffled by the earth itself and in the thick mild air all friction dropped out of contact and all shrillness out of talk – these things were much to the taste of our young lady, whose taste played a considerable part in her emotions.

It is a moving tribute to the culture of the English country house, rich in its suggestions of the refinements and accumulations of a whole way of life. There is also a curious unconsciousness of wealth and privilege, of the ways in which these enormously complicate the life of culture, problems which James would explore only later in his career. Missing is the ironic tribute that James will pay these complications in, for instance, *The Golden Bowl*, when he describes the beautiful and 'noble' drawing room of Maggie Verver, filled with the priceless treasures purchased for her by her millionaire-collector father. James then goes on to describe the Prince and Charlotte as 'the kind

9 James's relationship to this tradition is investigated in some detail in chapter 1. But it must not be thought that Isabel Archer ever articulates the nature of her quest in so rigid and explicit a manner. She responds to the concrete and the immediate; it is only the critic who conceptualizes these responses.

of human furniture required, aesthetically, by such a scene. The fusion of their presence with the decorative elements, their contribution to the triumph of selection, was complete and admirable; though, to a lingering view, a view more penetrating than the occasion really demanded, they also might have figured as concrete attestations of a rare power of purchase.'

That is to anticipate, however. For the moment I must stay with the issue of Gardencourt's vivid appeal to Isabel. The *Notebooks* are interesting in this connection. Almost the last entry, before the notes on *The Portrait of a Lady* (although a year elapsed between them), is this:

In a story, someone says – 'Oh yes, the United States – a country without a sovereign, without a court, without a nobility, without an army, without a church or a clergy, without a diplomatic ser-vice, without a picturesque peasantry, without palaces or castles, or country seats, or ruins, without a literature, without novels, without an Oxford or a Cambridge, without cathedrals or ivied churches, without latticed cottages or village ale-houses, without political society, without sport, without fox-hunting or country gentlemen, without an Epsom or an Ascot, an Eton or a Rugby...!!'

Although this passage was to appear almost word for word in James's biography of Hawthorne in 1879 as a list of the 'items of high civilization, as it exists in other countries, which are absent from the texture of American life', it is worth noting that the idea was first a fictional one. Isabel Archer may be taken as 'someone in a story' and, although she does not say these words, we feel their weight in seeing her response to Europe, and to Gardencourt as it represents a larger whole.

Initially, it is easy to suppose these things will win her for Lord Warburton. Her first impression of him is mixed with her first impressions of Europe. He is part of the set stage awaiting her initiations. She might well confuse his person with that image of high civilization which she seeks; and she does so confuse them at first. Ralph best describes Warburton's appeal:

'He occupies a position that appeals to my imagination. Great responsibilities, great opportunities, great consideration, great wealth, great power, a natural share in the public affairs of a great country.'

And later, Mr Touchett adds a few strokes of his own :

'Lord Warburton's a very amiable young man – a fine young man. He owns fifty thousand acres of the soil of this little island and ever so many other things besides. He has half a dozen houses to live in. He has a seat in Parliament as I have one at my own dinner-table. He has elegant tastes – cares for literature, for art, for science, for charming young ladies.'

The reader has no opportunity, interestingly enough, for verifying Warburton's elegant tastes (or those of the speaker) in literature, art and science, as he does, amply, with the charming young ladies.

Isabel is greatly taken by Warburton's two gentle sisters when they call on her. 'They're not morbid, at any rate, whatever they are', Isabel thinks,

and she deemed this a great charm, for two or three of the friends of her girlhood had been regrettably open to the charge . . . to say nothing of Isabel's having occasionally suspected it as a tendency of her own.

Embedded here is an invidious comparison with New England maidens of serious stamp, some of whom James will portray in *The Bostonians*. However, Warburton's sisters, the two Misses Molyneux, register more than that rather negative virtue for Isabel :

'I think it's lovely to be so quiet and reasonable and satisfied. I should like to be like that.'
'Heaven forbid !' cried Ralph with ardour.
'I mean to try and imitate them,' said Isabel.

Has she asked herself if she might imitate them best by becoming their sister-in-law ? She does speculate about the mode of life open to her as Lady Warburton. Here James gives us a splendid image in describing the two sisters that demonstrates clearly that despite her temporary infatuation with their sweet submissiveness Isabel will never really 'imitate' them, will never consent to a way of life so passive.

Isabel's visitors . . . [had] an extreme sweetness and shyness of demeanour, and . . . as she thought, eyes like the balanced basins, the circles of 'ornamental water', set, in parterres, among the geraniums.

Devastating in its mildness, the image can only foreshadow Isabel's ultimate reaction to Lord Warburton. Little enough time passes after this scene before she knows that Warburton wants to marry her; little enough for courtship, that is, but long enough for choice.

There is a long passage, worth quoting in full, on Isabel's feelings about marrying Warburton:

She had received a strong impression of his being a 'personage', and she had occupied herself in examining the image so conveyed. At the risk of adding to the evidence of her self-sufficiency it must be said that there had been moments when this possibility of admiration by a personage represented to her an aggression almost to the degree of an affront, quite to the degree of an inconvenience. She had never yet known a personage; there had been no personages, in this sense, in her life; there were probably none such at all in her native land. When she had thought of individual eminence she had thought of it on the basis of character and wit – of what one might like in a gentleman's mind and in his talk. She herself was a character – she couldn't help being aware of that; and hitherto *her visions of a completed consciousness had concerned themselves largely with moral images – things as to which the question would be whether they pleased her sublime soul* [my italics].

All of Isabel's suitors have their own kinds of 'individual eminence'. To say then that Isabel's conception of individual eminence has in it a strong moral bias implies not that any of them lack great virtues, but that only one of them – Osmond, whom at this point in the novel she has not yet met – will minister to her own 'sublime soul'. What in Osmond's character and wit speaks so to Isabel we shall have to look into; at the moment it is important to see why Warburton fails to do so:

Lord Warburton loomed up before her, largely and brightly, as a collection of attributes and powers which were not to be measured by this simple rule, but which demanded a different sort of appreciation – an appreciation that the girl, with her habit of judging quickly and freely, felt she lacked patience to bestow. . . What she felt was that a territorial, a political, a social magnate had conceived the design of drawing her into the system in which he rather invidiously lived and moved. A certain instinct, not imperious, but persuasive, told her to resist – murmured to her that virtually she had a system and an orbit of her own.

It is perhaps easier at this juncture to understand what Warburton's 'system' is than what Isabel thinks to be her own. That she is a young woman of independent mind and of bold spirit is clear enough, and we might assume only that she does not wish to be dominated by a territorial magnate. But if we remember the stress which James places on Isabel's sense of duty and on her 'moral bias', then something more positive must be at stake. The dislike of the idea of domination is rather the negative pole, while the positive is yet to be determined.

It is curious that in her careful examination of her feelings about Warburton, Isabel is not allowed the reflection that she simply does not love Warburton – or Goodwood. Recognizing that, she would want to conceptualize, or to rationalize, these failures of emotional response. That she may love neither is reasonable enough, obviously; but that she does not more explicitly deal with this primary fact tends to cast a somewhat dry tone of theory on these rejections of adoring men.

In any case, her rejection of Warburton is not coloured by a sense of commitment to Goodwood. Warburton has his great complicated system which will burden her freedom; Goodwood has a character dominant enough to pull her under also, as the image of drowning in her final meeting with Goodwood will remind us. The choice between the two men is simply not large enough; neither will minister to what she feels as a 'system and orbit of her own'. They do not please her sublime soul, which is to mean after all that they present her with no 'great and novel responsibilities'.[10]

It is perhaps worth mentioning that her rejection of Warburton is not determined by Warburton's radicalism, nor a

10 This is the expression James used in criticizing George Eliot's conventionally happy endings, which he saw as a serious limitation – the way in which she failed to please *his* sublime soul.

failure to take his position seriously enough. This *is* a reason for Bessie Alden in 'An International Episode' (1879). Miss Alden is the first Jamesian heroine to reject a Lord – this 'Bostonian nymph who rejects an English duke' – [11] and she has a certain kinship with Isabel in character and type. Warburton is allegedly a radical, whose hereditary position is said to embarrass him. But he has a strong sense of public responsibility, we are told, and if he works against his own hereditary interests this hardly makes him a dilettante, which is Bessie's complaint against Lord Lambeth.

Isabel's decision to reject Warburton, once granted her independence, has to do with her search for something different. He represents the world of power, of action, of position. He may, as an instrument of public office and of hereditary position, minister to civilization, but he cannot be said to represent it in the Jamesian sense, or to express it fully either in himself or in his way of life.

What I am suggesting is that Isabel, like James, is to place civilization primarily within the compass of the arts – as Culture – and outside the arena of what is commonly called history – outside the social, political, economic, institutional life of men. This fragmentation of the idea of civilization did not originate with James, of course.[12] Here it is important to see only that this disjunction is basic to the development of Isabel's story in *The Portrait of a Lady*. It can be seen more explicitly in *The Tragic Muse* (1890), where the major conflict is one between the world of public life and the world of art.

11 So wrote the reviewer of the *Pall Mall Gazette* on 'An International Episode'. James uses this sniffy attack for one of his rare excursions into satire in criticism: 'The writer in the *Pall Mall* opposes the delightful (as I suppose) novel of *Margot la Balafrée* to certain tales in which "Bostonian nymphs" appear to have "rejected English dukes for psychological reasons". I am not acquainted with the romance just designated, and can scarcely forgive the *Pall Mall* critic for not mentioning the name of the author, but the title appears to refer to a lady who may have received a scar in some heroic adventure. I am inconsolable at not being acquainted with this episode, but am utterly at a loss to see why it is a story when the rejection (or acceptance) of a duke is not, and why a reason, psychological or not, is not a subject when a cicatrix is' ('The Art of Fiction', *Partial Portraits*, p. 401).

12 See pp. 11ff. For a wider discussion of the general subject, see Raymond Williams, *Culture and Society* (London, 1958).

However, James is careful to separate himself from a *fin de siècle* aesthete's position. Crucial to his conception of culture is beauty of conduct and of character: of moral firmness, of integrity, of intelligence and proportion and grace. It is what Isabel has in mind when she speaks of individual eminence as based on 'character and wit'. Indeed, Isabel's ambition as a young heiress with all of Europe spread before her is larger than that of the aesthetic sight-seeker:

To look at life, – that is, to live, – freely, generously, handsomely.

For James, Europe was the very ground of culture, where this pursuit seemed most possible. But not because Warburton, or the public life even at its most imposing, represents the highest expression of human achievement, or provides the thrust for the 'free exploration of life' that Isabel seeks. If culture, or art, does, that is because first of all it is dedicated to the representation and even the exaltation of beauty – aesthetic, moral, natural, human, as in the metonymic image of Gardencourt in *The Portrait*, or in the old portraits in *The Tragic Muse*.[13] Second, it is a way of life which Isabel is to think she sees in the apparent dedications of Gilbert Osmond: art in itself, in its very profession, its disinterested devotion, is system and orbit of the highest human value.

Isabel does not, after all, want to be 'quiet and reasonable and satisfied' like the Misses Molyneux. She wants to live not as an appendage in Warburton's system, but as mistress of choice in her own.

EUROPE AND THE DEVELOPMENT OF TASTE

It has become customary to place the famous 'international theme' at the centre of interest in *The Portrait of a Lady*. Proper as this is within limits, it misses too easily other, more important, discriminations. James moves Isabel Archer from Albany to Europe, and this in favour of 'civilization'. But once this is accomplished, his later comparisons and contrasts are more

13 See p. 179.

important than simple distinctions between Americans and
Europeans. James is most concerned with questioning the
qualities most to be cared for in civilization. Not, first of all,
those of Lord Warburton. And not the mere acquisitive, collec-
tor-tourist's appreciation of art. For why else, if not to underline
this discrimination, does Edward Rosier enter the stage? To say
that he is needed as a suitor for Pansy is to beg the question, for
Pansy need not have just that particular kind of suitor. Pansy
does not need *him* at all – any pleasant young man will do. But
Isabel does need his presence, in terms of the novel's themes.
If Warburton characterizes the public, political, historical
aspect of what we commonly call civilization, Rosier represents
something else again, which although it too is commonly confused with a proper definition of culture, is less adequate to
Isabel's conception even than is Warburton. Rosier is the perpetual tourist-aesthete, the dilettante collector of pretty objects,
the worshipper of 'things', the devotee of art-as-commodity.
Civilization seems for him not a way of life, but an expensive
hobby. He lacks what Isabel thinks Osmond impressively has:
a 'high seriousness', a distinguished character. Rosier represents
the confusion of beauty with possessions, and of art with *things*
– the same confusion to which James devoted *The Spoils of
Poynton*, as well as the more complex, unfinished *The Ivory
Tower*. In *The Portrait* this confusion is not James's central
concern, except insofar as it is necessary to discriminate
between shallow conceptions of civilization and more substantial ones.

If it is an unkindness to feel that Rosier's great tragedy is not
so much his losing Pansy as his having sold his 'things' in vain,
it is a judgement made inevitable by James's presentation.
Luckily for Rosier's continued welfare, he withholds his enamels
from the auction block; although we know he will be unhappy
about Pansy, he has been left room for consolation. The appreciation of enamels involves a love of fine surfaces; Rosier, who
lacks depth of feeling and of taste, is not altogether devastated.
Isabel, in contrast, will come to wish that she could give her
fortune to Osmond as a small enough ransom for her freedom,
and will prove indifferent to the Roman palace which Osmond

decorates and furnishes with such painstaking care, such irreproachable taste.

Enough has been said already about Isabel's rejection of Warburton to help us on our way toward understanding her acceptance of Osmond. She has begun by wanting to *see*. Ralph challenges her just before her marriage:

'You wanted only to see life . . . I had an idea that you took a genial view of [liberty] and wanted to survey the whole field.'

Her answer is legitimate enough:

'I've seen that one can't do anything so general. One must choose a corner and cultivate that.'

She chooses her corner, a marriage with Osmond, for predictable reasons – for all those reasons adduced for her refusal of Warburton. But innocent idealist that she is, she fails to see that she uses the right reasons for the wrong choice. She has of course been taken in by Madame Merle, who strikes her as the most civilized creature she has ever known:

she had . . . to Isabel's imagination a sort of greatness. To be so cultivated and civilized, so wise and so easy, and still make so light of it – that was really to be a great lady, especially when one so carried and presented one's self. It was as if somehow she had all society under contribution, and all the arts and graces it practised . . .

All of this makes clear that 'really to be a great lady' involves consideration altogether different from those attached to the possibility of being the great Lady Warburton.

Mrs Touchett is also captivated by Madame Merle (though she recovers a proper vision long before Isabel does), and recommends her to Isabel without qualification: 'Serena Merle hasn't a fault.' But Isabel, for all her infatuation, has one interesting reservation:

If for Isabel she had a fault it was that she was not natural; by which the girl meant, not that she was either affected or pretentious, since from these vulgar vices no woman could have been more exempt, but that her nature had been too much overlaid by custom and her angles too much rubbed away. She had become too flexible, too useful, was too ripe and too final. She was in a word too perfectly the social animal that man and woman are supposed to have been intended to be; and she had rid herself of every remnant of that tonic wildness which we may assume to have belonged even to the most amiable persons in the ages before country-house living was the fashion.

This description is important for a discrimination too easily lost sight of in James (and, alas, sometimes later *by* James): the natural simplicity of one kind of Jamesian character (often his New Englanders), and the cultivated complexity of another (usually European) escape simple polarization. Hawthorne, given his habit of allegory, would have posed them as logically complete symbols. James gives us the antinomy of his fine moral discrimination, and this accounts in large measure for the tension to be found in most of his 'international' studies from *The Europeans* on. What James tends to lose later is not so much this complexity as his feeling for the 'natural' and for the 'tonic wildness' which he appreciates here. *The Portrait of a Lady*, given as it is to a study of modes of civilization, is full of reference to the natural; there is a constant interplay between types and shades of nature and cultivation, of innocence and experience.

Simply to recall some of the characters is to be made conscious of this: Henrietta Stackpole is the forthright American journalist searching always, as for a lost poodle, for the inner life, a burlesque variation, with her social gaucherie and her moral shrewdness, of Isabel's own search. Mr Bantling, her simple-minded English friend, pursues her in her intellectual scramble over Europe with all the delight of 'Twenty Questions', with marriage as the prize. The two Misses Molyneux are non-morbid 'simple' English gentlewomen, whose high breeding has left them, like hothouse tomatoes, all colour and no flavour. Pansy, the artfully cultivated *jeune fille*, is a consummate artefact of innocence. Mrs Touchett is the eccentrically innocent and selfish theorist of direct action, with action bounded only by her rigid sense of personal convenience. There is Caspar Goodwood, the American man of action not sicklied o'er with the pale cast of thought; and the vaguely bored, intensely preoccupied American expatriates of Paris (of whom Edward Rosier becomes the eminent example), who bemoan the loss of 'style' as the chief consequence of the Empire's fall. Daniel Touchett is the wise, urbane, gentle American banker who has lived in Europe for thirty years without surrendering his sense of nationality, of home-spun Americanism. When James's business men are 'good', they are very, very good, in the style of patriarch-philosophers, but when they are bad, they are horrid. The Countess Gemini, finally, is the 'ex-American' sister of Gilbert Osmond, a woman

who had so mismanaged her improprieties that they had ceased to hang together at all . . . and had become the mere floating fragments of a wrecked renown, incommoding social circulation.

Madame Merle touches a far extreme; she is too studied, too finally shaped, has too much art. Nature for James is always imitating art; that is one of the things that art is for. The question, with Madame Merle, is how deep the imitation may go. Isabel is conscious of the question :

Isabel found it difficult to think of her in any detachment or privacy, she existed only in her relations, direct or indirect, with her fellow mortals. One might wonder what commerce she could possibly hold with her own spirit.

Unfortunately, Isabel is so impressed by the visible signs of culture in Madame Merle that she reassures herself :

One always ended, however, by feeling that a charming surface doesn't necessarily prove one superficial; this was an illusion in which, in one's youth, one had but just escaped being nourished.

Isabel's Hebraic, New England inheritance has made her conscious of distinctions between superficiality and sincerity; but she is more innocent of the possible relationships between depth and depravity.

Madame Merle was not superficial – not she. She was deep, and her nature spoke none the less in her behaviour because it spoke a conventional tongue.

At the end of the novel a defeated Madame Merle exiles herself; she declares that she will go back to America. It is the less voluntary fate of Charlotte Stant in *The Golden Bowl*. What might appear to be all benignly a return to roots is in fact a harsh penance, as drastic as the distance between a natural American spontaneity and Madame Merle's contrived and cunning art. She pays a higher price than Osmond does for falseness, for she loses Isabel's friendship, and Osmond, *and* Pansy.

There is a significant scene in which Osmond reveals through a fine symbolic transaction the disdain in his relationship with Madame Merle:

He got up as he spoke and walked to the chimney, where he stood a moment bending his eye, as if he had seen them for the first time, on the delicate specimens of rare porcelain with which it was covered. He took up a small cup and held it in his hand; then, still holding it and leaning his arm on the mantel, he pursued: 'You always see too much in everything; you overdo it; you lose sight of the real. I'm much simpler than you think.'

'I think you're very simple.' And Madame Merle kept her eye on her cup. 'I've come to that with time. I judged you, as I say, of old; but it's only since your marriage that I've understood you. I've seen better what you have been to your wife than I ever saw what you were for me. Please be very careful of that precious object.'

'It already has a wee bit of a tiny crack,' said Osmond dryly as he put it down.

In the novel there is an interesting preparation for this scene that strengthens its bearing on Madame Merle. Fairly early in her friendship with Isabel, she had observed in response to a comment that many people give the impression of never having felt anything:

'It's very true; there are many more iron pots certainly than porcelain. But you may depend on it that everyone bears some mark; even the hardest iron pots have a little bruise, a little hole somewhere. I flatter myself that I'm rather stout, but if I must tell you the truth I've been shockingly chipped and cracked. I do very well for service yet, because I've been cleverly mended; and I try to remain in the cupboard – the quiet, dusky cupboard where there's an odour of stale spices – as much as I can. But when I've to come out and into a strong light – then, my dear, I'm a horror!'

The several modes of irony in this transaction are obvious enough; two are worth brief comment. There are signs that Madame Merle would like to be more open with Isabel, even to confide her secret, until Isabel becomes a wealthy woman and therefore usable in other ways. The other is to remind us that the later scene has its applications to Isabel as much as to Madame Merle. Her warning to 'be careful of that precious object' coming so close to her reference to Osmond's wife, together with our assumption that Isabel's character does have a crack – her self-willed vulnerability to the appeal of Osmond and Madame Merle – is combined richly with the easy distinction which has been suggested between porcelain (Isabel) and iron pots (Madame Merle).

Madame Merle has said to Osmond, 'I've seen better what you have been to your wife than I ever saw what you were for me.' That goes far in explaining her later action. I suggested earlier that one motive for Madame Merle's disclosure to Isabel that Ralph is the true source of her fortune is the desire to shift some of the blame for Isabel's marriage from herself. As complement to that, is there not another – a gesture of repentance – in her adding force to Isabel's desire to go to Gardencourt when Ralph is dying, knowing as Madame Merle does that such a move in the face of Osmond's strenuous objections may well lead to a break in the impossible marriage? There is no question of forgiving her, but in justice to Madame Merle one is led to believe that her idea of helping Osmond to a brilliant marriage did not carry with it an awareness of how terrible the marriage would prove to be. Isabel has discovered the true relationship of Madame Merle to Osmond and to Pansy; a defeated Madame Merle tries, in the only way she can, to give Isabel a leverage for escape.

The gradual uncovering or recognition of Madame Merle's character by Isabel plays an important part in the novel, and I want to return briefly to that process. Isabel, before her marriage, asks Ralph why he dislikes Madame Merle. He sees many of the same things that Isabel has seen, but with the important difference that he does not construe them as an epitome of the cultured life.

'Her merits are immense,' said Ralph. 'She's indescribably blameless; a pathless desert of virtue; the only woman I know who never gives one a chance . . . She pushes the search for perfection too far . . . her merits are in themselves too over-strained. She's too good, too kind, too clever, too learned, too accomplished, too everything. She's too complete, in a word.'

Ralph seems offended in his 'taste', rather than in what at first we might call his moral sense. Here one must deal with a common difficulty in understanding James, on an issue that is for him extremely important. Ralph is quite right in his taste, yet many readers have found it objectionable that so 'ornamental' a faculty should be the agency of such important judgements. But James is apt to mean more by 'taste' than we do when praising someone's drawing room or the selection of scarves and neckties. He uses the term in a cluster of ways, as he does 'civilization'. It can mean simply sensitivity and good judgement in matters of design, arrangement, proportion.[14] It can mean these things but with additional intimations of high sensibility and imagination, as when we learn that Gardencourt

14 On this first level, the exercise of taste might be said to be like that of Esther Lyon in George Eliot's *Felix Holt*, whose undue concentration on taste is one of the novel's themes. '[Esther] was alive to the finest shades of manner, to the nicest distinctions of tone and accent; she had a little code of her own about scents and colours, textures and behaviour, by which she secretly condemned or sanctioned all things and persons' (p. 69). George Eliot anticipates James's usage when she has Holt describe Esther's taste as 'thoughts about small [subjects]: dress, behaviour, amusements, ornaments', and then goes on to relate these to thoughts on great subjects: 'It comes to the same thing; thoughts, opinions, knowledge, are only a sensibility to facts and ideas. If I understand a geometrical problem, it is because I have a sensibility to the way in which lines and figures are related to each other; and I want you to see that the creature who has the sensibilities that you call taste, and not the sensibilities that you call opinions, is simply a lower, pettier sort of being' (p. 111). Still, when Esther is converted by Felix, she seems to lose or drop her earlier awareness of manners, colours, behaviour, etc. In James, the heroine would hold on to both 'tastes' *and* 'opinions' as part of a single sensibility.

E

was much to Isabel's 'taste'. James adds to this description the comment, 'Taste played a considerable part in her emotions', so that we sense in Isabel a complexity of response beyond the superficially aesthetic.

But 'taste' comes to mean still more in James: it is synonymous with 'sensibility', as 'culture' is with 'civilization'. Thus we find Isabel weighing the propriety of visiting the ailing Ralph against her husband's wishes:

The measure of propriety was in the canon of taste, and there couldn't have been a better proof that morality was, so to speak, a matter of earnest appreciation.

It is worth insisting upon, because for James 'taste' is a function of civilization or culture; their relationships are central to *The Portrait of a Lady*. 'Taste' comes to mean the response of the unified sensibility to all of experience, to the largest moral issues as well as to aesthetic objects. Two critical statements will reveal how taste and sensibility are interchangeable and will suggest again the ways in which James's comments about the novel have their close application to what he feels about character. The first is from the preface to *The Golden Bowl*, where he speaks of

the whole growth of one's 'taste' . . . a blessed comprehensive name for many of the things deepest in us. The 'taste' of the poet is, at bottom and so far as the poet in him prevails over everything else, his active sense of life: in accordance with which truth to keep one's hand on it is to hold the silver clue to the whole labyrinth of his consciousness.[15]

The second is from the preface to *The Portrait of a Lady*:

There is . . . no more nutritive or suggestive truth . . . than that of the perfect dependence of the 'moral' sense of a work of art on the amount of felt life concerned in producing it. The question comes back thus, obviously, to the kind and the degree of the artist's prime sensibility, which is the soil out of which his subject springs.[16]

15 Preface to *The Golden Bowl*, pp. xix–xx.
16 Preface to *The Portrait of a Lady*, p. xiii.

This Jamesian identification has been noted before, of course, but the tradition of interpretation has not always been fortunate. Thus, Eric Bentley writes, 'Is not one of the meanings of Henry James's work that, if we become more civilized, morals will become an aesthetic matter?'[17] This is true, but only if attached to its corollary – that aesthetics will become a moral matter – without which the formulation becomes rather precious, if not insidious. For despite the pointing toward the aesthetic of so much criticism on James, the whole point of James's conception is that both, aesthetics and morals, are expressions of a single sensibility. Civilization can improve both only insofar as they are both expressions of what ideally is the same thing, whether called sensibility or taste.

Even Ralph thinks that Madame Merle can do Isabel 'no harm'. If Ralph's taste, the most highly developed in the novel, fails to uncover adequately Madame Merle's careful mask, it is no wonder that Isabel's taste, which is considerably less formed, sees even less of what lies underneath.

I have taken so long with Madame Merle because the impression she makes on Isabel Archer leads directly to Isabel's impressions of Gilbert Osmond. Isabel could not feel she knew him half so well did she not know Madame Merle more, admire her and accept her representation of the civilized. Osmond assumes much of that representation, as with the logic of a syllogism. During his brief courtship of Isabel he has mainly to demonstrate that he does in fact fall into an established category. Osmond is a more extremely finished and polished specimen even than Madame Merle, and this lady serves the function, among others, of acting as a bridge in the development of Isabel's taste – from Gardencourt, Ralph Touchett and Lord Warburton (and even earlier, of course, from Albany, Caspar Goodwood and romantic German novels), to the appeal of a marriage to Osmond. When Isabel is courted by Lord Warburton, the Misses Molyneux provide her with first a temptation, and then a warning. When Isabel is courted by Gilbert Osmond, Madame Merle provides her with first a temptation, and then a trap. Isabel's independence of choice leads her into both.

17 E. Bentley, *The Importance of Scrutiny* (New York, 1948), p. xix.

THE BETRAYAL OF CHOICE

Isabel may have been changing as a result of her initiations in England and in Europe, but she is never more recognizably the young American girl, with her earnestness even of enjoyment, than in her early relations with Osmond. James describes Osmond's first visit, in the company of Madame Merle:

Isabel took on this occasion little part in the talk; she scarcely even smiled when the others turned to her invitingly; she sat there as if she had been at the play and had paid even a large sum for her place.

The others are Madame Merle and Osmond; Isabel, like a child who has long heard about the pantomime before attending one, has at last discovered the real thing, the representation before her very eyes of the civilized life. James develops his image:

They might have been distinguished performers figuring for a charity. It all had the rich readiness that would have come from rehearsal.

The irony of course is that the humorously exaggerated metaphors point to the literal truth: they *are* performing, and the charity is the one that proverbially begins at home.

Whether this performance is of an art that holds a mirror up to nature, or whether it is merely the baseless fabric of a vision,[18] Isabel is clearly fascinated. What fascinates her most, as she comes to know Osmond, is *his* taste:

He had consulted his taste in everything – his taste alone perhaps, as a sick man consciously incurable consults at last only his lawyer: that was what made him different from everyone else.

18 Since the reader knows more than Isabel does about Madame Merle and Gilbert Osmond, these tropes work in both ways. Equally suggestive to the reader is James's first description of Osmond's villa, which precedes Isabel's meeting: 'The villa was a long, rather blank-looking structure . . . The house had a front . . . pierced with a few windows in irregular relations and furnished with a stone bench . . . useful as a lounging-place to one or two persons wearing more or less of that air of undervalued merit which in Italy, for some reason or other, always gracefully invests any one who confidently assumes a perfectly passive attitude – this antique, solid, weather-worn, yet imposing front had a somewhat incommunicative character. It was the mask, not the face of the house.'

There is an ominous note in this simile, but it does not alert Isabel. Her sense of Osmond's 'difference' is followed by a comparison between Ralph and Osmond, as Isabel sees them:

Ralph had something of this same quality, this appearance of thinking that life was a matter of connoisseurship, but in Ralph it was an anomaly, a kind of humorous excrescence, whereas in Mr. Osmond it was the keynote, and everything was in harmony with it.

Her weighting the balance in Osmond's favour is a delusion; the reality is that there is a radical imperfection in Osmond, rather than an anomaly in Ralph. Ralph's taste is fine, yet has in it something of 'nature' and of 'tonic wildness'. His characteristic hands-in-pocket stance, his refusal to take himself too seriously, his warm friendliness together with his detachment and humour, all bespeak a healthy taken-for-grantedness in his relationship to culture.[19] However he has acquired it, he need not worry over it since it is a genuine quality rather than a studied and rehearsed role. Isabel's failure to take Ralph more seriously is simply another measure of her peculiar earnestness.[20]

Osmond's culture, in contrast, is calculated, a mask adopted for self-seeking purposes, measured to his own uses. Ralph's sensibility, his taste, has travelled the whole ambit that James staked out for this faculty, while Osmond's has stopped short, been deflected. His sensibility is devoid of moral fineness, of the 'disinterested and generous', of the humane. His taste is only in his appearance of connoisseurship, his sense of manners and forms. In James's vision these elements are *parts* of the taste developed by civilization, through which a high morality can

19 cf. F. R. Leavis, *The Great Tradition*, p. 150: '[Touchett] is the centre, the key-figure, of James's "system" . . . He is neither American nor English – or he is both; that is, he combined the advantages, while being free from the limitations. He can place everyone, and represents the ideal civilization that James found in no country.'

20 The same earnestness can be seen in Charlotte Wentworth, in *The Europeans*, who has great difficulty in seeing that the high culture of Felix Young is not belied by his cheerful good spirits.

also develop and flourish. Osmond's feeling for manners and forms, however, is a feeling for the things-in-themselves as recognized attributes of high estate, the mastery of which ministers not to morality but to ego. His integrity is intense, but incomplete, limited, a studied devotion to the narrow compass of his forms. His early renunciation, his plan to 'resign myself . . . to be content with little' is not motivated by disinterestedness, or by a scorn of ambition or of material values, but by an indolent cynicism which sees the coveted prizes beyond its reach and so determines to snub them rather than to suffer the possible humiliation of defeat. His cool urbanity disguises a restless, dissatisfied egotism whose private ambitions are tremendous, are megalomaniacal: he would like to be an Emperor, or Pope. Short of that, the happiest alternative is the pose of indifference.

Nevertheless, he is moved to effort when Madame Merle brings him game he had not thought of: an immense fortune at the command of an attractive charming intelligent woman, a combination his cynicism apparently had despaired of encountering. Further, her conquest will involve no great trouble – and Madame Merle has to 'guarantee' this when she proposes the match – for she has already done half his courting for him, has led his prey within easy range.

It is obvious enough what Osmond sees in Isabel; more complex is Isabel's seeing him as the most cultivated, the most 'beautiful', the most civilized person she has known. Nevertheless, it is clear that Isabel's (and indeed James's) conception of taste is not wrong, but rather her reading of Osmond's embodiment of it. That this is so is confirmed by comparing her admiration for Osmond's taste before their marriage with her later estimate. After she comes really to know him, she no longer thinks of his 'taste'. Rather, her real contempt for the pettiness and the severe limitation of that faculty in Osmond is revealed when Warburton praises the decoration of her Roman palace. She doesn't commend his taste now, but comments drily: 'He has a genius for upholstery.'

Isabel's infatuation with Osmond's high culture is a determining cause of her marriage. But there is a contributory cause as well. The central irony of the novel (what the Aristotelians would call the novel's *peripety* or reversal) is that her fortune, the very gift which Ralph has arranged so that she might live 'freely, generously, disinterestedly', is what makes her marriage with Osmond actually possible. It is not just that Osmond would never have married her had she not been wealthy; that is too easy an irony. It is that the money has determined *her*, has worked on her through her sense of duty. For Isabel's sensibility does have a high moral tone.

She would launch his boat for him; she would be his providence; it would be a good thing to love him. And she had loved him, she had so anxiously and yet so ardently given herself – a good deal for what she found in him, but a good deal also for what she brought him and what might enrich the gift. As she looked back at the passion of those full weeks she perceived in it a kind of maternal strain – the happiness of a woman who felt that she was a contributor, that she came with charged hands. *But for her money*, as she saw today, *she would never have done it*. And then her mind wandered off to poor Mr. Touchett, sleeping under English turf, the beneficent author of infinite woe! For this was the fantastic fact. At bottom her money had been a burden, had been on her mind, which was filled with the desire to transfer the weight of it to some other conscience, to some more prepared receptacle. *What would lighten her own conscience more effectually than to make it over to the man with the best taste in the world?* . . . He would use her fortune in a way that would make her think better of it and rub off a certain grossness attaching to the good look of an unexpected inheritance [my italics].[21]

This is what she comes to understand on the occasion of the all-night vigil which James thought the 'best thing in the book', Isabel's long soliloquy in which she recounts for herself all the motives for her marriage, and the tragically inconsequent results. To be allowed, she had thought, to discover at last the 'civilized' is wonderful enough; still, she had in a sense done that much already in discovering Madame Merle. But to be

21 Compare this with the passage from Pater's *Marius the Epicurean* (discussed on p. 26, above): 'the precept of "culture", as it is called – that is, of a complete education – might at least save him from the heaviness and vulgarity of a generation, certainly of no general fineness of temper, but with much material well-being'.

allowed to contribute to it, to help to bring it about as well as to participate in it, this might well appear to the young lady from Albany to be a very rich fulfilment of the ideal so eloquently expressed by Ralph : to live 'freely, generously, disinterestedly'. Surely half the reader's wonder that Isabel should act consciously in terms of *duty* at the end of the novel, when she returns to her marriage, is explained when it is realized that the marriage has from its inception involved the same moral terms.

Mr Touchett's fortune proves to be the 'curse in disguise' that Henrietta Stackpole has predicted it will become. Her satirically presented 'Americanism' does not prevent James from giving her also her own deep moral insights.[22] She is afraid that the money will confirm Isabel's 'dangerous tendencies'. Significantly, Henrietta sees these not as the love of luxury or of high living, but Isabel's 'exposure on the moral side'. Henrietta thinks Isabel is 'not enough in contact with reality'. 'You're too fastidious', she says, 'you've too many graceful illusions.' Nothing could be more clever than the way James gets in this foreshadowing – the ominous beat of drums offstage – without spoiling for us the freshness and directness of Isabel's later responses. So relevant a warning from the author, or even from a 'deep' character like Ralph, might make Isabel's actions seem too blind and foolhardy. It comes instead from Henrietta, and we smile at her provincialism; only later do we recognize her accuracy. As in the novels of Jane Austen, complex characters (Emma, Elizabeth Bennet), more intelligent than their companions, are also more prone to complex mistakes in judgement.

The history of Isabel's mistake is built up carefully and gradually, until we get the full statement of her tragic fallibility in the all-night vigil referred to earlier. What sets this long soliloquy off is a little scene from which Isabel carries

22 One of the sub-plots of Trollope's *He Knew He Was Right* (1869) concerns a young American girl who has become engaged to an English aristocrat despite the disapproval of her good friend Wallachia Petrie, satirized as 'the American Byron', whose exaggerated Americanism causes her to predict various catastrophes as the result of European entanglements. Nowhere is James's richness of imagination, his superior claims as a novelist, more evident than in comparing his portrayal of such characters as Henrietta Stackpole and Isabel Archer with Trollope's comfortably simplified characterizations.

away a vague, scarcely articulated suspicion that Madame Merle
has some closer relation with Osmond than she had understood.
It is a classic example of the way James uses his 'forms' as
guides to truths, manners as index to morals. Isabel has discovered Madame Merle and Osmond together. She has no
ground for any particular suspicion, but their present image is
vastly disquieting. Madame Merle stands while Osmond sits.
Further, they are engaged not in the flow of polite conversation,
but in the pause of a familiar silence. Osmond is too much the
studied gentleman to ignore the ordinary amenities except for
some extraordinary cause.

Isabel's pondering of this caught image of Madame Merle and
her husband becomes larger than its occasion, for it gives rise
to a rehearsal of her whole married career. The scene is particularly important because James has skipped the interval of four
years between her betrothal and the later short period when the
dénouement takes place. This trick of foreshortening, brilliant
in some ways, has certain unfortunate consequences. For one
thing we never see directly the period of real love between
Isabel and Osmond. This love does not easily inspire a willing
suspension of disbelief. For another, we are told in cavalier
fashion that Isabel has had a child and lost it, an event presumably of some emotional importance, but never mentioned again.
The natural attraction of Osmond for Isabel is legitimate enough
in terms of theme, but the flowering of this attraction into love
occurs in a hiatus of narrative, and of emotion. The thematic
infatuation with civilization is not the same thing (even, one
hopes, for the exegetical critic) as the literal, dramatic involvement of one person with another. The absence of this representation will make the later scene when Goodwood does make
love to Isabel seem out of focus with the rest of the novel.

But the soliloquy is done magnificently, and her 'discovery'
of Osmond, even in retrospect, is treated so well as partially to
redeem the absence of earlier representation.

Under all his culture, his cleverness, his amenity, under his good-
nature, his facility, his knowledge of life, his egotism lay hidden
like a serpent in a bank of flowers.

There is an ironic reference here to her earlier rejection of Warburton, whom she had judged by her touchstone:

When she had thought of individual eminence she had thought of it on the basis of character and wit – of what one might like in a gentleman's mind and in his talk.

In judging Osmond by that touchstone, she has failed to go beyond the appearance of the thing, to what Melville might have called 'the little lower layer'.

Isabel is honest enough in thinking back to recognize that in the normal way of courtship Osmond had dissembled no more than she. Eager to anticipate the other's expectation, Isabel was too ready to appear to rely sweetly on masculine authority, Osmond too ready to appear cultivated, disinterested, and gentle. At the time of this soliloquy she does not yet know that there has been collusion in the concealment of Madame Merle's old relationship with Osmond or of their tacit pact of mutual assistance. This knowledge will come later, as a further blow. Now, there is ground enough for knowing that she has made a great mistake. In Osmond she thought to have found her Eden; she has overlooked only the serpent.[23] He was to be the new Adam of a new civilization, and she its Eve. She had intended the lofty, the fullest expression of herself in the service of a high civilization; she has realized instead a confined and base adherence to empty forms. The very embodiment of the life which was to be free and generous and disinterested proves to be the 'mill of the conventional' – Gilbert Osmond with his cold egotism, his worldliness, his snobbery.

She had taken him seriously . . . She was to think of him as he thought of himself – as the first gentleman in Europe . . . But when she began to see what it implied she drew back . . . It implied a sovereign contempt for everyone but some three or four very exalted people whom he envied . . . he pointed out to her so much

23 James comes closest to Hawthorne when he is portraying deep evil: egotism as a 'serpent in a bank of flowers' is a symbol from the heart of Hawthorne's manner. The distance, however, even in this closeness, is the contrast in characterization between the dramatized Osmond and the allegorized Chillingworth of *The Scarlet Letter* or the protagonist of 'The Bosom Serpent'.

of the baseness and shabbiness of life, opened her eyes so wide to the stupidity, the depravity, the ignorance of mankind, that she had been properly impressed with the infinite vulgarity of things and of the virtue of keeping one's self unspotted by it. But this base, ignoble world, it appeared, was after all what one was to live for; one was to keep it for ever in one's eye, in order not to enlighten or convert or redeem it, but to extract from it some recognition of one's own superiority.

Isabel's own idea of the civilized life which she has sought is presented in contrast to the shabby reality which she finds herself possessed of:

His ideal was a conception of high prosperity and propriety, of the aristocratic life . . . That again was very well; here too she would have agreed; but they attached such different ideas, such different associations and desires, to the same formulas. Her notion of the aristocratic life was simply the union of great knowledge with great liberty; the knowledge would give one a sense of duty and the liberty a sense of enjoyment.[24] But for Osmond it was altogether a thing of forms, a conscious, calculated attitude.

The indictment is clearly not of high civilization itself, but against the confiscation of its forms for base ends. For there is always Ralph Touchett in the background.

Ralph Touchett is necessary to the novel as a representative of the real thing; his very name suggests the Arnoldian touchstone. At the same time, it is just as necessary that he be eliminated as the goal of Isabel's quest. Isabel does not take Ralph seriously enough, her very earnestness, paradoxically, preventing her from recognizing his claims. But an equally important fact is that he is simply unavailable. That Ralph Touchett is an invalid, and thus prevented from playing a more active role, seems to me more than a convenience of plot, or a fortuitous accident. We touch again the tendency of too many of James's protagonists to see themselves as on the outside of life, looking

24 Thus Marcellus Cockerel, in 'The Point of View' (first published in 1882): 'If this general efficiency and spontaneity of the people – the union of the sense of freedom with the love of knowledge – isn't the very essence of a high civilization I don't know what a high civilization is.'

in, men who appreciate passionately life's great possibilities, but mainly as these involve someone else. If Ralph is the most appealing, and central, representative of the civilized among the men who surround Isabel, he is also the most passive.

Still, Touchett's passivity is not complete. Like the novelist who must determine which actions will constitute his character's experience, Touchett arranges things for Isabel. James's first conception of the novel, according to the later preface, was the image of a figure awaiting a setting and a sequence that would best express her possibilities. And does not Ralph exercise the same initial curiosity, and the same later prerogative, by arranging a fortune for Isabel? He does so in order to set her free to follow her own bent. His reward is to be simply that of *seeing*, of watching her develop under the pressure of his idea. That he will to that degree participate vicariously in her life is, though not articulated, perhaps a further inducement.

The somewhat Byronic note of concealed suffering in Ralph's characterization escapes autobiographical reference at first glance. It has as parallel James's own attitude toward his mysterious though frequently discussed pre-Civil War injury which presumably kept him from sharing the short life of his own particularly engaging cousin, Minny Temple. Her affronting of *her* destiny ended with an early death. James's first great celebration of her memory is Isabel Archer, whose story ends with a death of hope and of aspiration, if not of the body. His last and more rhapsodic treatment of a similar heroine is Milly Theale, whose story ends with both.

THE SIGNIFICANCE OF RENUNCIATION

That James intended us to see that Isabel must carry much of the blame, as well as the burden, of her marriage is obvious enough. It is equally obvious that he intended that our criticism of Isabel should be tempered by as strong a sympathy. She has been tampered with, been tricked; we cannot altogether blame her for her loss of happiness. Further, the destiny of another young woman is juxtaposed with hers, compared and contrasted and seen, finally, as subject to the same betrayals. Pansy

Osmond, the *jeune fille* whose frequently invoked image is that of the 'blank page', the Lockean *tabula rasa*, is a contrast in modes of innocence. Isabel's is the innocence of nature, of a spontaneous spirit nurtured by a young society lacking forms and traditions. Pansy's, however, is the innocence of achieved art, the nurtured and controlled product of a system. Isabel's is the innocence of a nineteenth-century New World; Pansy's of an eighteenth-century Pastoral. Pansy is 'cultivated' in the most literal sense; her simplicity is the product of a sophistication as intense as a child's portrait by Fragonard or Watteau. It can be the groundwork for an achieved happiness and beauty in the expression of a nature directed, not eliminated, by art. Or it can be used, as a fortune can be used, for deceitful purposes. Osmond chooses that Pansy's innocence, which *is* her fortune, shall be used to achieve a profitable marriage, however little the profit might be Pansy's. The poor girl is betrayed, and her smaller drama throws many lights on the larger one of her step-mother. Isabel's is the fate dispensed by a shammed civilization to the dupe from outside, the innocent abroad; Pansy's that of the victim who is a product of the very civilization that uses her.

Again, it is portentous that Pansy, as aristocratic innocence, should become only the tool, just as Ralph, as aristocratic experience, becomes only the passive spectator, of a thoroughly spurious form. About Pansy's and Ralph's predicament there is something particularly modern in its emphasis. Each represents a failure of will, while their opponents, Madame Merle and Gilbert Osmond, represent the growth of will as the instrument of ego, the weapon of power. We recognize it as one of the themes of D. H. Lawrence, one that has been anticipated by Henry James.

Isabel's predicament is not the same. It is the surrender to a factitious civilization of a genuine spontaneity and a genuine will – genuine in that it ministers to an enlightened intelligence and a generous imagination in the pursuit of the good life.

James's Good Life, it needs to be said, is a light never seen on land or sea. It is an ideal, elevated above the tangled and contingent in human life. If it is an ideal the realization of which he thought most possible in Europe, that does not mean, alas, that he ever found it there. The distance travelled by Isabel between Albany and Rome is of a different measure from the geographical, or even social distances involved. Whether his novels deploy characters in an American setting, or an English or European, or in international groupings, his primary concern, as I have argued, is the search for, and the defence of, a postulated high civilization, the moral and aesthetic demands of which set off his characters in its pursuit or its betrayal, in search of its realization, or of its loot. Even when the canvas is smaller, when the pursuit of civilization is not central to the novel, as in *The Europeans*, we are conscious still of the same implicit problem: the search for a way of life conducive to 'the union of great knowledge with great liberty'.[25] If it is never realized in the actualities of Europe, neither is it available in America.

That long parenthesis allows me to turn, at last, to a figure in the novel who so far has received scant attention in this study. Caspar Goodwood has waited all this time, even as he does in the novel (and for the same reasons) for a resolution. Isabel comes to feel that he is the one person she has injured, possibly even wronged, in refusing his proposal. She feels that he has no 'compensations' as Lord Warburton has in his position and his public career. It is an over-simplification to say that Goodwood represents Isabel's sense of America; still, there is a rough justice in the idea, and a rough usefulness as well. It helps to explain, for one thing, Isabel's special sense of obligation, even of guilt, as well as the particular quality of his appeal.

Whatever else James conceived his American characters as being, particularly when they happened also to live in Europe, he always considered them on dangerous ground when they left America too far behind. His attitude about expatriation was certainly not Van Wyck Brooks's attitude in considering

---

25 Interestingly enough, James is most apt to describe those novels as 'slight' or as 'small' when they do not take up in some fairly central way his problem of civilization. *Washington Square*, *The Awkward Age*, and *What Maisie Knew* are all novels which James described in this way. In each of them the theme is not unrelated to the central concern I have been discussing but at a tangent to it.

James himself.[26] But James was conscious of the dangers of *deracination* – of, literally, the destruction of roots, especially when new roots did not take, or were planted only superficially. At its worst, the result was a Gilbert Osmond, a Madame Merle, who adopted traditions and forms separate from deep personal commitment, deep moral foundation. Madame Merle, in the time before Isabel's acquired fortune made her the target less of frankness than of policy, has told Isabel about 'her kind' of American:

'If we're not good Americans we're certainly poor Europeans; we've no natural place here. We're mere parasites, crawling over the surface; we haven't our feet in the soil.'

It is not too fanciful to see in the contrast between Goodwood and Osmond an inverted variation of the theme of 'The Jolly Corner'. Goodwood, like Osmond, is possessed of tremendous ambition and tremendous will. Goodwood has given it expression in the manner his country and his time best allow: he has become a magnate, a titan of industry. Osmond has not lost this drive in his exile, but only its American expression. Even Rosier, with so much less intense an ambition, significantly defends his continued expatriation just in terms of *career*:

'You think I ought to do something, and so do I, so long as you leave it vague. But when you come to the point you see you have to stop. I can't go home and be a shopkeeper . . . I can't be a clergyman; I haven't got convictions. And then I can't pronounce the names right in the Bible . . . I can't be a lawyer; I don't understand – how do you call it? – the *procédure*. Is there anything else? There's nothing for a gentleman in America.'

It's comic and satirical, of course, but not without foundation.[27]

26 Van Wyck Brooks, *The Ordeal of Henry James* (New York, 1925), argues that James was ruined as a novelist by his expatriation. While I think Brooks's thesis has come to be dismissed *too* glibly, his argument about James is as problematic as the argument that Roderick Hudson should have stayed home.

27 The situation, more soberly seen, is not unlike the experience related in *The Education of Henry Adams*. Adams had the advantage of intelligence, and he became for a while at least a distinguished professor. Rosier has not the mind; Osmond has not the disinterestedness.

Unlike the Parisian expatriates, however, Osmond retains an ego made monstrous by its very rootlessness. The irony is that Osmond patronizes Goodwood as a blasé, world-weary ancient patronizes the recollected image of his own raw and zealous youth.

Less dramatic, perhaps, but dangerous too, are the pitfalls of judgement for an expatriated American like Winterbourne in 'Daisy Miller', whose diagnosis of *his* mistake is that he has lived too long in foreign parts, and so was 'booked to make a mistake'. Mrs Touchett's expatriation (like Isabel's) shares in this effect. She accepts Madame Merle without reservation, and recommends her to her niece as one of the very few people she would honour by her choice. At the same time, Mrs Touchett dismisses Henrietta Stackpole as 'both an adventuress and a bore – adventuresses usually giving one more of a thrill'. An American 'fact' that might guard Isabel against these pitfalls, Caspar Goodwood hovers always near as a constant prod of conscience and of memory. In the event, Isabel's insistence on her independence renders his service rather useless.

Her reasons for not marrying Goodwood when she might, and for refusing to go away with him at the end, have a certain consistency, of course, but are not quite the same. Much of her reasoning in rejecting him as suitor has already been implied; only a little is needed to fill out the picture. Goodwood intimidates Isabel; he is too direct, his onslaught too downright. If forms are an index of civilization then he is still of the frontier :

If he extended his business – that, to the best of her belief, was the only form exertion could take with him – it would be because it was an enterprising thing . . . not in the least because he might hope it would overlay the past. This gave his figure a kind of bareness and bleakness which made the accident of meeting it in memory or in apprehension a peculiar concussion; it was deficient in the social drapery commonly muffling, in an over-civilized age, the sharpness of human contacts.

Early in the novel, Isabel thinks :

Sometimes Caspar Goodwood had seemed to range himself on the side of her destiny, to be the stubbornnest fact she knew; she said to herself at such moments that she might evade him for a time, but that she must make terms with him at last – terms which would be certain to be favourable to himself.

She puts him off temporarily at first, 'dazzled as she was by the great immediate opening of her aunt's offer of "Europe" ', and then forever (as she thinks) with her marriage to Osmond. She has chosen Osmond in preference to Goodwood because, simply put, in her quest Goodwood represents what she is moving from, rather than toward.

He seems to her to be a strong character, a 'natural' force, nurtured by and serving nothing but what James elsewhere calls the 'world of grab'. His power is too little shaped or nurtured by the complex structure of civilization which might realize his spiritual and moral possibilities. He represents a tremendous energy hurled at a world she sees to be limited by the goals of money, of business, of power. Consequently she finds in him a 'want of easy consonance with the deeper rhythms of life'. He is the product, if not the embodiment, of the boldest, most prominent aspect of emerging American society: the cult of 'doing', the worship of success. His figure represents the modern theme (which James himself returned to several times, but never really mastered) of Capitalist-as-Hero. He is an early manifestation of what was to become a familiar pattern in American life.

The American woman of strong character was left relatively free to cultivate 'an easy consonance with the deeper rhythms of life' – which is to say, to represent the amenities generously allowed to be the pleasant by-products of material success. The more pragmatic dedication of her husband was to the *essential* business of life, to the bedrock of material prosperity, on the comfortable surface of which his wife might erect as many ivory towers as she pleased. Business was masculine, culture feminine, and the occasional young American men who emerged as 'passionate pilgrims' to Europe represented a confusion of publicly sanctioned sex roles that exposed them to scorn. From that danger Goodwood appears staunchly immune. He is young and personable, but there is nothing about him to prevent his development into another Abner Gaw (in *The Ivory Tower*), James's truest, if most brutal, characterization of the type.

Isabel thinks Goodwood to be not only unlike her ideal of civilization, but inimical to its discovery. He makes her fear for her independence, for her liberty, in seeking out this fulfilment. Her account to him of why she will not marry him, and why she wishes him away from Europe, is portentous:

'I . . . am not bound to be timid and conventional; indeed, I can't afford such luxuries. Besides, I try to judge things for myself; to judge wrong, I think, is more honourable than not to judge at all. I don't wish to be a mere sheep in the flock; I wish to choose my fate and know something of human affairs beyond what other people think it compatible with propriety to tell me.'

This argument is remarkably close to her grounds for rejecting Warburton, and the resemblance helps us to recognize how both men represent powerful social values incompatible with her pursuit of high civilization.

When Isabel at last discovers that her own particular ambition has played her false, and has allowed her no more liberty than she feared she might have with Goodwood, it is inevitably Goodwood who must appeal to her. He represents the beginning of her odyssey, and the long journey home. He will make a last powerful bid for her loyalty; and thematically at least we can now understand its strong direct physical emphasis. She resists this appeal because she cannot go back on her commitment, not so much to Osmond, as to her own pledge to what he is supposed to have represented. We must remember that she had had her final interview with Ralph, when she comes to realize for the first time how very dear to her he is, and how much closer to the truly civilized than is Osmond. If she can have loved Ralph, and in loving him have participated in the civilization she has all along sought, how can she possibly return to Goodwood? Going back to Goodwood now is an admission that not only her choice, but the ideal underlying it, have been wrong. Her scene with Ralph, I suggested earlier, is the true climax of the novel, while the rather false love scene with Goodwood afterwards represents a falling away. The scene with Ralph makes her refusal to escape the 'civilized' by returning home with Goodwood seem inevitable and right, while the interest and credibility of 'story' are perfectly maintained.

She has chosen: She has staked her whole life on her need and her right to choose. When Osmond warns her that she must not go to Gardencourt at her cousin's bidding, she thinks him sophistical in saying:

'I think we should accept the consequences of our actions, and what I value most in life is the honour of a thing.'

We know how great is the disparity between Osmond's surfaces and the reality beneath. But the argument is not a sophistry for *her*. If by 'honour' he may mean only its appearance and its form, Isabel accepts it, but with her own infusion of the moral reality which justifies the appearance and the form. She is quick to see that he speaks not only for himself, but for her, 'in the name of something sacred and precious – the observance of a magnificent form'. It is easy enough to see where the appeal lies for both of them in invoking the authority of 'magnificent form'. Isabel has given up Goodwood because of her belief in 'magnificent form'; she cannot violate it now in order to return to him.

Is it Isabel's *pride* which determines her final decision to return to Osmond, as a number of critics have argued? Henrietta Stackpole appears to think so, when she asks Isabel why she doesn't leave Osmond:

'I can't change that way,' Isabel said.
'Why not, I should like to know? You won't confess that you've made a mistake. You're too proud.'
'I don't know whether I'm too proud. But I can't publish my mistake. I don't think that's decent. I'd much rather die.'

And in a later scene Henrietta chides Isabel for keeping her unhappiness so secret, asking, 'Don't you think you're rather *too* considerate?' – to which Isabel answers, 'It's not of him that I'm considerate – it's of myself!'

Her pride *is* strong, and plays its part in her decisions. But I think it quite wrong to see it as a conventional pride which blushes to admit a mistake. Rather, it is a pride that refuses to go back on one's deepest commitments; it is *that* which is not decent. Even though her choice has not been as free as she had thought, before her discovery of the snares set for her, Isabel cannot deny her own responsibility. If Madame Merle has arranged the marriage, she has herself consented to it. If much evidence has been withheld, there should still have been enough, in her own perceptions and in her friends' warnings, to show her that she was wrong. Isabel's is a pride one comes to recognize as characteristically Jamesian: a pride that insists on seeing wrong and on accepting its consequences.

In an earlier chapter of this study I have proposed that central to James's renunciations (as resolutions to fictional conflict – renunciations most frequently linked to the cause of civilization) is the pride of preserving, at whatever cost to happiness, one's moral identity. James consistently asserted the close relation of moral sensibility with true culture, and indeed this relationship forms an important article of faith. Isabel, like so many other of his characters, renounces with all the self-justification, even exaltation, that a religious code might provide.

She has herself recognized that nineteen of any twenty women would leap at such an offer of marriage as Warburton's. So must we recognize that at least the same number of women would, in Isabel's circumstances, break with Osmond at the end. Many readers still find it impossible to give their assent to this exception. Too often a compounding of this difficulty has resulted from the reading that Isabel does act simply out of pride in a conventional sense, and out of duty in its parochial and limited sense. But this finally may be no justification at all, since it can be argued that pride might take the form of refusing to be made a tool of, while duty might be cancelled out, righteously, in the face of deceit. That Isabel is proud constitutes only a strength of character that must accompany, but which in itself does not sufficiently explain, her act of renunciation.

A more substantial difficulty in accepting Isabel's rejection of

Goodwood is the problematic nature of their final encounter. The scene, as I have suggested, presents the only physical, sexually passionate note in the novel. One is made uneasy by James's polarization here of the physical and passionate on one side, and of the civilized and cultured on the other. *Must* Isabel's consistent fear of the physical attend a consistent love of the cultured? The same kind of polarity occurs frequently in James and constitutes, I think, one of his greatest weaknesses. It is probably not altogether conscious, nor yet, as the psychoanalytical critics would have us believe, altogether unconscious – else why should we be told that Isabel has had a child and lost it, if not to establish her marriage as a matter of 'themes' and 'definitions' only, but as a physical fact? But James is too delicate and too oblique; the point is not registered with convincing dramatic force.[28]

With its interesting variation on Osmond's words, Goodwood's challenge to Isabel, 'Why should you go back – why should you go through that ghastly form?' is apt to win the twentieth-century reader's support. Nurtured on a literature that has lost faith in forms and in the bearings of culture or civilization on our moral lives, most readers expect that Isabel will renounce her fond, mistaken illusions about the good life, and go off with Goodwood. Such readers would prefer Isabel to act in the name of self-expression, and fail to see that in fact this is what Isabel has done. Uncertain that there is any reality in the idea of moral identity, our touchstones have changed.

Again, a reader nurtured on nineteenth-century novels – even on the moral realism of George Eliot – might well have expected Osmond considerately to die (as Causabon and Grandcourt die), and thus save Isabel for a chastened but still visible happiness. James seems to satisfy nobody, and though I suspect that many people dislike James's ending for the wrong reasons, the general dissatisfaction may not reflect only on a capricious public.

As James managed it, the final scene between Isabel and

28 The representation of physical passion is usually attended by deep moral ambiguities, as for Kate Croy and Merton Densher in *The Wings of the Dove*, or Charlotte and Prince Amerigo in *The Golden Bowl*. Even the Prince's love-making to his wife Maggie is mentioned only when his affair with Charlotte is being discovered.

Goodwood must be considered an artistic flaw in terms of dramatic credibility and emotional conviction. At his best, James gives us renunciations which have intrinsic justifications on moral and thematic levels. Isabel's renunciation has them: in terms of the theme of *The Portrait of a Lady*, her decision to leave Goodwood is legitimate and right, even though its dramatic, narrative-level embodiment seems rather hollow. But a dramatically weak ending does not of itself condemn a novel. Nor does it cancel out this novel's claim to a very high place not only in James's achievements, but in the whole tradition of the novel in English.

Whatever Isabel's frailties, it is worth remembering that she has the dignity of being the first woman in English fiction to sustain the entire weight of a major novel without the supports of parallel stories or sub-plots. Nor is she simply the object of pity or condemnation, in the manner of the frequently invoked fallen woman of nineteenth-century fiction. This 'young woman affronting her destiny' – as James called her in his preface – commands the interest and respect traditionally reserved for male protagonists, and she stands without diminution in the company of Stendhal's or Balzac's young men from the provinces confronting the large cultural issues of their times.[29]

Thematically there is nothing quite like it in the English-speaking tradition, ending and all. To Goodwood's challenge, 'why should you go through that ghastly form', Isabel's own answer is unique. It cuts deeper than all the oversimplified cant about pride and duty: she goes back 'in the name of something sacred and precious – the observance of a magnificent form'. Tautological as they superficially seem, his question and her implied answer – a secular litany – constitute Isabel's story.

Isabel learns that Osmond has betrayed her great ideal. She knows, as we know, that Osmond is damned by the very values whose outward appearances he has so mastered. The difference,

29 See Diana Trilling, 'The liberated heroine', *Times Literary Supplement*, 13 October 1978, pp. 1163–7. Her claim for the novel is more generous even than my own: 'Isabel Archer's story, *The Portrait of a Lady*, remains, to my view, the best novel not of female liberation but *about* female liberation that has yet been written, indeed the only great one. That it was written by a man is striking but irrelevant here.'

which must mark the distance between Isabel and us, is that we seem no longer certain of what to make of the ideal itself. Isabel clings still to this ideal, on which she has staked her life. To betray it in turn would be to suffer her own kind of damnation, beside which her continued unhappiness with Osmond must be accepted as the lesser evil. The greater – the greatest – would be the destruction of her cause, her quest, her own sacred identity.

5

The defence of culture and the claims of history

After *The Portrait of a Lady*, James's next three novels[1] – *The Bostonians* (1886), *The Princess Casamassima* (1886), and *The Tragic Muse* (1890) – have a common concern despite their substantial differences of situation and setting. They all dramatize conflicting views of what may be considered of greatest worth to man in the widely divergent conceptions of civilization current in James's time. These novels advance James's own view of civilization as culture despite the strong claims made for social-political commitment.

The sequence known traditionally as James's 'middle period' was launched with *The Bostonians*. The novel is primarily a critique of assumptions about civilization popular in the New England of the post-Civil War era, assumptions present also in England in the Victorian campaigns for Philanthropy and Progress. These are views which James regarded (with Matthew Arnold) mainly as a confusion of 'machinery' with civilization or culture. The novel is a satire on the machinery of social agitation and reform, and of such wayward paths to salvation as vegetarianism, nudism, and spiritualism. Possibly as a consequence of the novel's setting in time and place, it places little stress on the conception of high culture which James championed. The relative absence of this stress gives to *The Bostonians* a rather negative insistence which is unique to the major works of this period. It assumes therefore a special relationship to *The Princess Casamassima*, which, although it

1 *The Reverberator* (1888) precedes *The Tragic Muse*. Although it is sometimes cited as a novel, it is actually a longish *nouvelle*, a slight but humorous 'international' story which satirizes the growth of yellow journalism.

was written shortly after *The Bostonians*, I shall discuss first for reasons which I trust will become apparent.[2]

'THE PRINCESS CASAMASSIMA': CULTURE AND ANARCHY

One consequence of James's continued residence in London, which began in 1876, was a growing awareness of its extension beyond the West End. Fog in Hyde Park might limit the sensuous appeal that London represented, but it provided its own consolations: of novelty, of mystery, and, more important perhaps, of the comfortable sense that abiding verities were hidden by but a transient shade. But James's pleasure in walking the streets, an inveterate occupation, he tells us, of his early London years,[3] led him past the happy emblems of Kensington and Park Lane and Belgravia into that larger area, as yet uncharted in his fictional world, of Islington and Pentonville and Soho. There, pondering his cherished ideas on the correspondence between material and spiritual beauty, he must have asked himself questions very new, and very deep. What was perhaps most obvious was that so long as one remained an observer only, the transition from the splendid to the sordid was a matter simply of peripatetic energy. What of the reverse, however – the movement from east to west, or from north and south – what would that involve? Any individual from those regions whose sensibility was of the kind to interest James must fail to accept mere spectatorship. So long as such an individual had from the first any 'fineness', how could he help but want to have for himself the life of high civilization? If such a desire could motivate a young lady from Albany, New York, why not a young man from Soho? The finer the organism, the more passionately must he want a life that could express and develop it. The *donnée* for a new fiction that James conceived in his perambulations was exactly

that of some individual nature or fine mind, some small obscure intelligent creature whose education should have been almost wholly

2 A reading of *The Princess Casamassima* is not illuminated by a prior consideration of *The Bostonians*, whereas the special problems of the earlier novel *are* made clearer by the discussion of *The Princess*.
3 Preface to *The Princess Casamassima*, p. v. See also *Letters*, I, p. 209.

derived from them [the London streets], capable of profiting by all the civilization, all the accumulations to which they testify, yet condemned to see those things only from outside – in mere quickened considerations, mere wistfulness and envy and despair.

James identifies this process with his own initiations, as the reader may identify them with Isabel Archer's, but with one crucial difference:

so far as all the swarming facts should speak of freedom and ease, knowledge and power, money, opportunity and satiety, he should be able to revolve round them but at the most respectful of distances and with every door of approach shut in his face. For one's self, all conveniently, there had been doors that opened – opened into light and warmth and cheer, into good and charming relations.[4]

Here once more is the passionate pilgrimage made familiar to us first through Roderick Hudson's youthful statue, 'Thirst'. But now the cup is out of reach. Eager but deprived, James's 'small obscure intelligent creature', Hyacinth Robinson, is to involve himself in a revolutionary programme sworn to abolish those splendours the cost of which, he comes to believe, is his own disinheritance.

There is no full or final sense in which *The Princess Casamassima* resolves the basic problem raised by James's opposition of social revolution to high culture. The novel's genius resides in the way the problem is embedded in an artistically convincing vision of experience.[5] The evidence which this experience represents – dramatic, contradictory, ambivalent, personal – in its very particularity retains much of its cogency some ninety years later. Taken literally as a sociological document, there are several openings in James's argument large enough, no doubt, to admit an opponent's dialectic wedge. But there is no reason why anyone should take the novel as document. Better by far to take it as fiction, recognizing its sociological or political

4 Preface to *The Princess Casamassima*, p. viii.
5 I think that *The Princess*, which has generally been underrated, is the best of the novels discussed in this chapter. None of the three seems to me as good as the two novels in which the 'sacred quest' is most important, *The Portrait of a Lady* and *The Ambassadors*.

implications as one part of its burden.[6] In the end, assent must be given as an act of faith to one side or the other of James's argument, with the knowledge that something of value is sacrificed in each. That James gives his assent to high culture will come as no surprise. What may appear surprising is that he should entertain on so large a scale the theme of a profound conflict between his own cherished ideal and a programme looming large in the social climate of his time which he saw as not only most opposed, but most hostile, to civilization.

Hyacinth Robinson is the illegitimate and unacknowledged son of an English lord murdered by his French mistress, Hyacinth's mother. There is perhaps too literal a grounding in the very nature of his violently divided heredity for the conflict which is so to torment him: his identification with the people and his 'French' taste for revolution on the one hand, and on the other, his 'natural' response to the appeals of high culture. Elsewhere James has written:

No themes are so human as those that reflect for us, out of the confusion of life, the close connection of bliss and bale, of the things that help with the things that hurt, so dangling before us for ever that bright, hard medal, of so strange an alloy, one face of which is somebody's right and ease and the other somebody's pain and wrong.[7]

The opposition of the things that help to the things that hurt is the unifying principle of the novel, the dramatic base which supports the thematic opposition between *Cause* and *Culture*. Hyacinth Robinson must mediate the divergent, the hostile claims of elitist culture and of social justice. There is no such conflict to perplex the earlier protagonists in James's novels who set out on the sacred quest: Roderick Hudson has a wealthy sponsor; Christopher Newman is a millionaire; Isabel Archer

---

6 I want to avoid on the other hand the mistaken critical tradition which interprets James's interest in and command of contemporary revolutionary movements as vague or shallow. See especially W. H. Tilley, *The Background of The Princess Casamassima* (Florida, 1960) and Oscar Cargill, *The Novels of Henry James* (New York, 1961), for evidence of James's interest and awareness that contradicts these earlier assumptions.

7 Preface to *What Maisie Knew*, p. ix.

inherits a handsome fortune. Nowhere else in James has the outside world of economic hardship or poverty intruded, either to prevent his characters from aspiring to the life of culture or to challenge the goal itself.[8] In *The Princess Casamassima*, this is just what does happen, and a large part of the novel's considerable energy is derived from the dramatic power of the arguments adduced both for Culture *and* for Cause.

James was more intensely aware of the social evils of his time than were the *fin de siècle* aesthetes with whom he is sometimes confused. In 1886 James wrote to his friend, Charles Eliot Norton:

The condition of that body [the English upper class] seems to me to be in many ways much the same rotten and *collapsable* one as that of the French aristocracy before the revolution – minus cleverness and conversation; or perhaps it's more like the heavy, congested and depraved Roman world upon which the barbarians came down. In England the Huns and Vandals will have to come *up* – from the black depths of the (in the people) enormous misery, though I don't think the Attila is quite yet found ... At all events, much of English life is grossly materialistic and wants blood-letting.[9]

This might appear at first glance as an eloquence more extreme than James's actual beliefs would justify. The eloquence in fact echoes *The Princess Casamassima*, newly published,[10] in which the Princess herself exclaims:

It is the old regime again, the rottenness and extravagance; bristling with every iniquity and every abuse, over which the French revolution passed like a whirlwind; or perhaps even more a reproduction of Roman society in its decadence, gouty, apoplectic, depraved,

8 In the fine story 'Four Meetings' (1877), Caroline Spencer is defrauded of her meagre life-savings within 24 hours of her arrival in Europe, and deprived of her long-cherished initiation into the life of culture. But the issue is not one of social justice, and the idea of culture remains unchallenged.

9 *Letters*, I, p. 125. It is interesting that this letter, reflecting James's preoccupation with the ideas of the novel, should include also one of James's rare personal references to Matthew Arnold, who is mentioned with a singular note of intimacy as 'Matt Arnold'.

10 It is easy to assume that the letter came first, with its eloquence then appropriated for the novel, as does for instance Brian Lee (*The Novels of Henry James*, London, 1978, p. 44), but the reverse is true.

gorged and clogged with wealth and spoils, selfishness and scepticism, and waiting for the onset of the barbarians.

The even more flamboyant style *here* is justified not only by its fictional setting, but by the fact that it is the Princess who is speaking. Her lack of deep personal conviction may need the bolstering of additional rhetoric. James says of her :

She would be world-weary – that was another of her notes; and the extravagance of her attitude in these new relations would have its root and its apparent logic in her need to feel freshly about something or other – it might scarce matter what. She can, or she believes she can, feel freshly about the 'people' and their wrongs and their sorrows and their perpetual smothered ferment; for these things are furthest removed from those others among which she has hitherto tried to make her life.[11]

I do not mean to imply a corresponding artificiality in James; I think that his recognition of materialism and decay in the upper classes is sincere enough. But his political and social commitments, even in response to his radical discontent with European civilization, were deeply conservative. The only period in James's life when politics or public affairs became an active concern was at the outbreak of the First World War, and then precisely because he shared the not uncommon belief that European civilization was in peril.

Against the rottenness and extravagance James speaks of in describing the aristocracy, he has no salutary contrast among his revolutionists.[12] They are either humorously ineffectual, if amiable, or else power-hungry in subtle and sinister ways. His aristocratic radicals are far less impressive than Lord Warburton, and are seen either as adventurers, like the Princess and Captain Sholto, or as unmarriageable maidens with a genius for altruistic sublimations, like Lady Langrish (it is the Princess who forces the inevitable pun with Lydia Languish). Indeed, everyone in the novel except Hyacinth Robinson is seen not only

---

11 Preface to *The Princess Casamassima*, p. xxiv–xxv.
12 It would be easy to accuse James of stacking his cards against the revolutionists were it not for the fact that there are no fictional representatives of culture who fare any better.

satirically or ironically – sometimes even viciously – but from the outside. I rather like Hyacinth's foster-mother, Miss Pynsent, and her musical friend, Mr Vetch, both of whom are brilliant characterizations of the ineffectual but admirable poor. But they come close to being Dickensian character-caricatures, with little force on the level of the novel's ideas. James's canvas is very large, and few of his novels give more the sense of the heterogeneity of character and of life. It is the novel, more than any other of James's, which has close and obvious affinities with the Victorian tradition. While we are conscious always of James's own voice, we seem often to catch the echoes of Dickens and of Thackeray.[13] Moreover, there is a most wonderful air of invention all through the novel, a sense of improvisation so free, and often so masterful, as to challenge criticism.

The sense of improvisation relates especially to Hyacinth's revolutionary activities. James's account of his treatment of these, he cunningly tells us, was thought out in advance as a defence of his 'artistic position' against possible charges of vagueness:

the value I wished most to render and the effect I wished most to produce were precisely those of our not knowing, of society's not knowing, but only guessing and suspecting and trying to ignore, what 'goes on' irreconcileably, subversively, beneath the vast smug surface.[14]

However wonderful in its effects James's *tour de force* on London's revolutionary underground may be, what most compels the reader's interest is the novel's intense involvement with Hyacinth Robinson, with the growth of his experience and imagination. James makes us feel sometimes that Hyacinth is *too* fine an organism for the account given of him, too frequently a sensitively vibrating victim of experience rather than an active agent. He tends to be a passive receptacle of choices, rather than (like Isabel Archer, for instance) a maker of choices. At the same time, he is eager, intense, touching in his loyalties

13 There are echoes also of Turgenev, especially of *Virgin Soil*, and, in a more generalized way, of Balzac.
14 Preface to *The Princess Casamassima*, pp. xxv–xxvi.

and in his aspirations. It is a shrewd observation on James's part that it would be just such a person as Hyacinth, ordinarily passive in outward action, but tightly wound in his inner life, who alone among the revolutionists leaps to take the solemn pledge for an act of terrorism, thus marking the passion of a commitment that goes beyond words, words, words.

Lionel Trilling has suggested biographical motivations for James's concern with Hyacinth. Trilling sees him especially as a spokesman for James's own dedication to European culture, as opposed to his brother William's demands for an American life of action.[15] This seems to me a sound, if only partially relevant speculation, at least to the degree that William might have stood in Henry James's mind as representative of the opposition in America to the culture he was defending.

More interesting than a dialogue between two fictionally disguised brothers, however, is the spectacle of Hyacinth Robinson himself, for whom the conflict is single and internal. The other characters embody alternatives which exist within Hyacinth, rather than in opposition to him. The Princess represents the magnetism of a magnificent way of life (however much she thinks she wants to disown it); and the revolutionists, the mechanism of a powerful social action. Novels most often present central characters who represent unique modes of action and of thought which are in conflict with the opposing modes of other characters. But the main characters in *The Princess Casamassima* are seen as symbols or personifications of possible types of action or thought that meet and clash within the protagonist, Hyacinth.[16] For this reason I think *The Princess*

15 Lionel Trilling, *The Liberal Imagination* (New York, 1951), pp. 58–92. What Trilling omits in his biographical speculations (as does Quentin Anderson in his studies of James's uses of his father's thought) is that this novel opposes the social philosophy of James Senior. He was a socialist strongly influenced by Fourier. One of his best-known lectures, 'Socialism and Civilization' (in *Moralism and Christianity*, Boston, 1850, pp. 39–94), expressly advocated socialist programmes as an antidote to the evils of civilization.

16 The most obvious descendant in the English tradition is Joyce's *Portrait of the Artist as a Young Man*, the theme of which – the conflict of alternative vocations or definitions of life, resolved in favour of art – is not so unlike that of *The Princess*. One remembers also Thomas Mann's *The Magic Mountain*, with Hans Castorp caught between Settembrini and Naphta in the 'Great Debate'. They all belong loosely to the tradition of the *Bildungsroman*.

Casamassima is much less a novel about politics than has frequently been argued, and much more a novel of education, in the long loose tradition that begins with Goethe's *Wilhelm Meister*.

The development of Hyacinth's education, and of his conflict, is expressed and reinforced in a number of ways. His opposed parentage is dramatized on the one hand by Miss Pynsent's constant intimations of his 'noble blood' and on the other by his terrifying (and dramatically powerful) visit as a child to Millbank Prison, where his mother is dying. His attraction to Millicent Henning, a vulgar and vital London product, is contrasted with his attraction to the dazzlingly elegant Princess, who is never more aristocratic than when she is acting the revolutionary. Even his craft of book-binding, combining as it does the domain of manual labour with that of aesthetic creation, serves its contributing function.[17]

Hyacinth is made to vibrate to these contradictions with remarkable intensity. It is useful to remember James's classic formulation on fictional character, and that it is Hyacinth Robinson who is called upon to be 'finely aware and richly responsible'. It is Hyacinth whom we are to see as

the person capable of feeling in the given case more than another of what is to be felt for it, and so serving in the highest degree to *record* it, dramatically and objectively . . . the only sort of person on whom we can count not to betray, to cheapen or, as we say, give away, the value and beauty of the thing.[18]

As a person capable of feeling, Hyacinth responds strongly to the squalor of Lomax Place, and to the wrong done him by his noble father and his family. He extends the personal to principle, and becomes a radical, determined to avenge the general wrong done to all the poor by all the rich. But his very capability of feeling will give rise to contradiction; for by James's logic it is inevitable that so fine a sensibility must

17 I wonder if James had William Morris in mind, since Morris dedicated himself to 'arts and crafts' and to a socialism impatient with elite views of culture.

18 Preface to *The Princess Casamassima*, p. xv.

respond eventually to the appeal of culture. James recounts his conception of this contradiction:

The complication most interesting then would be that he should fall in love with the beauty of the world, actual order and all, at the moment of his most feeling and most hating the famous 'iniquity of its social arrangements'; so that his position as an irreconcilable pledged enemy to it, thus rendered false by something more personal than his opinions and his vows, becomes the sharpest of his torments.[19]

The 'something more personal' will be his falling in love, first with the Princess, and then with the *civilized* which she and her magnificent home at Medley represent for him.

The Princess has opinions also. She has decided to turn her back on civilization and has become interested in the revolutionary party which Hyacinth has embraced. She now takes so radical a view of the wickedness of culture that with all the strenuousness of a new convert she scorns even his offered tokens of love, his beautifully bound books. She sees them only as typical products of the rotten existing order of things which awaits destruction. One cannot serve both God and Mammon, she sententiously, if rather irrelevantly, explains. The revolutionists are sworn not simply to change existing civilization, but to destroy it. There is enough in contemporary history to demonstrate that we have our own extravagant versions of apocalypse, but so all-embracing is the anarchists' programme for complete destruction that it helps to explain not only the acuteness of Hyacinth's developing conflict, but paradoxically, the tremendous infatuation of the Princess with such possibilities of obliteration.

She is, of course, the Christina Light of *Roderick Hudson*, whose love for Rowland Mallett had gone unrequited. She had succumbed to the established scheme of things, as represented most immediately by her ruthlessly ambitious mother, and had accepted marriage with a wealthy and stupid Italian Prince for whom she feels neither love nor respect. At the end of the earlier novel it is clear that she has no illusions about the kind of barter that has taken place. She emerges some years later

19 Preface to *The Princess Casamassima*, p. xv.

F

as the wondrously glamorous Princess Casamassima, bored and desperate in her boredom, ready for Causes. Her friend and companion, Madame Grandoni, explains :

'the Princess considers that in the darkest hour of her life she sold herself for a title and a fortune. She regards her doing so as such a horrible piece of frivolity that she can't for the rest of her days be serious enough to make up for it.'

One example of the queer and wonderful combinations and effects of the novel is that this explanation is offered to the very person to whom Christina has sold herself, to Prince Casamassima himself.

The Princess comes to abandon her old way of (high) living for an intense interval of (plain) thinking in an ugly little house in Paddington. With a consummate sense of theatre, she chooses a setting in which presumably the revolutionary muses are more accessible. Hyacinth, whose sense of irony is sometimes blunted by infatuation, sees this in the true Emersonian perspective, if with less awe than the Princess wishes to inspire :

Hyacinth lost himself in worship of the Princess's housewifely ways and of the exquisite figure she made as a small bourgeoise; judging that if her attempt to combine plain living with high thinking were all a burlesque it was at least the most finished entertainment she had yet offered him.

It seems curiously reminiscent of Marie Antoinette, walking among real lambs in imaginary pastures just out of sight of Versailles. The reader has no doubt, ever, that this is all a charming little intermezzo for her, and may note that she is never more capriciously individualistic than when she is most caught up with the social question. It is a singular feat of James's skill that we can be sceptical and amused at the Princess during this sham renunciation at the same time as we catch ourselves admiring the boldness of imagination which it demonstrates. Hyacinth's less romantic revolutionary friend Paul Muniment becomes first politically, and then personally, involved with the Princess, but he is detached enough to predict coolly that she will return to the Prince when he has cut off her funds. His prophecy is in the process of being realized at the novel's end.

Her brief but intense romance with revolution is capricious, but not without probability. Remembering her American blood we may wonder if James naïvely wants us to make something of it, as he does of Hyacinth's French (therefore republican) antecedents. But the Princess's moral deracination is extreme, and her zeal has been perverted into irresponsible adventurism. Her way of getting back at society, and at herself, for the stupidity of her life is really breath-taking. She feels the need for bringing down all civilization in her fall. Incapable of violence herself, she inspires it in others. However, she proves to be not the high-priestess of the day of judgement, but only of the suicides of Roderick Hudson and Hyacinth Robinson. The activities of the revolutionists prove to be neither as exciting nor as productive as she had hoped, and besides they make it clear that what they trust her for is mainly the ability to write large cheques. The Prince does embarrass her by cutting off his financial support, and she withdraws. She will not, after all, experience annihilation. And the civilization which has both shaped her and alienated her survives all her conspiracies.

Despite her adventurism, James manages to give to her characterization an element of personal dignity and worth throughout the novel. At the end, we see that her concern for Hyacinth has become, if not passionate, at least sincere. And she suffers, ironically enough, the same treatment at the hands of the revolutionists that she had condemned herself for: they use her for her money, while the question of her worth, her intelligence, her devotion – her *personal* values – affect them as little as personal values had counted in her marriage to Prince Casamassima.

If the Princess's motivations are unusual, they are nevertheless convincing. Her burning desire to 'know' the poor leads her to Hyacinth, the first of the incidental paradoxes in her adventure, since Hyacinth is the most civilized creature in the novel. If she drops him later on, it is not so much because he is insufficiently proletarian as that he tends too much to dote on her, as too many fine young men have done in the past. This is a weakness notably absent in Paul Muniment, who is no more poor than Hyacinth, but who is consistently more brutal. Similarly, Hyacinth's admiration for her has nothing to do with her class consciousness, but with the nobility of her beauty and her 'form'. Her grace, her cleverness, her gentleness, her tact, her emancipated imagination – these are the ideal attributes of the cultured person, as much for Hyacinth as they have been for Isabel Archer. Because of these attributes Hyacinth is even at the end of his career unable to condemn that in her which falls so drastically short of the ideal and which contributes so poignantly to his own catastrophe.[20]

In contrast to the Princess is the figure of Millicent Henning, the daughter of the people, the opposite pole of Hyacinth's experience:

> there was something about her indescribably fresh, successful and satisfying. She was to her blunt, expanded finger-tips a daughter of London, of the crowded streets and bustling traffic of the great city; she had drawn her health and strength from its dingy courts and foggy thoroughfares and peopled its parks and squares and crescents with her ambitions; it had entered into her blood and her bone, the sound of her voice and the carriage of her head; she understood it by instinct and loved it with passion; she represented its immense vulgarities and curiosities, its brutality and its knowingness, its good-nature and its impudence, and might have figured, in an allegorical procession as a kind of glorified towns-woman, a nymph of the wilderness of Middlesex, a flower of the clustered parishes, the genius of urban civilization, the muse of cockneyism.

The very vitality and buoyancy of James's description registers her appeal for Hyacinth. He is immensely attracted, and yet apprehensive. He is like the Hans Castorp of Mann's *The Magic*

20 Madame Grandoni offers an illuminating analysis of Christina in *Roderick Hudson*: 'She needs to think well of herself; she knows a fine character easily when she meets one; she hates to suffer by comparison, even though the comparison be made by herself alone; and when the figure she makes, to her own imagination, ceases to please or to amuse her she has to do something to brighten it up and give it a more striking turn. But of course she must always do that at somebody's expense – not one of her friends but must sooner or later pay, and the best of them doubtless the oftenest. Her attitudes and pretences may sometimes worry one, but I think we have most to pray to be guarded from her sincerities.'

Mountain, who recognizes and admires the vitality and hearty forthrightness of the burghers of the plains, but at the same time fears the accompanying indifference to scruples, to fine discriminations, to the suffering of refined, or over-refined, sensibilities such as his own. As Hans is drawn contradictorily to the world of spirit and the world of nature, so is Hyacinth drawn both to the Princess and to Millicent. Divided in consciousness and in loyalty, he cannot reconcile himself to a single mode of experience.

In a similarly contrasting way we are given both his deep immersion in the revolutionary cause and his experience at Medley. There he discovers the great appeal of the English country house to his taste for civilized forms. This appeal is larger than any single quotation can convey, though perhaps it may be suggested by his very anticipations :

He would go there . . . because a man must be gallant, especially if he be a poor little bookbinder; but after he should be there he would insist at every step on knowing what he was in for . . . All warnings, reflexions, considerations of verisimilitude, of the delicate, the natural and the possible, of the value of his independence, had become as nothing to him. The cup of an exquisite experience – a week of such immunity from Lomax Place and old Crook as he had never dreamed of – was at his lips; it was purple with the wine of romance, of reality, of civilization, and he couldn't push it aside without drinking.[21]

But a few pages after this account of the solicitations of Medley, we are given Hyacinth's impressions of the revolutionary underground, which has its own divisive appeal :

'It's beyond anything I can say. Nothing of it appears above the surface; but there's an immense underworld peopled with a thousand forms of revolutionary passion and devotion . . . And on top of it all society lives. People go and come, and buy and sell, and drink and dance, and make money and make love, and seem to know nothing; iniquities flourish, and the misery of half the world is prated about as a "necessary evil," and generations rot away and starve in the midst of it, and day follows day, and everything is

21 James is, yet again, drawing on the symbolism of Roderick Hudson's early statue, 'Thirst'.

for the best in the best of all possible worlds. All that's one half of it; the other half is doomed! In silence, in darkness, but under the feet of each one of us, the revolution lives and works. It's a wonderful, immeasurable trap, on the lid of which society performs its antics.'

The Princess's attraction proves stronger in her person and her possessions than in her professions; Medley stronger than the bold, bright picture of revolution, stronger than Millicent Henning. Hyacinth is more and more disaffected, even though he has taken a sacred vow to undertake some act of terrorism at any time he may receive a command. Indeed, his anxious passion in taking this vow, in itself sincere enough, is perhaps a measure of his fear that his revolutionary zeal is being undermined by his new experiences.

His growing disaffection from the cause reaches its climax when he travels on the Continent with the modest funds left him by Miss Pynsent's death and Mr Vetch's strained generosity. Heretofore his French heritage has been associated mainly with an affinity for the people, but republicanism is not what most excites Hyacinth in Paris. Now his blood vibrates to the spectacle of present beauty. Although he imagines for himself the barricades where his maternal grandfather must have fallen in the Revolution, this event represents for him simply the grandeur of history and the heroism of *character*, rather than a spur to revolutionary passion or devotion:

He recognized, he greeted with a thousand palpitations, the seat of his maternal ancestors – he was proud to be associated with so much of the superb, so many proofs of a civilization that had no visible rough spots.

The image of France as a civilization with no visible rough spots is surely remarkable for a social critic, and leads directly to the ceremonies of Medley rather than to the cell meetings at the Sun and Moon pub. Hyacinth is well aware of the shift:

He had his perplexities and even now and then a revulsion for which he had made no allowance, as when it came over him that the most brilliant city in the world was also the most blood-stained;

but the great sense that he understood and sympathised was prepon-
derant, and his comprehension gave him wings – appeared to trans-
port him to still wider fields of knowledge, still higher sensations.

His French inheritance, which has linked him previously with
Revolution, undergoes a profound sea-change in the face of an
achieved civilization, a brilliant culture. It is this spectacle of
French culture which now solicits his passions. His radical
commitments are not altogether supplanted, but seriously con-
founded.

The Princess's great denunciation of existing society, echoed
later in James's letter to Charles Eliot Norton, is not the only
expression of radical sentiment which James gives us in the
novel, but it may be taken as the dramatic focus of radicalism
in the novel's dialectic. If her speech is a thesis, the antithesis
is in the moving letter which Hyacinth writes to the Princess
from Venice. Here we see him trying to work out the implications of his initiations and discoveries. It marks a crucial stage
in Hyacinth's development, and is worth quoting from at some
length:

Dear Princess, I may have done you good, but you haven't done
me much . . . I may have helped you to understand and enter into
the misery of the people . . . but you've led my imagination into
quite another train. Nevertheless I'm not wholly pretending it's all
your fault if I've lost sight of the sacred cause almost altogether in
my recent adventures. It's not that it hasn't been there to see, for
that perhaps is the clearest result of extending one's horizon – the
sense, increasing as we go, that want and toil and suffering are the
constant lot of the immense majority of the human race . . . What
struck me is the great achievements of which man has been capable
in spite of them – the splendid accumulations of the happier few,
to which doubtless the miserable many have also in their degree
contributed . . . They seem to me inestimably precious and beautiful
and I've become conscious more than ever before of how little I
understand what in the great rectification you and Poupin propose
to do with them . . . The monuments and treasures of art, the great
palaces and properties, the conquests of learning and taste, the
general fabric of civilization as we know it, based if you will upon
all the despotisms, the cruelties, the exclusions, the monopolies and
the rapacities of the past, but thanks to which, all the same, the

world is less of a 'bloody sell' and life more of a lark[22] – our friend Hoffendahl seems to me to hold them too cheap and to wish to substitute for them something in which I can't somehow believe as I do in things with which the yearnings and the tears of generations have been mixed.

This is the sum, as it is the climax, of Hyacinth's experiencing of the world. It has all the intensity, and the implied sanction, of a religious conversion. What remains to be known is how Hyacinth's revelation affects his future experience. He has had his epiphany; what can he do with it?

What happens, in brief, is the closing of the circle, the demonstrated fulfilment in the betrayal of Hyacinth. The Princess, restlessly searching always for stronger draughts of the rare and the 'real', takes up Paul Muniment who, with an unruffled ease inconceivable in Hyacinth, can accept the favours of a foolishly inconsistent aristocrat. This brilliantly portrayed young chemist has no difficulty in seeing a future which is steady if not necessarily whole; but he is not so myopic as to recognize the need for scruples in the present. It is made abundantly clear that in the relationship of Muniment with the Princess more than a meeting of radical minds has occurred. I have spoken earlier of the way that James is able to describe manners in order to reveal morals. There is a beautiful instance of such a revelation here.

Madame Grandoni has served the Princess as companion for some years, disapproving strongly of her caprices, but remaining loyal. She makes it clear that she will serve as *duenna* only so long as the Princess, however unconventional, remains 'respectable'. Her remaining all through the Princess's experi-

---

22 This conviction, that the monuments and treasures of art make the world somehow less a 'bloody sell' – is echoed significantly many years later, in a letter to G. B. Shaw in 1909: 'Works of art are capable of saying more things to man about himself than any other "works" whatever are capable of doing – and it's only by thus saying as much to him as possible, by saying, as nearly as we can, all there is, and in as many ways and on as many sides, and with a vividness of presentation that "art" and art alone, is adequate mistress of, that we enable him to pick and choose, and compare and know, enable him to arrive at any sort of synthesis that isn't, through all its superficialities and vacancies, a base and illusive humbug' (*The Complete Plays of Henry James*, ed. Leon Edel (London, 1949), p. 645).

mental flirtation with Hyacinth acts as a demonstration not of Hyacinth's virginity, of which we have no doubt, but rather of Madame Grandoni's frame of reference. When, near the end of the novel, we come to suspect that the Princess has gone far in her friendship with Muniment, we discover *how* far by learning that Madame Grandoni has suddenly departed. We need no further demonstration, and the effect is more evocative than any direct word to Hyacinth, or to us, could be.

Thus betrayed, Hyacinth hopes to find some final resource in Millicent Henning. Such resources have become crucial, for Hyacinth has at last received his command: he has been given his instructions for a political assassination. But if the Princess, that false messenger of civilization, has betrayed him, so too will Millicent, the 'muse of cockneyism'. On his last desperate day he thinks of Millicent, whose commonness and vulgarity have alienated him despite the appeal of her warmth and vitality. He hopes now that she may be a last refuge from both his commitment to culture and his commitment to destroy it. He looks to her, at least, for some reassurance, some comfort, some sanction that might justify the assassination he has been ordered to undertake:

she was such a strong obvious simple nature, with such a generous breast and such a freedom from the sophistries of civilization . . . Again and again . . . he indulged in the reflection that spontaneous, uncultivated minds often have inventions, inspirations.

He discovers that he is not mistaken; Millicent does have inventions. For on entering the shop where Millicent puts her body to good use by working as a model, he encounters the adventurer Captain Sholto, who has preceded him.

She was showing off this treasure to the Captain, who was lost in contemplation. He had been beforehand with Hyacinth as a false purchaser, but he imitated a real one better than our young man [he is a false purchaser not of gowns only, but of Millicent – he has imitated the lover better than Hyacinth] as with his eyes travelling up and down the front of their beautiful friend's person, he frowned consideringly and rubbed his lower lip slowly with his walking-stick. Millicent stood admirably still – the back view of the garment she displayed was magnificent. Hyacinth stood for a minute as still as she. By the end of that minute he was convinced that Sholto saw him, and for an instant he thought him about to make Milly do as much. But Sholto only looked at him very hard a few seconds, not telling her he was there; to enjoy that satisfaction he would wait till the interloper had gone. Hyacinth gazed back at him for the same length of time – what these two pairs of eyes said to each other requires perhaps no definite mention – and then turned away.

The next words of the novel, in a new paragraph, are these: 'That evening at nine o'clock the Princess Casamassima drove in a hansom to Hyacinth's lodgings in Westminster.'

They are striking because first, the Princess has never before come to Hyacinth's lodgings, and second because in her republican phase she had forsworn the luxury of hansoms. We know that this phase is now ending: the Prince has cut off her funds. Exactly why the Princess has come we are not told, although it is safe to guess that she has come to take her farewell of the revolution and of Hyacinth. In an unexpected way, this is exactly what she does. For what finally makes the passage particularly interesting is that she has some difficulty in gaining entrance to Hyacinth's room, and must employ the services of a newly arrived visitor, one Herr Schinkel (a fellow revolutionist, one of the 'fools who minister') to break down the door:

The Princess was anxious, was in a fever, but she could still relish the romance of standing in a species of back slum and fraternising with a personage so like a very tame horse whose collar galled him.

The door is broken down, and she discovers that Hyacinth, given a pistol for his anarchic blow against civilization, has used it instead to kill himself.[23]

Betrayed by both the Princess and Millicent, we might expect in Hyacinth a reaction of cynicism, and an assent to anarchist

---

23 There is a heightening of horror for the Princess, as for Hedda Gabler, in the discovery that Hyacinth has killed himself not with a 'clean' bullet in the head, but with a 'mess of blood, on the counterpane, in his side, in his heart'. The tendency of the idealizing and romanticizing mind to forget about blood is terrifying.

terrorism. But the direction which Hyacinth's actual renunciation takes is a refusal to betray either his high ideal of culture,
or – what is so often in James involved in this ideal – his sacred
moral identity.

Together with his defence of culture, James takes up another
thematic issue. Action in terms of black-and-white absolutes,
the novel suggests, is destructive and self-defeating, even if like
Hyacinth one may be given no finer choice. The richness of
life fully lived – which for James means lived on the civilized
crest – is good. Any tampering with another's life is evil, is
indeed the defining attribute of the Jamesian villain. If this
novel has a villain, it is the Princess, who was manipulated
Hyacinth too casually and for selfish motives.

However, Hyacinth's fate cannot be seen as the effect of so
single a cause as the Princess's irresponsibility. Hyacinth begins
with a fixed, arbitrary set of values (as does Lambert Strether
in *The Ambassadors*) which experience and the free intelligence,
aspiring toward the 'civilized', prove to be inadequate. No
absolute system, James implies, can be superimposed on human
experience, neither on individual men nor on the collective
group of their fellows in society, even for the achievement of
benevolent ends. So far as salvation may be possible, it must
derive from lived experience, from a free involvement with
the best that human beings have thought and said, from the
effort of converting as wide an experience as possible into consciousness. Finally, James suggests, the human quest for amelioration cannot ignore the central human need for culture
without damage to the integrity of the whole man.

So far as all this goes I find it easy to assent. What is disquieting here – as in much of James – is the dangerously
individualistic emphasis which is placed on self-awareness, the
heightening of sensibility, and the eager search for beauty. Noble
as are such goals, they too much ignore the sense of community,
of commonweal, without which even these goals must be undermined. No civilization is conceivable without some social base
and without reference to a community of relationships beyond
the personal. And to the degree that James's conception of
culture is so detached from – if not opposed to – a broader con-

cept of civilization, his vision has an excessively narrow focus.[24]

Elsewhere in this study I have discussed a suggestive and important difference in James's world-view from that of George Eliot, which was rooted in her own experience of an organic community with a specific social history and sense of continuity. James came to feel himself liberated from parochial ties by the educational philosophy of his father which led to a nomadic early life, by his family's wealth, and his own later wanderings. All of these contributed to make him admirably cosmopolitan in culture, but also cut off from any strong and intimate sense of social community. While he prized responsible moral commitment – a quality which makes his own individualism preferable to that of the acquisitive society of the later nineteenth century – even moral commitment for James's typical protagonists has as its most persuasive sanction not publically shared values or a sense of commonweal, but rather the sacredness of their own moral identity.

Virginia Woolf, writing of James's essays on the First World War, says: 'A moralist perhaps might object that terms of beauty and ugliness are not the terms in which to speak of so vast a catastrophe.'[25] But we have seen James use the same terms with a greater richness of reference in *The Princess Casamassima*. His appeal to the aesthetic-ethical wholeness of culture, so basic to his vision of the world, seems to me not false, but limited. His conception of culture was idealized, abstracted from the social facts which themselves could lead to 'so vast a catastrophe' as the First World War, the advent of which so astonished and defeated him. Within its limits, James's appeal to culture has its own integrity, and its own great power. While it has evidently proved to be no solution

24 A later commentator on civilization, Kenneth Clark, defines what he thinks are the qualities of a civilized society: order, creation (as opposed to destruction), gentleness, forgiveness, knowledge (as opposed to ignorance), human sympathy (as opposed to ideology), courtesy, a dependence on nature, the existence of geniuses. But he also states: 'Even in the darkest ages, it was institutions that made society work, and if civilization is to survive, society must somehow be made to work' (*Civilization* (London, 1969), pp. 346–7).

25 Virginia Woolf, *The Death of the Moth* (London, 1942), p. 85.

for the evils of civilization or of its discontents, it remains a moral challenge of the highest order.[26]

'THE BOSTONIANS': CHARACTER WITHOUT CULTURE

In both *The Princess Casamassima* and *The Bostonians* James takes up social themes more explicitly than elsewhere in his fiction. In each novel there is conflict between established tradition and radical unorthodoxies. These conflicts are not altogether resolved, although through them James's greater sympathy with tradition becomes evident.

Nevertheless, the novels differ from each other in theme in a way which may have something to do with the interesting closeness of their composition. *The Bostonians* was written first and serialized (in *The Century Magazine*) from February 1885 to February 1886, while *The Princess Casamassima* appeared (in *The Atlantic Monthly*) from September 1885 to October 1886. Both were published in book form in 1886. Both, it must be admitted, were great failures with critics and readers alike.[27] When the New York edition was being developed the publishers thought it best to omit *The Bostonians* for reasons of space. James accepted this edict, under protest. He felt it never to have 'received any sort of justice', even though he admitted at the same time that the novel was too diffuse. The writing of *The Princess Casamassima* so close on the heels of

26 The unresolved tensions in James's novel recur frequently in our confusing intellectual history, and can be seen again as recently as 1967, for instance, in a writer whose commitments one does not readily associate with James. Herbert Marcuse in 'Art in the One-Dimensional Society' writes: 'I remember the familiar statement made long ago about the futility and perhaps even about the crime of art: that the Parthenon wasn't worth the blood and tears of a single Greek slave. And equally futile is the contrary statement that only a Parthenon justified slave society. Now, which one of the two statements is correct? If I look at Western civilization and culture today, at the wholesale slaughter and brutality it is engaged in, it seems to me that the first statement is probably more correct than the second. And still, the survival of art may turn out to be the only weak link that today connects the present with hope for the future' (*Radical Perspectives in the Arts*, ed. L. Baxandall (Pelican Books, 1972), pp. 53–67).

27 'I have entered upon evil days . . . I am still staggering a good deal under the mysterious and (to me) inexplicable injury wrought – apparently – upon my situation by my two last novels . . . from which I expected so much and derived so little. They have reduced the desire, and the demand, for my productions to zero.' Letter to W. D. Howells (*Letters*, I, p. 136).

the earlier novel may have seemed urgent to James because of the relative absence of a positive argument in *The Bostonians*. He wrote to Edmund Gosse:

The immediate inclusion of the 'Bostonians' was rather deprecated by the publishers . . . and there were reasons for which I also wanted to wait . . . Revision of it loomed particularly formidable and time-consuming (for intrinsic reasons) and as other things were more pressing and more promptly feasible I allowed it to stand over – with the best intentions.[28]

Why this novel should have struck him as especially difficult to revise is not easy to say; the writing itself is no more diffuse than that of *The Princess Casamassima*, and less so than *The Tragic Muse*. Were the 'intrinsic reasons' in some way related to the absence in *The Bostonians* of a characteristically positive alternative to its satirized programmes and personages? The New York edition, at any rate, failed in popularity, and the novel was not revised for subsequent addition, as James had hoped. How he might have changed the novel it is impossible to say; he might, perhaps, have forced the conflict of ideas to a more decisive conclusion.

The novel portrays a world of New England reformers and suffragettes, mesmeric healers and spiritualists and journalists, all frenetically eager to sustain the flagging idealism of the Transcendentalist movement and the Abolitionist cause. Into this world, thought to be illuminated by a New Dawn – though in fact it is the lurid twilight of a dying day – James introduces the opposing figure of Basil Ransom. Originally conceived of as a conservative and a distant relative of Olive Chancellor, unknown to her because of his long residence in the West,[29] he is finally given a persona more formally opposed to the world Olive inhabits. James must have felt a certain inadequacy in the idea of opposing an individual conservative to the radical Bostonians. He usually preferred the individual who represented a type *and* a tradition. In the novel Ransom becomes a representative Southerner, James's single eminent example.

Basil Ransom has fought in the Civil War on the side which

28 *Letters*, II, pp. 515–16.
29 *Notebooks*, p. 47.

his New England relative and friends regard as morally repre-
hensible. He has been bred in the complex neo-aristocratic
society of the pre-Civil War South which some historians
regard as the most homogeneous and highly developed culture
America has known. One effect of this change of background
in Ransom's characterization is the opportunity for humour in
the encounters between such a creature – the veritable enemy
– and the Boston ladies in whom, long after the war, Abolitionist
passions still run strong. There is, moreover, a remarkable pres-
cience in James's characterization, for Ransom anticipates
(lacking perhaps only the passion for agrarianism) the figures
who stand out in twentieth-century American intellectual life
as Southern Traditionalists: John Crowe Ransom, Allen Tate,
Donald Davidson, Andrew Lytle.[30] Basil Ransom is a bold conservative, and a stoic. He is, if anything, more extreme as a
'critic of life' than the New England reformers he detests:

The whole generation is womanised; the masculine tone is passing
out of the world; it's a feminine, a nervous, hysterical, chattering,
canting age, an age of hollow phrases and false delicacy and exaggerated solicitudes and coddled sensibilities, which, if we don't soon
look out, will usher in the reign of mediocrity, of the feeblest and
flattest and most pretentious that has ever been. The masculine
character, the ability to dare and endure, to know and yet not fear
reality, to look the world in the face and take it for what it is – a
very queer and partly very base mixture – that is what I want to
preserve, or rather, as I may say, to recover.

Basil Ransom has left the bankrupted South, despite his strong
loyalties, to make his way as a lawyer in New York. His distant
cousin, Olive Chancellor, has written to him out of a super-
abundant sense of duty, simply as to an unknown relative in
the vanquished South. Olive, as we are to learn, functions always
in terms of duty. Then sense of duty is frequently prominent in
James's American heroines, but Olive's is notable as the most
intense, and the most tragic in its confusions.

Ransom concludes a first visit to his Boston cousin, whom he
is not sure he likes, by accompanying her to a meeting of
reformers. There he hears an extemporized speech on the

30 This correspondence has been noted by Philip Rahv in his introduction
to *The Bostonians* (New York, 1945), p. ix.

suffragist cause by a young lady with a great natural gift for eloquence. Before she speaks, her father, a gold-toothed spiritualist, 'lays hands' for inspirational purposes on the young lady's head, which has the added advantage of magnificent red hair. Ransom recognizes at once that Verena Tarrant's eloquence has nothing to do with her ideas; he loves her eloquence and despises her opinions. He regards her with just the approval he might give to a beautiful and gifted actress or singer – she seems to be a little of both – but he has nothing but scorn for those who regard her as a thinker :

The sort of thing she was able to do, to say, was an article for which there was more and more demand – fluent, pretty, third-rate palaver, conscious or unconscious, perfected humbug; the stupid, gregarious, gullible public, the enlightened democracy of his native land, could swallow unlimited draughts of it.

She sounds as if she would be irresistible even at a contemporary political convention. Ransom falls in love with her, convinced that he can provide better uses for her gifts.

Although James is obviously sympathetic to the character of Basil Ransom, the sympathy is by no means unconditional. The reader must be wary of accepting Ransom as an auctorial voice. James does not identify himself at all with Ransom's positive ideas, which he separates himself from by 'confessing' them to be Ransom's remarkable ideas. There is, however, ample evidence that James does sympathize with his negative critique of the Boston machinery. Ransom's positive values express an exaggeratedly aggressive view of 'masculine' character that anticipates not so much modern Southern Traditionalism as a more general modern defensiveness about sex differentiation, whether that of Philip Wylie or the more symptomatic search for Spartan masculinity of Ernest Hemingway and his followers. That James was not committed to a similar flight from the feminine principle needs no demonstration; one need only remember Isabel Archer and Milly Theale, Mme de Vionnet and Maggie Verver.

In any case, Ransom is given fine opportunities for the firing of broadsides at some of the assumptions of James's age (and of our own) :

You had a right to an education only if you had an intelligence
. . . an intelligence was a very rare luxury, the attribute of one
person in a hundred.

. . . he was sick of all the modern cant about freedom and had no
sympathy with those who wanted an extension of it. What was
needed for the good of the world was that people should make a
better use of the liberty they possessed.

He, too, had a private vision of reform, but the first principle of
it was to reform the reformers.

This austere young man delivers these assaults from the bastion
of a 'severe, hard, unique stoicism'. Stoicism is invoked frequently in *The Bostonians*. But what is distinctive in this novel
is that stoicism is not a corollary of a belief in civilization or
high culture, as is usual in James, but rather is an end in itself.
As the sole alternative even to the 'machinery' of social reform
it may seem a little hollow. Consequently the novel is, more
profoundly than in its surface political observations, a curiously
reactionary one.

Never in James does the word 'renunciation' so bravely ring.
The paradox is that there is in the novel so little actual renunciation. Basil Ransom's kinswomen, we are told, face their
Mississippi impoverishment with a stoicism scarcely less yielding
than Basil's own. But it is not clear, however they face their
impoverishment, what alternatives are open to them to renounce. Olive Chancellor and Verena Tarrant dedicate themselves to a selfless battle for feminism with frequent and
passionate avowals of renunciation. But Verena goes off with
Basil in the end. She gives up what is presented as a false career
in the advancement of causes, and a false friendship under the
domination of Olive Chancellor, for what is proposed as a 'true'
career of home and hearth. Olive Chancellor, the one tragic
figure in the novel, is tragic not because she deserves what she
loses, but because we feel that she deserves more than her own
twisted nature can ever give her. She suffers not as she chooses,
but as she must. Basil Ransom renounces nothing but Mrs Luna,
Olive's widowed and infatuated sister; but no one, except perhaps Mrs Luna, can possibly regard this as a sacrifice. It requires
less than heroic stoicism to give up the moon, or at least it did
before 1968.

Miss Birdseye near the end of her brave, foolish, selfless life waits for its close:

There was, to Ransom, something almost august in the trustful renunciation of her countenance; something in it seemed to say that she had been ready long before, but as the time was not ripe she had waited, with her usual faith that all was for the best.

This particular renunciation we all must face, with but little allowance for choice. Still, Miss Birdseye rises to the dignity of death touchingly, and Ransom's reflections bypass the specific conflicts of the novel to recall, in a modest way, that very great stoical pronouncement:

> Men must endure
> Their going hence, even as their coming hither.
> Ripeness is all.

Hyacinth Robinson's suicide in *The Princess Casamassima* is a deliberate act clearly related to the idea of stoicism. It is clearly related also to the ideal of culture, which Hyacinth feels he cannot betray. His act is contrasted to other, and ironic, references to stoicism. The Princess's renunciation of the privileges of her wealth and position in favour of her brief proletarian make-believe in Paddington represents only the privilege and luxury of her distorted will. The explicit naming of stoicism occurs in two places in the novel, and in each the irony is marked. Hyacinth at first admires the stoicism of Rosy Muniment, the invalid whom he (with the reader) comes to dislike for her positive maliciousness of unfailing good spirits, her arrogance, her exasperating and patronizingly egotistical gratitude. Hyacinth also admires the stoicism of her brother Paul when he seems with such sublime ease able to accept the sacrifice of his dearest friend, Hyacinth, for the good of the Cause. Hyacinth at this point in his development trustingly believes this act of brave disinterestedness to be more difficult than the mere sacrifice of self. Muniment's later relationship with the Princess, however, will throw a different light on the limits of Paul's selflessness. In the end, when Hyacinth takes his life, surrendering both revolution and civilization, these ironic invocations of the stoic spirit serve to highlight his own renunciation. But in *The Bostonians*, stoicism serves no end but itself, and despite the frequent reiteration of the ideal, no one in fact renounces.

The New England sense of Cause – the burlesqued dissipation of New England's 'heroic age' – is exposed brilliantly by James's satiric treatment. He presents us with a great carnival of genuine freaks and spurious saints, among them Verena's father, Selah Tarrant, the spiritualist with an enthusiasm for nature camps sorely trying to his tremulously trusting wife; and Mrs Farrinder who affects large hats and larger views and who sails through the shoals and shallows of social movements like a launched frigate; and Miss Birdseye, sweet and vague and suffering from the battle fatigue of innumerable campaigns, of whom it is definitively said that 'the whole moral history of Boston was reflected in her displaced spectacles'. This gallery of eccentrics which James placed so conspicuously on view deeply antagonized James's American public.

Beyond the satire, however, we have the remarkably penetrating study of Olive Chancellor, whose repressed loves and sublimated passions, whose aggressions and shynesses, anguishes and altruisms, constitute a vivid rendering of a profoundly wounded psyche. James leaves little for a later science of psychiatry to add but the jargon of labels.

James's *Notebooks* record his determination that *The Bostonians* should be 'as local, as American, as possible, and as full of Boston, an attempt to show that I *can* write an American story'.[31] The brilliant if satirical representation of certain American types is one aspect of this ambition. But perhaps we may find another consequence of James's intention in his suppression of his usual emphasis on civilization as culture. The insidious suggestion is that an 'American story' would have but little to do with such an ideal.[32]

---

31 *Notebooks*, p. 42.
32 Even *Washington Square* uses Europe as an idea within an American setting, both in the figure of the deracinated Morris Townsend, and in the significant failure of Catherine Sloper's European pilgrimage to liberate her sensibility and to shake her single passion.

In *The Bostonians* some use is made of the idea of Europe, and the familiar ideal of culture is introduced as well. But these motifs are not extensively developed or integrated with the central conflicts of the novel. Although Olive *hates* Europe, as we are told more than once, she does take Verena there to study the 'woman question' – the *idée fixe* that limits Olive so narrowly. Verena, on the other hand, responds to Europe in the way that James's free sensibilities are supposed to, and it is open to us to feel how easily she might become another of James's passionate pilgrims, but for the dominating influence of her friend:

Olive had always rated high the native refinement of her country-women, their latent 'adaptability', their talent for accommodating themselves at a glance to changed conditions; but the way her companion rose with the level of the civilization that surrounded her, the way she assimilated all delicacies and absorbed all traditions, left this friendly theory halting behind.

Olive is sadly insensible of the irony that the qualities which she rates so highly are just those qualities which she herself most lacks: adaptability and accommodation. Most important to the novel's development, however, is a related irony. Verena's new experiences, generously provided through the patronage of Olive in forms broader and more liberal than those offered by her early environment, are just the experiences which will lead to her eventual disaffection from Olive's tyrannies. We remember that Hyacinth Robinson's exposure to a wider experience has similar effects on him, including a growing scepticism about over-simplified absolutes. 'There was enough of the epicurean in Verena's composition', we are told, 'to make it easy for her in certain conditions to live only for the hour.' Olive's sensitive awareness of this developing sensibility in Verena makes her fear the civilizing process, and she dreads the possibility of Verena's fondness even for New York, with its dangerous appeals to the senses and its low regard for duty.

If the novel does not involve Europe extensively in a process of enrichment, Boston and New York provide Verena with more openings to culture than she has known, or than Olive

would choose. We are introduced to a more Jamesian figure
than Basil Ransom in the person of Henry Burrage, a wealthy
Harvard undergraduate who represents the familiar values of
developed taste and high culture. Burrage comes to the Tarrants'
peculiar household in Cambridge for the amusement of the
thing, but stays to fall in love with Verena. He is a young man
who 'collected beautiful things, pictures and antiques and
objects that he sent for to Europe on purpose, many of which
were arranged in his rooms at Cambridge'. Verena is persuaded,
not too easily, to agree with Olive's rejection of Burrage's appeal.
'Taste and art were good', Olive explains, 'when they enlarged
the mind, not when they narrowed it.' The formula is irreproachable, so long as one agrees on its applications. Olive's own
application is the thesis that all history is the record and per-
petuation of pain and persecution for the 'sisterhood of women',
a history in which culture has offended no less frequently than
any other of insidious man's activities. Here we come close to
a similar conflict of culture versus cause to that in *The Princess
Casamassima*.

  Olive is given to certain contradictions in her responses to
culture, contradictions which are one symptom of her distorted
psyche. It is not just that she can quote Goethe's *Faust* in support
of aspiration while unaware of her own narrowness, but that
she is a sensitive and intelligent woman in flight from her
vulnerability to the appeals of beauty. Henry Burrage enter-
tains Olive and Verena in his beautiful rooms and performs for
them at the piano. The scene is worth quoting at some length
because it gives us the Jamesian touchstone which is so missing
in the 'American' conflict between Olive and Basil Ransom,
between New England austerity and pious stoicism:

His guests sat scattered in the red firelight, listening, silent, in comfortable attitudes; there was a faint fragrance from the burning logs,
which mingled with the perfume of Schubert and Mendelssohn; the
covered lamps made a glow here and there, and the cabinets and
brackets produced brown shadows, out of which some precious
object gleamed – some ivory carving or *cinquecento* cup. It was
given to Olive, under these circumstances, for half an hour, to
enjoy the music, to admit that Mr. Burrage played with exquisite

taste, to feel as if the situation were a kind of truce. Her nerves were calmed, her problems – for the time – subsided. *Civilization, under such an influence, in such a setting, appeared to have done its work; harmony ruled the scene; human life ceased to be a battle.* She went so far as to ask herself why one should have a quarrel with it; the relations of men and women, in that picturesque group-ing, had not the air of being internecine [my italics].

The spell does not last long beyond its inspiration, however, for Olive deliberately throws it off, for the sake of the Cause. Later in the history of causes, Lenin confessed that he loved the music of Beethoven, but felt it dangerous to listen to such things too much lest they soften and undermine the dissident will, tempt one to 'fondle' and 'say nice things' to the oppressors of men.

Paradoxically, even Olive's sensibility has to acknowledge to some extent the power of culture; the uses to which she puts it are something else again. The extreme bias of her personality may be related to the peculiar malaise of late-nineteenth-century New England, where a dynamic potential of spiritual energy was cut off from meaningful expression or release. Olive's doctrinal suspicion of culture denies crucial elements of her own sensibility. A spiritual and aesthetic deprivation forces her authentic needs into strange and ultimately unfulfilling substi-tutions. James describes Olive's morbid but unrecognized rela-tionship with Verena as common among New England women of that kind. If this is so it bespeaks a society with serious biases and deprivations. New England moral intensity, without what Matthew Arnold had called sweetness and light or what James in a larger context called culture, distorts the human personality. Olive Chancellor must be seen, if not as a victim of this society, at least as an expression of its dangerous possibilities. While other Jamesian heroines may come to grief because, like Isabel Archer, they aspire to a high culture which eludes them, Olive Chancellor becomes a tragic figure because the very nature of such an aspiration has been poisoned at its source.

Olive mortifies her person by dressing deliberately beneath her own taste, although her family home is very handsome. She detests horse-cars, but (like Princess Casamassima) denies herself the luxury of private conveyance because her 'sisters' must do without. She has a real passion for learning, but it has been narrowed to the single track of her researches on oppression. She dreams of conditions of worldly bliss for her down-trodden sisters, and at the same time

in a career in which she was constantly exposing herself to offence and laceration, her most poignant suffering came from the injury to her taste. She had tried to kill that nerve, to persuade herself that taste was only frivolity in the disguise of knowledge; but her susceptibility was constantly blooming afresh and making her wonder whether an absence of nice arrangements were a necessary part of the enthusiasm for humanity.[33]

As a kind of counterweight to the scene in Henry Burrage's rooms, where Olive yields briefly to the temptations of culture, James gives us another in Mrs Luna's elegantly prosperous New York mansion. Here Basil Ransom is offered the temptation of surrendering his unsuccessful struggle to redeem his family's fallen fortunes through hard work, by yielding to Mrs Luna's obvious readiness to marry him. At first glance the choice offered Basil might seem to invalidate the point of the earlier scene, where Olive's rejection of temptation reveals the mutilation of so large a part of her sensibility. But the temptation offered Basil is not in the direction of wholeness and liberation, but of a surrender of independence and integrity. What Mrs Luna offers is wealth, not culture.[34] Her values and her Europe are as worldly, as superficial, as she is herself. She is not, that is, a spokesman for culture at all.

In despair of understanding the complex relations around her, Miss Birdseye says – with 'a little ineffectual sigh' – 'Well, I suppose everyone must act out their ideal.' We must attribute to this least acute and responsible of Jamesian figures the central statement of the novel's idea. In the dramatic clash of ideals represented by Olive and Basil, with Verena as the prize, both

33 One must confess that there are times, as in this instance, when James seems to be speaking less of the values of culture than of the prejudices of class snobbery.

34 The theme of acquisition, of 'Things', in relation to culture is discussed more fully in chapter 6.

of these bigoted characters prove incapable of any compromise of ideal or of action throughout the novel. The opponents enact their ideals with a relentless logic. For even if Verena renounces Basil, as at several points she determines to do, she cannot renounce her emotions, or return to an earlier singleness of devotion which alone can satisfy Olive. Long before Verena goes off with Basil she has succumbed to his influence. Her final passionate struggle is the consequence not of uncertainty in her feelings for him, but of her consideration for Olive, whose pain in losing Verena will be even greater with the victory of her hated Southern, male, reactionary kinsman.

But Verena does go off with Basil, and she leaves Olive very like a martyr in the arena to face alone the angry crowd that has come to hear Verena speak at a major feminist rally. The only alternative to the actual ending (at that hypothetical juncture where such alternatives may occur in the creative process) is for Verena to give up Basil out of loyalty to Olive, and then to give up Olive out of loyalty to herself.[35] This has the ring of a classic Jamesian renunciation, stoicism and all. James's *Notebooks*, however, make it clear that he intended from the first to have Verena surrender to the young man, even when his character was still imperfectly determined. Why in this case James desired a happy ending is itself interesting. Was it because he was determined to write an '*American* story'? – to deal with what William Dean Howells argued was the proper province of the American novel: 'the smiling aspects of life'? In any case, happy it was intended to be. But given James's reservations about the particular young man who emerges in the novel, it was perhaps inevitable that some complication to happiness should colour his original intention.

Does Verena conform to the fatality of Ransom's grim vision – 'We are born to suffer – and to bear it, like decent people'? Or does she instead fulfil the more liberal prophecy of Olive (whose own genius for suffering is unalloyed): 'You were not

35 A similar alternative might have presented itself to Isabel Archer; that is, to give up Goodwood out of loyalty to Osmond, and then to give up Osmond out of loyalty to herself. In neither case does James believe such alternatives acceptable, and both novels employ theatrical final scenes to clinch the issue.

made to suffer – you were made to enjoy'? The novel's conclusion might appear to support Olive's prediction, were it not
for the very last lines. They follow Basil Ransom's theatrical
last-minute rescue of Verena from the Boston Music Hall, where,
he feels, she has been about to sell her soul to the populace in
some final and definitive way. These are the novel's last lines:

'Ah, now I am glad!' said Verena, when they reached the street.
But though she was glad, he presently discovered that, beneath her
hood, she was in tears. It is to be feared that with the union, so
far from brilliant, into which she was about to enter, these were
not the last she was destined to shed.

This uneasy union of an epicureanism foretold by Olive – 'You
were made to enjoy' – with a stoicism insisted upon by Basil –
'we are born to suffer and to bear it' – makes for a somewhat
ambiguous ending. Verena's suffering is presumably mitigated
by the happy conjunction of Basil's specification for feminine
happiness – 'to be as pleasant as a woman can be, in the functions of a wife' – with the winning of the very man she loves,
the man whom in all the world she most wants to be pleasant
for. However we interpret the tears to be shed in a union 'so
far from brilliant', however, Verena's future of enjoyment
appears to be met with a very meagre diet.

Olive's words to Verena – 'You were not made to suffer –
you were made to enjoy' – strike a responsive echo, for they
resound from *The Portrait of a Lady*. There, Ralph has said to
Isabel early in her career, 'But you haven't suffered, and you're
not made to suffer', to which Isabel has added her own affirmation: 'It's not absolutely necessary to suffer; we were not made
for that.'

Much could be made of the similarities between Verena
Tarrant and Isabel Archer, but what interests me now, especially
for the light it sheds on James's most characteristic themes, is
their essential difference. Verena, after all, was *not* made to
suffer, if for no other reason than that she was not destined, as
Isabel Archer was, to embrace the ideal image of civilization
for the sake of which James's characters most ambitiously aspire
and most tragically fall. This ideal image causes Isabel to re-

nounce a last possibility of happiness, for it is the only ideal by which she can live, even while it has proved to be unattainable in her marriage. The search for high culture as a way of life is not the representative New England ideal (and even Henry Burrage is not a New Englander), and such a search is likely to be regarded as irrelevant to – if not destructive of – more narrowly seen ideals of moral character and conduct. Instead of the ideal image of civilization as culture, Verena is asked to embrace Ransom's dubious stoicism, which is only another version of the idealization of moral conduct. Its spiritual and aesthetic vacuum is no more generously filled than in Olive's alternatives. The choice would seem to confirm the 'terrible paucity of alternatives' in New England that James identified in his fine essay on Emerson. There he had praised Emerson's 'genius for seeing character as a real and supreme thing'.[36] But it is a conception of character that does not provide for the wholeness of human potentiality: it is the genius of Character without Culture.[37]

'The use of a truly amiable woman is to make some honest man happy', Ransom has told Verena, with intimations of personal convenience sufficient to make his professions of austere stoicism appear suspect. Verena has evidently been converted to this ideal, and the more we think about Ransom's pronouncement, the less stoical becomes the novel's ambiguous resolution. Obviously, James found it difficult to assent to Ransom's views. If Verena is destined to shed tears, glad as she is at the moment of choosing Ransom, it will be because Ransom's stoicism will prove to be less rewarding, less 'brilliant' as a way of life than the requirements of her own developing sensibility. What she is likely to require is more generously

36 *Partial Portraits*, pp. 1–32.
37 In his early review of George Eliot (*Atlantic Monthly*, October 1866), James tempers admiration with two reservations. The first is that the author is 'in morals and aesthetics essentially a conservative'. He says, 'she has made no attempt to depict a conscience taking upon itself great and novel responsibilities'. The second is that she tends to 'compromise' with the old tradition which 'exacts that a serious story of manners shall close with the factitious happiness of a fairy-tale'. The two reservations together provide just the critique needed for illuminating the difference between *The Portrait of a Lady* and *The Bostonians*.

embodied in the statue which James invented in his first novel to symbolize the passionate pilgrim, Roderick Hudson's 'Thirst'. A youthful, innocent, eager figure holds a cup which Roderick says represents 'knowledge, pleasure, experience'. Of the figure itself, Roderick says, 'Aye, poor fellow, he's thirsty.'

At the end of *The Bostonians* we may safely assume that Ransom achieves most of the things he wants, short of a resurrection of the fallen South. We are not likely to feel the same assurance about Verena, for all her fairy-tale escape from the cave of the wicked witch. Her cup is a fairly dry one, and as we get past the bustling dramatic scene in which she makes her choice, we may feel some sense of anti-climax in its results.

Perhaps the relative absence of the ideal of civilization in *The Bostonians* suggested to James the desirability of dealing with a comparable conflict in which the opposition to 'machinery' or social upheaval might be more positive – might, indeed, involve his own convictions about the highest good. The positive value of stoicism in the earlier novel proves to be an insufficiently convincing contribution to fictional conflict and resolution; it lacks the superior dramatic and thematic possibilities James saw in the pursuit of culture.

The *Notebooks*, unfortunately, do not reveal James's conceptions of *The Princess Casamassima*. But we have at least the corroboration of the novels themselves, following one so closely upon the other. Moving beyond the conflict of stoic conservatism with social reform, in the later novel the conflict is between culture and social revolution, between the preservation of ideals that James truly believed in, and their complete destruction.

'THE TRAGIC MUSE': CULTURE AND COMMONWEAL

The third of the novels of this period, *The Tragic Muse*, also invokes forces divergent from civilization; in this case not from civilization as we may normally regard it, but from culture as James rather specially defined it. The central conflict in the novel is whether or not Nick Dormer will give up the 'life of history' for the 'life of art'. The case is often made for seeing civilization primarily as the embodiment and product of public and political life, as a process of history, with a social end.[38] In distinction from this emphasis, James advances his own higher claim for culture as art in its moral, intellectual, and aesthetic wholeness. It is possible, if not inevitable, to confuse definitions of what high civilization essentially *is* and to assign quite different values to it. *The Tragic Muse* has little to do with the labels of reformer, revolutionary, or reactionary. Its burden is that of deciding which values – those of public history or of art – should command man's highest loyalty and commitment. But the extreme separation which is developed in the novel between these values will prove to be fatal.

There are two trains of action in *The Tragic Muse*: first, Miriam Rooth's development as a brilliant and dedicated actress, together with her less preoccupying relationship with Peter Sherringham, a diplomat by profession and an art devotee by inclination; and second, Nick Dormer's conflict between a brilliant public life which includes Parliament and marriage with a great heiress, Julia Dallow, on the one hand, and on the other, the prospect of an obscure and lonely life as an artist. The two stories are obviously related, and one is supposed to illuminate the other. Nick's decision to renounce his career as a politician in order to paint is given greater emphasis by Peter Sherringham's refusal to renounce *his* career to marry Miriam Rooth.

James discusses the two separate *données* which launched this work in his preface to the novel, and recalls his concern that they might not join properly. He assures himself that they do, and that his canvas is not too ample.[39] It is not too ample, perhaps, but it *is* disjointed. The two movements refuse to coalesce as one. The development of each of these elements tends too frequently to be suspended while the other is taken

38 Toynbee, for example, defines civilization as 'an endeavour to create a state of society in which the whole of Mankind will be able to live together in harmony, as members of a single all-inclusive family . . . This is, I believe, the goal at which all civilizations so far known have been aiming unconsciously, if not consciously' (*A Study of History*, revised edition, London, 1972, p. 44).
39 Preface to *The Tragic Muse*, p. ix.

up, in mechanical alteration, rather like Scott's technique for increasing suspense. But here there is little narrative suspense, and at the thematic level a counterpoint which should lead to a unifying resolution contributes instead to a forced discord.

History and the public life as the central focus of civilization is a theme touched on in *The Portrait of a Lady*, in the values assigned to Lord Warburton. But Warburton was not asked to choose between his life of high responsibility, of political power and prestige, and a life both removed absolutely from the world and without material reward or public honour – the life of the artist. The conflict for Nick Dormer is defined in just this way. A number of external forces, in combination with certain talents of his own, conspire to push him toward a public life. For the life of art there are no external temptations – whether of money or fame – and even the question of his native talent is left rather vague. There is one argument only, one reiterated often in the novel: 'the idea itself', the classic *ding an sich*, as it speaks to the private sensibility. This conflict of Dormer's is announced quite early in the novel with some energy; its development and resolution are much more falteringly accomplished.

In contrast with Dormer's velleities, we have the unambiguous, undivided determination of Miriam Rooth to become a great actress. But the light which her steadily advancing career sheds on the difficult choices confronting Nick Dormer is unclear. Indeed, her contrasting story bristles with ironies. For in pursuing her ambition she will appear to give up nothing which she visibly yearns for. Since her private life is a matter of comparative indifference to her, even her renunciation of Peter Sherringham costs her little, however it might affect Sherringham.[40] I am uncomfortably reminded of a less attaching character in James, the over-sophisticated and brittle Lady John of *The Sacred Fount*, of whom it is said that she

didn't want a lover; this would have been, as people say, a larger order than, given the other complications of her existence, she could meet; but she wanted, in a high degree, the appearance of carrying

---

40 Peter Sherringham, however, is said to love representation more than the thing itself.

on a passion that imposed alike fearful realisations and conscious renouncements.

Moreover, whatever in her life Miriam may be said to renounce is given up not *only* for the pure state of being an artist, for 'the idea itself', but as much for just what Nick cannot look to have: success, power, fame – the triumphant actor's public justification for the not-so-private act.

The invoked moral of her tale, in contrast with Dormer's, would appear to be that the mark of the true artist is to have *no* temptations or distractions, even from the beginning, that might interfere with the singleness of dedication required for a sacred calling. Even if this were true – which is by no means self-evident – it would scarcely help illuminate the dilemmas of Nick Dormer. Because of conflicts both of background and of talent he must make a *choice*, the necessity for which seems almost to disqualify him from serious consideration. The novel suggests what I doubt was James's deliberate intention, that one does not chose to become an artist, but is chosen. If this is true, we can only sigh for Dormer, remembering that many are called but few are chosen.

When Peter Sherringham in turn chooses, his choice proves to be mainly a diversion rather than a significant contrast; and in the last half of the novel it is damaging to the form as well as to the idea, since his choices seem finally unimportant, and all too predictable even from the beginning.

And yet *The Tragic Muse* begins with tremendous promise. At the first we are conscious of a suggestive and interesting interaction in the grouped figures of Nick Dormer, Peter Sherringham, and Gabriel Nash. James avoids giving them too much the sense merely of forces or symbols until later in the novel, when they tend to become all too obviously just that. In Gabriel Nash, the completely convinced aesthete, and in Peter Sherringham, the intelligent but over-worldly dilletante, we have the alternatives which Nick must choose between. We want from the first to know which way his choice will go. The characterizations of Miriam Rooth and of her ubiquitous mother are brilliantly managed. How James's irony shone when it was exercised on elderly ladies! Miriam is still the best study of an actress in English fiction. She convinces us completely of her devotion to her art which, unusually for James, is not idealized or embedded in a wider conception of culture, but is literally professional. Acting for her is an exacting and challenging craft. She sets out ambitiously to master it with great talent and in-defatigable work, and not much intelligence – an ideal com-bination, James conceives, for the actress. She has a communi-cated vitality rare in James's artists, and her vitality reflects by very contrast unfavourably (though I think unintentionally) on Nick Dormer's career.

Part of this contrast comes from the fact that Miriam's ambitions in art are mainly internal, self-generated, while much of Dormer's pull towards art is seen to come from Gabriel Nash. James appears to have wanted to 'do' the *fin de siècle* aesthete then coming into prominence. But how we are to take him is unclear, as unclear as the strange disposition which James makes of him at the end. While early in the novel Nash has served as the impassioned champion of art (mainly, it should be added, for art's sake), he becomes a hopelessly mechanical presence in the latter part, and then disappears. The point made even of his disappearance is unsatisfactory. James invents a play-fully coy episode about a portrait of Nash which is fading on the canvas, 'as in some delicate Hawthorne tale', and suggests that it will vanish completely on the day Nash returns in the flesh. It is a false note, lacking what the Hawthorne tale would characteristically embody: an objective moral point or truth. The episode is more evocative of the Oscar Wilde mode than of Hawthorne, even as Gabriel Nash himself suggests Wilde – especially Wilde's generally over-praised use of the painting in *The Picture of Dorian Gray*.[41]

In the dialectic established between the 'whole, wide world'

41 *The Tragic Muse* precedes both *The Picture of Dorian Gray* (1891), and the appearance of *The Yellow Book*, to which James contributed 'The Death of the Lion' in 1894. The case for seeing Nash as a representation of Wilde, with some composite elements, is argued in Oscar Cargill's *The Novels of Henry James*, pp. 191–3. Leon Edel sees Dormer as modelled largely on Cyril Flower (later Lord Battersea), and Nash as modelled on Herbert Pratt, in *Henry James: The Middle Years* (London, 1963), pp. 192–3 and 198–9.

of a successful public life and the 'little corner' of art, neither term is dealt with convincingly. Nick Dormer does choose: he leaves Parliament and takes up portrait painting. But the significance of his choice is vitiated by weakness of specification. The political world, the arena of practical history, is not re-created in a way convincing in itself, nor as having sufficiently powerful temptation for Dormer. Moreover, it is not clear that what he rejects is a public life so much as it is personal acquisition and gratification. He rejects the appeals of his mother, and his father's ghostly solicitations, the wealth and love of Julia Dallow (although how much he prizes these is rather ambiguous in the end). He rejects all these so that he can paint, knowing that he probably has not genius, but only passion. But even his passion is rendered dubious to the reader by the example of Gabriel Nash. We are likely to have the uncomfortable feeling that Dormer gives up life itself for an abstraction, a displacement which is as likely to prove fatal for the artist as for the man. I am not concerned to vindicate the public life. I do not object to his renunciations; but to the degree that he seems to give up temptations insufficiently urgent to himself, any poignancy in his renunciations is lost on us, and seems rather lost on him. What is lacking is a more convincing internal drama – Faust's 'two worlds at war within' – so vividly depicted by James (if on a lesser scale) in Hyacinth Robinson. There seems a great loss of vitality in Dormer by the end of the novel, and one fears that he is not so much moving toward a significant area of life as a consequence of his choice as he is retreating from life altogether.

Some of the problems of the novel may possibly be attributed to the circumstances of serialized publication. James was committed to twelve instalments for *Atlantic*, but the novel ran into a desperate seventeen, some of them mercilessly foreshortened. Compressed into the latter parts are great blocks of exposition and summary, and the very end – the last fifty pages or so – seems a frantic packing of luggage into the groaning trunk, the whole banged shut with sleeves and snippets bulging out still, and the train gates closing. James's ends often have a way of falling below the standards of his beginnings; his complications are generally more convincing than his unravellings. Readers of Shakespeare know the kind of dénouement which is held back until the penultimate moment, and then exploded for its full impact in the fifth act. In *The Tragic Muse*, something of the same holding off appears to be developing, but the explosion is absent.

Opposing Nick Dormer's friend Gabriel Nash as an influence is Mr Carteret, who acts as Nick's patron so long as Nick remains in politics. In the earlier part of the novel this characterization of a representative Victorian liberal is very good. But Carteret lingers on in sickness and silence through most of the second part. There is no canvas from which he may picturesquely fade, but he does die at last, long after it is abundantly evident even to the casual reader that he has disowned Nick – dies mainly in obedience to the mechanical fate that disposes of the actor when he is no longer of use to the author. And what had begun as an approach to a more fully realized physical passion than is usually to be found in James – there is a remarkable love scene between Julia Dallow and Nick Dormer on the little island on Julia's estate – dwindles, quite literally, to nothing. Even the thrust provided by Miriam Rooth's fine energy seems somehow dissipated by the end.

I have already argued that the world of ideas, of actions, of practical significances which should be represented as attaching to the life of politics or social history is curiously thin, lacking in any of the power that might make Dormer's ambivalences vivid to us. The effect is not only to invalidate the novel as argument, but as art. James lacks a certain intensity of imagination in creating the two worlds of Nick Dormer's choice. 'Without intensity', we remember James saying in one of his prefaces, 'where is vividness, and without vividness where is presentability?'

If any reader persists in believing that James's novels may be read as tracts, with transparent garments of fiction perfectly clothing the bodies of conscious or deliberate intention, then *The Tragic Muse* will prove incapable of explication. It is perhaps no accident that this novel was to be James's last for some six years; its reception was scarcely less depressing than that of the two social novels of 1886. As though inspired by the successes of Miriam Rooth, James turned to the theatre with a similar passion, unrequited though it proved to be.

Given the themes of *The Bostonians* and *The Princess Casa-massima*, one might suppose James's further explorations in *The Tragic Muse* capable of inspiring a more brilliant treatment. But something has gone wrong, something for which the seeds have already been sown in the earlier novels, where culture is too drastically removed from its social and communal context. His sympathies have become engaged not too strongly with art, but with too limited and sterile a conception of art. James's identification with Dormer – perhaps a kind of self-justification – is excessive, and its effect on the novel is warping. And in the later novels a certain clear energy and vitality which one has felt in the earlier works is absent.

The point worth making here is that Nick Dormer's *art* has become so rarefied, so etiolated in conception, that it can no longer be felt to be the 'criticism of life' which Arnold had convinced James that art must be. It is, rather, an escape from life. *The Tragic Muse* is the only extended work by James dealing with the life of art which seems less related to a conception of its intellectual, moral, and aesthetic wholeness – a conception which one associates with the examples and influences of George Eliot and Matthew Arnold – than to the more precious tradition of the aesthetes, of the *art pour l'art* which burgeons from Walter Pater into Oscar Wilde and the 'yellow nineties'.[42]

There is persuasive evidence that James's intention was more vigorous. The central passage in Nick Dormer's development has great suggestiveness in supporting the high importance which James gives to culture, and it stands out from too much

42 I think it is this tradition which leads to the disturbing questions raised by Rajah Amar in L. H. Myers's *The Near and the Far* (London, 1956): 'At what point between barbarism and decadence does civilization reign? If a civilized community be defined as one where you find aesthetic preoccupations, subtle thought, and polished intercourse, is civilization necessarily desirable? Aesthetic preoccupations are not inconsistent with a wholly inadequate conception of the range and power of art; thought may be subtle and yet trivial; and polished intercourse may be singularly uninteresting' (p. 404).

else in the novel in its vigorous conception and eloquence. Nick is reflecting on some portraits in the National Gallery:

These were the things most inspiring, in the sense that while generations, while worlds had come and gone, they seemed far most to prevail and survive and testify. As he stood before them the perfection of their survival often struck him as the supreme eloquence, the virtue that included all others, thanks to the language of art, the richest and most universal. Empires and systems and conquests had rolled over the globe and every kind of greatness had passed away, but the beauty of the great pictures had known nothing of death or change, and the tragic centuries had only sweetened their freshness. The same faces, the same figures looked out at different worlds, knowing so many secrets the particular world didn't, and when they joined hands they made the indestructible thread on which the pearls of history were strung.[43]

In itself this is an impressive enough credo. But the crucial failure of *The Tragic Muse* is just the absence of a persuasive objectification in fiction for this passionate belief. There is a gap between explicit pronouncement and dramatic fulfilment that disappoints expectation.

When Nick Dormer asks Gabriel Nash what matters most in life, Nash replies, 'To be on the right side – on the side of

---

43 The passage has clear affinities with Gautier's famous poem 'L'Art', from *Emaux et Camées*, which James had singled out for full quotation and praise in his study of Gautier (*French Poets and Novelists*, London, 1884). The poem, especially in its latter part, became an early manifesto of the aesthetes:

> Tout passe. – L'art robuste
> Seul a l'éternité,
>   Le buste
> Survit à la cité.
>
> Et la médaille austère
> Que trouve un laboureur
>   Sous terre
> Révèle un empereur.
>
> Les dieux eux-mêmes meurent,
> Mais les vers souverains
>   Demeurent
> Plus forts que les airains.
>
> Sculpte, lime, ciselle;
> Que ton rêve flottant
>   Se scelle
> Dans le bloc résistant!

beauty.' He amplifies his statement in a way that will sound both impressive and familiar :

the beauty of having been disinterested and independent; of having taken the world in the free, brave, personal way.

If the ideal is promising, the practice as we get it in the novel is not. In consequence, the quotation above is almost embarrassing in its echoing of Isabel Archer's ideal, which was described in *The Portrait of a Lady* in such similar terms : 'To look at life – that is to live – freely, generously, handsomely'.[44] The embarrassment attaches to Nick Dormer, for Isabel Archer at least lives with a good deal of intensity, tries fully to meet the ideal of 'having taken the world in the free, brave, generous way'. Nick Dormer strikes us, finally, as just not having taken the world at all.

I stress all this because there is ample evidence that James knew that the life of art, while disinterested, requires both personal passion and power. It is a knowledge which Balzac and Flaubert might well have confirmed for him. As a way of life, art posits an ideal which needs both commitment and ambition; the making of art implies *force*. The ideal of beauty must transcend the picturesque and pretty, and even the well-made; the artist is not only maker, but seer. James may portray the artist as mere struggling mortal or – sometimes – as saint; but in either role he is usually compelled by an ideal imbued with the sense of glory, the sense of power. James had a vision about the connection between art and power, but in *The Tragic Muse* he avoids the implications of this vision, or pretends that it does not exist. An episode in his own autobiography will best demonstrate the vision so lacking in the novel.

James tells us that during an early visit to Europe (1859–60), he was roused to a great 'awakening' in the Galerie d'Apollon in the Louvre. The Galerie d'Apollon breathed for him 'a general sense of *glory*' :

44 It is interesting how James echoes, in weaker novels like *The Bostonians* and *The Tragic Muse*, the very strength of his characterization of Isabel Archer.

The glory meant ever so many things at once, not only beauty and art and supreme design, but history and fame and power, the world in fine raised to the richest and noblest expression.[45]

This seminal experience in the Louvre had begun with an awakening to *style*, but it ended with a more general vision, with the seed and sense of his central fictional theme :

The beginning, in short, was with Géricault and David, but it went on and on and slowly spread; so that one's stretched, one's even strained, perceptions, one's discoveries and extensions piece by piece, come back, on the great premises, almost as so many explorations of the house of life, so many circlings and hoverings round the image of the world.[46]

These two passages give us not only James's vision of the world he most cared about, but of the artist's high place in it.

But there is more. James tells of a dream many years later, which he describes as the 'most appalling yet most admirable nightmare of my life'. His account of it deserves a rather lengthy quotation :

The climax of this extraordinary experience – which stands alone for me as a dream-adventure founded in the deepest, quickest, clearest act of cogitation and comparison, act indeed of life-saving energy, as well as in unutterable fear – was the sudden pursuit, through an open door, along a huge high saloon, of a just dimly-descried figure that retreated in terror before my rush and dash (a glare of inspired reaction from irresistible but shameful dread), out of the room I had a moment before been desperately, and all the more abjectly, defending by the push of my shoulder against hard pressure on lock and bar from the other side. The lucidity, not to say the sublimity, of the crisis had consisted of the great thought that I, in my appalled state, was probably still more appalling than the awful agent, creature or presence, whatever he was, whom I

45 *A Small Boy and Others* (London, 1913), p. 361. Curiously, Theophile Gautier, whose poem 'L'Art' I have already quoted from, in 1867 found his inspiration also in the same gallery of the Louvre: 'Traversons à présent la Galerie d'Apollon . . . le milieu est rempli par des vitrines renfermant des vases d'argent, des coupes d'or, des onyx, des jades, des bijoux, des émaux et tous ces joyaux où le travail dépasse encore la matière quelque précieuse qu'elle soit.'

46 *A Small Boy and Others*, p. 366.

had guessed, in the suddenest wild start from sleep, the sleep within my sleep, to be making for my place of rest. The triumph of my impulse, perceived in a flash as I acted on it by myself at a bound, forcing the door outward, was the grand thing, but the great point of the whole was the wonder of my final recognition. Routed, dismayed, the tables turned upon him by my so surpassing him for straight aggression and dire intention, my visitant was already but a diminished spot in the long perspective, the tremendous, glorious hall . . . over the far-gleaming floor of which . . . he sped for *his* life, while a great storm of thunder and lightning played through the deep embrasures of high windows at the right. The lightning that revealed the retreat revealed also the wondrous place and, by the same amazing play, my young imaginative life in it of long before, the sense of which, deep within me, had kept it whole, preserved it to this thrilling use; for what in the world were the deep embrasures and the so polished floor but those of the Galerie d'Apollon of my childhood? The 'scene of something' I had vaguely then felt it? Well I might, since it was to be the scene of that immense hallucination.[47]

This felt sense of power, this 'straight aggression and dire intention' in the life of art is just what is missing, to its injury, in *The Tragic Muse*. The commitment to art *is* an assault on life, the pursued turning and becoming the pursuer through the house of life. It is the audacity of genius which imposes its own image of reality on other men, and claims its own reality to be 'the world in fine raised to the richest and noblest expression'.

Some small portion of this vision is suggested in Miriam Rooth's relationship to her art. But both Nick Dormer and Gabriel Nash fall far below it in characterization, still more in action. Both fail to represent the passion either of creation itself or of the vital energy, the spiritual and moral integrity that ideally informs the aesthetic adventure. Nick Dormer's reflection on the great portraits, quoted above, does imply some of this, but it remains an isolated passage of which not enough is made in the working out of the novel's conflicts. In such portraits it is the vividness of their art that they persuade us of the felt life of their subjects, life rich in its intimations of 'history and fame and power'. The portraits may transcend

47 *Ibid.*, pp. 362–4.

history, but do not deny it. Dormer's fading portrait of Gabriel Nash, in contrast, fails us on both counts.

A commitment to art, however intense, is still a commitment *in* life, not an escape from it. James was aware of some of the ambiguities which can confound the life of art in society, the terrible contradictions in the relationships of money with art, status with sensibility, opportunity with appreciation.[48] They are the ambiguities which give tension to real – as opposed to theoretical – human conflicts and choices. But when Nick Dormer gives up his career in Parliament and loses Julia Dallow, in giving up all worldly things he appears to give up all personal feeling as well, and his embracing of art causes him to move through the rest of the novel like a man anaesthetized. My admiration gives way to sympathy, sympathy to pity, and pity finally to indifference. The novel does not enlighten me with its suggestion that the disinterested service of art should be indistinguishable from dull martyrdom. The final justification of martyrdom – or even of renunciation, if you will – is not in what has been lost, but in what has been gained; not in what has been sacrificed, but to what end. Even the martyr may see great reward in service to a high ideal, and may know exaltation.

However, what finally (and unintentionally) holds the central position in the novel is not the conflict between passion and vocation, public career or private, commonweal or culture, but the more vivid representation of the power of acquisition, of 'Things', in comparison with which the other conflicts pale. It is Things finally that one does or does not give up. Things shape Miriam's career, they loom endlessly in Nick's loss of public position, of his patron's support, of his mother's fond aspirations to social standing, of Julia Dallow (wealthy as *she* is!) James seems unaware of the ubiquity of 'Things' in the novel, and ignores their potency in his attempted resolutions, as he seems finally to ignore or to obscure almost every force in life, even in the life of art.

Nick Dormer has given too unqualified an assent to the

---

48 It is just these ambiguities which more and more troubled James, and which he tried to deal with most directly, albeit unsuccessfully, in *The Golden Bowl* and *The Ivory Tower*.

narrow aestheticism of Gabriel Nash. He has moved close to that insidious solipsism which eliminates all the world beyond the figure of the artist and the whiteness of his canvas.[49] It is obvious then why Dormer's portrait of Nash completely displaces his physical reality. Dormer expects the fading image to disappear absolutely when Gabriel Nash returns as 'life'. But Gabriel Nash does *not* return; the door that opens on to life from the studio has been closed and locked. Nick Dormer is left with a representation only, faded and dead. Regretfully, one remembers James's own earlier judgement:

In life without art you can find your account; but art without life is a poor affair.[50]

---

49 James would appear to have forgotten his own early story, 'The Madonna of the Future' (1873), in which an American painter in Florence squanders his life in endless talk about a great Madonna he will one day paint, until he dies, leaving 'a canvas that was a mere dead blank, cracked and discoloured by time'.
50 'Daniel Deronda: A Conversation', *Partial Portraits*, p. 92.

6

Americans and ambassadors: the whole man

THE GENESIS OF 'THE AMBASSADORS'

Any reader wishing to investigate *The Ambassadors* has the rare privilege of tracing the creative process that shapes a novel. The stages of conception and development can be observed in notebooks and letters, and in the retrospections of the preface to the New York edition. These materials are available, however, in studying many of James's novels. What is unique in this case is the discovery of a detailed synopsis which James wrote (probably in 1900) for Harper's in anticipation of the novel's serialization.[1] Harper's did not accept the novel at that time, and it waited until 1903 for publication.

James thought that he had derived from his otherwise fruitless years in the theatre certain technical or formal principles which he could apply to the novel. One of them was a renewed emphasis on 'dramatization'; another, the practice of preparing scenarios for the novels as he had done for his plays. Although James believed the synopsis for *The Ambassadors* to have been destroyed,[2] it was discovered many years later and printed in part in the James issue of *Hound and Horn* (1934), and in its entirety as an appendix to the *Notebooks* (1947).

Tracing the development of *The Ambassadors* allows for a fascinating participation in what is probably the most useful of all forms of criticism – the self-criticism of the artist in the process of creation. I shall trace just one element of this process for the light it sheds on my subject.

In his notebooks, James describes the encounter of Jonathan

1 James's synopsis and notes for his two unfinished novels, *The Ivory Tower* and *The Sense of the Past*, have also been published; it is the completed works themselves which we miss.
2 See letter to H. G. Wells in *Letters*, I, pp. 412–14.

Sturges (who related the episode to him) with William Dean
Howells in Paris. Howells had 'scarcely been in Paris', even in
former days:

Virtually in the evening, as it were, of life, it was all new to him;
all, all, all. Sturges said he seemed sad – rather brooding; and I asked
him what gave him (Sturges) that impression. 'Oh – somewhere –
I forget, when I was with him – he laid his hand on my shoulder
and said *à propos* of some remark of mine: "Oh, you are young,
you are young – be glad of it; be glad of it and *live*. Live all you can;
it's a mistake not to. It doesn't so much matter what you do – but
live. This place makes it all come over me. I see it now. I haven't
done so – and now I'm too old. It's too late. It has gone past me –
I've lost it. You have time. You are young. Live!" '

James ponders over the possibilities of this touching picture:

the little idea of the figure of an elderly man who hasn't 'lived',
hasn't at all, in the sense of sensations, passions, impulses, pleasures
– and to whom, in the presence of some great human spectacle,
some great organization for the Immediate, the Agreeable, for curiosity, and experiment and perception, for Enjoyment, in a word,
becomes, *sur la fin*, or toward it, sorrowfully aware. He has never
really enjoyed – he has lived only for Duty and conscience – his
conception of them; for pure appearances and daily tasks – lived for
effort, for surrender, abstention, sacrifice.[3]

That notebook entry is dated October, 1895. A year later, in
November, 1896, there is an oblique reference to the Howells
matter in a letter to Sturges: 'What you said about Howells
most true – he is very touching.'[4] The impact of Howells's
regretful apostrophe to life can be seen in another letter, one
of consolation to A. C. Benson, written in December, 1896:

If there be a wisdom in not feeling – to the last throb – the great
things that happen to us, it is a wisdom I shall never either know
or esteem. Let your Soul live – it's the only life that isn't on the
whole a sell.[5]

The next step in the development of the novel was to find

3 *Notebooks*, pp. 226–7.
4 *Letters*, I, p. 257.
5 *Ibid.*, p. 258.

an 'action' that would best express his idea. James speculates in the notebooks that the protagonist may be either English or American. It becomes obvious soon enough that he will be American, in order to represent the familiar Jamesian associations with the life of 'duty and conscience' making its pilgrimage to a world of 'the Immediate, the Agreeable . . . curiosity, and experiment and perception'. James worries about some circumstance which will help to explain his character's special sensitivity to, or his re-awakened awareness of, the possibilities of a fuller and richer life:

He has sacrificed some one, some friend, some son, some younger brother, to his failure to feel, to understand, all that his new experience causes to come home to him in a wave of reaction, of compunction. He has not allowed for these things, the new things, new sources of emotion, new influences and appeals . . . It was in communication with *them* that the spirit, the sense, the nature, the temperament of this victim (as now seems to him) of his old ignorance, struggled and suffered. He was wild – he was free – he was passionate . . . Our friend never saw it – never, never; he perceives that – ever so sadly, so bitterly, now. The young man is dead; it's all over. Was he a son, was he a ward, a younger brother – or an elder one? Points to settle: though I'm not quite sure I like the *son*.[6]

The Harper's synopsis lays stress on the same tragedy, so that it is clear that James's intention remains the same until the actual writing of the novel, where a higher logic takes over. In the novel itself it *is* a son who is lost. But the emphasis has become so changed that the meaning of this circumstance is radically altered. And the very nature of the change from notebook and synopsis to the novel itself is significant to James's theme.

For in the novel we are told that Lambert Strether has had a son who died of diphtheria some years after the death of his mother, and whose nature Strether had never fully appreciated. Strether had cut himself off from the son in his grief for his wife. But his son was still a young child, not the young man who is wild, free, passionate. And the memory of his son's death is

6 *Notebooks*, p. 227.

barely touched on, and then mainly as one cause of Strether's lonely life. It explains very little about the direction or intensity of Strether's present participations.

Strether has come to Paris to rescue Chad Newsome from the influence of a 'wicked woman' and to bring him home to his mother and to a flourishing family business in Woollett, Massachusetts. We learn that Mrs Newsome is a wealthy widow who devotes much of her life and her apparently inexhaustible moral energy to philanthropic expiations for her wealth (and for the suggested 'vulgarity' of its source). She is in love with, or at least accustomed to, Lambert Strether and will marry him when he returns successfully from his mission as her ambassador. Strether has been her adviser and consultant in philanthropy, and of recent years has been the editor of the 'green' review which she subsidizes, a journal which James describes in the notebooks sardonically as 'devoted to serious questions and inquiries, economic, social, sanitary, humanitary'. It evokes strongly Emerson's New England, which James had once described as the world of the lecture hall and podium.

Mrs Newsome's physical fortitude is less heroic than her moral; formidable as she is in the walks of Duty, she is notoriously given to bodily collapses of an indeterminate nature. She cannot possibly undertake herself the harrowing task of confronting the Wicked Woman and of reclaiming her son Chad; hence Lambert Strether's ambassadorship.

The essence of the novel is that Strether, under the pressure of new experiences, shall act in a way directly opposite to Mrs Newsome's ideas or his own original concurrence in them. Strether arrives at a new conception of Chad's responsibilities which contradicts the old strict New England definitions. As in *The Portrait of a Lady*, the plot hinges on a reversal, a proper Aristotelian *peripety*.[7] The intensity of the plot's reversal depends, obviously, on the presence of its elements within the created fiction. And everything that will determine the reversal *is* present – even the prodigious figure of Mrs Newsome. She never appears in the novel except as represented by her am-

---

7 Technically, the reversal of *The Ambassadors* is further complicated and enriched by an opposite reversal on the part of Chad Newsome.

bassadors; yet her force is dramatically imposed throughout the action.

The credibility, as well as the intensity, of Strether's rapid and unexpected responses to his European initiations depend on our seeing their ground in the special sensitivities and circumstances of Strether's life. That is why the notebooks and synopsis lay stress on some crucial earlier loss or tragedy. Yet, James must have felt that to place so much weight on the invoked moral of a dead son would be to bring too much pressure to bear from outside the central action. James's solution to his problem is barely intimated in the synopsis, and is found only in the novel itself. It depends upon Strether's relations in the past not with some other person – son or brother – but with himself. The person who proves to have been sacrificed to 'his failure to feel, to understand, all that his new experience causes to come home to him' is not a young son, but the young Lambert Strether : the child is father to the man. For the strongest note in the tremendous appeal of Paris for him now is the revival of old memories, the memories of the alternatives which he has lost. His failure to achieve the life of high civilization is precisely what has made Strether 'this victim (as now seems to him) of his old ignorance'.

The significant history had begun with Strether's early visit to Europe with his young bride, with their eager promise then to live the 'life of culture'. He had carried back a dozen yellow novels like some holy grail, as a promise in itself of the civilized life, as an initial instalment on further and deeper initiations to come. Strether had tried to bring 'Europe' back to New England, but had failed. Instead of fulfilling these brave intentions, Strether had succumbed to the immediate pressures of the New England milieu. His dedication was weakened further, perhaps, by the early death of his wife; yet again by the subsequent death of his son. The measure of his inability to keep his promise during the long New England years is the fact that he has forgotten even the promise itself. Sitting in the Luxembourg Gardens in a kind of Proustian surrender to memory, he is appalled now by the very failure of any conscious remembrance of his sacred vow. Yet he feels, under the renewed spell of Paris, that some such memory, however repressed, must have been a strong element in the emptiness and unhappiness of all those years.

Failing in his early dedication, he has failed in the American sense as well. Unlike Waymarsh, who *is* an American success, and who hates Europe, Strether has done badly for himself in the American 'world of grab'. Strether says of Waymarsh: 'He's a success of a kind that I haven't approached.' Maria Gostrey, Strether's new friend who elicits these confidences, asks, 'Do you mean he has made money?' Strether answers: 'He makes it . . . to my belief. And I . . . though with a back quite as bent, have never made anything. I'm a perfectly equipped failure.' Maria Gostrey has her answer ready: 'Thank goodness you're a failure – it's why I distinguish you. Anything else today is too hideous. Look about you – look at the successes. Would you *be* one, on your honour?' Waymarsh has had his success, in any case. He appears to have preserved the old New England morality as well. What he lacks, however, is what Strether now most covets: curiosity, freedom, the ability to live in the moment, to 'take things as they come', to triumph over what Strether calls the 'failure of Woollett': the failure to enjoy.

Waymarsh, admirable enough within his own limits, makes obvious just what those limits are. What we need to learn is what limitations Strether's own vocation imposes, and this of course is the central burden of the novel. The idea of limitations is an important motif in *The Ambassadors*. When in the autumn of his life Strether tells the young American Bilham to 'live', the sense seems far more vital than Gabriel Nash's or Nick Dormer's formulations in *The Tragic Muse*. Strether tells Bilham: 'It doesn't so much matter what you do in particular . . .' but the second part of this statement goes uneasily with the first: '. . . so long as you have your life'. It does after all matter what in particular one does.[8] Waymarsh, Mrs Newsome, Chad,

8 The theme of looking back with the sense of waste over one's life, of seeking out the springs of failure and, in consequence, of searching for a key to life's essential point or meaning, is common both to *The Ambassadors* and to Tolstoy's *The Death of Ivan Ilyich*. What is remarkable, given this similarity of situation, is the radically different conclusions to which the philosophies of the two authors take these works.

Strether himself in his past life, in committing themselves to their particulars have lost the whole. And the central vision of the novel, the vision that shapes its characterizations and its setting, its plot and its narrative technique, is the vision of the Whole Man. Lambert Strether is Henry James's study of the truly civilized human being. His story is of the conjunction of the moral *and* aesthetic, the Hebraic – to look back to Matthew Arnold – and the Hellenic. He represents the complete merging of 'character' and 'culture' which until now James's protagonists have striven for, but never attained. And even his wholeness, as we shall see, is achieved too late.

THE WORLD OF ACQUISITION

It is significant that by the time of *The Ambassadors* the American ambassador to Europe has at last stopped being the anomalous millionaire-saint. Strether, unlike Christopher Newman in *The American* (1877), is a failure economically, and we understand a good deal from this fact. Newman was a success, and we are asked to believe that he was also a paragon of the major virtues, a confusion of James's own premises. To add to the confusion, Newman 'adopts' the most sympathetic member of the aristocratic Bellegarde family and decides to take him back to America to launch *him* as a business success. The distance James has travelled by the time of the writing of *The Ambassadors* may be measured by comparing Newman's idea for Valentine, and Strether's reactions to Chad's desire to go back to the Woollett dollars.

The American dollar is the most important single explanation for the fact that James's passionate pilgrims are so often women. Their sensibilities have neither been brought into conflict with, nor been subverted by, the 'world of grab'. His most sympathetic men are those young enough to have escaped it altogether, or old enough to represent (with perhaps dubious authenticity) an older, pre-Civil War New England where business was thought to flourish in closer harmony with traditional Puritan moral imperatives. The sense of a division in American life that dates from the time of the Civil War has been commented on widely enough, and may be seen in such disparate works as William Dean Howells's *The Rise of Silas Lapham*, Walt Whitman's *Democratic Vistas*, and Mark Twain's *Life on the Mississippi*. With the development of a more nakedly acquisitive society in the years following the Civil War – the era that Mark Twain in *The Gilded Age* called 'The Great Barbecue' – there came a distinct division between men and women in their relationships to culture. This division has been well described by George Santayana:

One-half of the American mind, that not occupied intensely in practical affairs, has remained . . . slightly becalmed; it has floated gently in the back-water, while, alongside, in invention and industry and social organization, the other half of the mind was leaping down a sort of Niagara Rapids . . . The American Will inhabits the skyscraper; the American Intellect inhabits the colonial mansion. The one is the sphere of the American man; the other, at least predominantly, of the American woman.[9]

Curiously enough, James returned in *The Golden Bowl* (1904) to a major study of an American millionaire, the new Newman, Adam Verver. Between *The Golden Bowl* and the unfinished *The Ivory Tower*, James had revived or renewed his impressions of the United States through his grand tour of 1904–5 which was to be commemorated in the brilliant *The American Scene* (1907). It leaves little doubt as to the low regard in which James held the American cult of success. Neither does the story 'The Jolly Corner' (1909), in which an expatriated American returns from Europe to confront the ghost of an *alter ego* – of himself as he might have become had he stayed in America to play the game of grab:

Horror, with the sight, had leaped into Brydon's throat, gasping there in a sound he couldn't utter; for the bared identity was too hideous as *his*, and the glare was the passion of his protest. The face, *that* face, Spencer Brydon's? . . . It was unknown, inconceivable, awful, disconnected from any possibility – ! Such an identity filled his at *no* point, made its alternative monstrous . . . the face was the face of a stranger . . . the stranger, whoever it might be,

9 G. Santayana, *The Winds of Doctrine* (London, 1926), p. 188.

evil, odious, blatant, vulgar, had advanced as for aggression, and
he knew himself give ground.

Another part of this commemoration is in the harsh portraits
of American men of business, Gaw and Betterman, in *The Ivory
Tower*.[10] The novel's protagonist, Graham Fielder, is a Europeanized and cultured American who, James tells us in his notes
on the novel:

I have felt my instinct to make . . . definitely and frankly as complete a case as possible of the sort of thing that will make him an
anomaly and an outsider in the New York world of business, the
New York world of ferocious acquisition, and the world there of
enormities of expenditure and extravagance.

James seems nervous of repeating previous characterizations
of young passionate pilgrims:

I want to steer clear of the tiresome 'artistic' associations hanging
about the usual type of young Anglo-Saxon 'brought up abroad';
though only indeed so far as they *are* tiresome.

But the associations considered tiresome are left for the reader's
judgement; Graham Fielder remains a typical Jamesian representative of culture,

by reason of course of certain things, certain ideas, possibilities,
inclinations, and dispositions, that he *has* cared about and felt, in
his way, the fermentation of. Of course the trouble with him is a
sort of excess of 'culture', so far as the form taken by his existence
up to then has represented the growth of that article.

His culture is in 'excess' presumably in relation to his new
American experiences, which makes him an 'anomaly and an
outsider alike'.

His experience springs from the elements embodied in the

---

10 The completed fragment of *The Ivory Tower* – about one-third of the
novel – was published posthumously in 1917, although it was written in
1914, together with his 'scenario' and notes. A quite dissimilar story, using
many of the same names, was sketched out as early as 1910. See *Notebooks*,
pp. 343–60.

symbolic ivory tower, a magnificently carved pagoda. This fine work of art which has been given Fielder by Rosanna, the sympathetic daughter of the corrupt Abner Gaw, is clearly both in its subject as well as its form a symbol of the life of art, rather like Yeats's

> such a form as Grecian goldsmiths make
> Of hammered gold and gold enamelling.

Inside the pagoda, in a secret drawer, Graham has placed, unread, a document written by old Abner Gaw, the one-time partner of Fielder's uncle and benefactor, the ironically named Betterman. This document is the confession or description of the swindles, extortions, malpractices which are the basis of Betterman's (and therefore of Fielder's) fortune. The document is in the base of the ivory tower, which symbolically rises from it : it is what the life of culture is built upon.

Fielder is confronted with the complex social facts that lie behind art-as-commodity, that lead not to the relatively easy dichotomizing of art and culture on the one hand with materialism on the other, but to the far more difficult challenge of facing up to their interdependence. He is not well-equipped for the task.

His 'culture', his initiations of intelligence and experience, his possibilities of imagination, if one will, to say nothing of other things, make for me a sort of figure of a floating island on which he drifts and bumps and coasts about, wanting to get alongside as much as possible, yet always with the gap of water, the little island *fact*, to be somewhat bridged over.

The island fact – the fact of money[11] – proves to be not little at all, and Fielder's determination to allow his avaricious friends, Cissy Foy and Horton Vint, to swindle from him the money that has been accumulated by swindle raises more problems than James managed to solve. He knew, more or less, what he

11 James's metaphor of a 'floating island' here has an interesting resemblance to the 'golden islands' of money and privilege which Margaret Schlegel speaks of in E. M. Forster's *Howards End*.

wanted of the life of culture, as a great many of his novels will testify; and he knew what he did *not* want of the world of acquisition. But he seemed uncertain about their actual connections, and about the kind of connections which might justify a continued defence of culture. No mere accident of time will explain the novel's remaining unfinished. It deals with a conflict which vexed James and which continues to vex serious artists, as well as theorists and social critics of art, even today.

I do not wish to be taken as scolding James for thematic falterings or uncertainties except insofar as these damaged the actual fabric of his novels. The great literary artists are those able to command a deep understanding of the prevailing ideology of their own time and to embody this understanding in convincing fictional or dramatic form. The mark of their greatness is not to be found in their ability to resolve the apparent tensions, inconsistencies, or contradictions in public ideology, as these inevitably appear in any epoch, by the application of a 'penetrating' deeper analysis – such as those for example of Marxists or Freudians – but rather in their ability to dramatize them, to give them effective artistic form. This ability is brilliantly manifested in Balzac's *La Comedie Humaine*, for instance, even while his social theories are largely questionable. The same ability will be found in novelists with far less ambitious intentions than Balzac's, as Jane Austen demonstrates with such distinction.

James's difficulty in such works as *The Ivory Tower*, then, is after all his inability to find a coherent dramatic pattern for the tensions between prevailing social and economic forces in his own society and the ideal working power of culture. My additional point is that systematic cultural criticism has not fared much better than James did in relating these elements.[12]

12 See, for example, Theodor Adorno, *Minima Moralia* (trans, E. F. N. Jephcott, London, 1978), pp. 43–4: 'Among the motifs of cultural criticism one of the most long-established and central is that of the lie: that culture creates the illusion of a society worthy of man which does not exist; that it conceals the material conditions upon which all human works arise, and that, comforting and lulling, it serves to keep alive the bad economic determination of existence. This is the notion of culture as ideology, which appears at first sight common to both the bourgeois doctrine of violence and its adversary,

Uncertain as James showed himself to be in dealing with the relationship of acquisition and art in *The Ivory Tower*, his feelings about acquisition itself are never more unambiguously expressed than in his characterization of Abner Gaw. He represents the logical fulfilment of a given Jamesian type. To what end can the young Caspar Goodwood of *The Portrait of a Lady* be moving, from what end does Christopher Newman of *The American* hope to save himself by his sudden and dramatic departure for Europe, but that end represented by Abner Gaw?

He was a person without an alternative, and if any had ever been open to him, at an odd hour or two, somewhere in his inner dimness, he had long since closed the gate against it and now revolved in the hard-rimmed circle from which he had not a single issue. You couldn't retire without something or somewhere to retire to, you must have planted a single tree at least for shade or be able to turn a key in some yielding door; but to say that [he] was surrounded by the desert was almost to flatter the void into which he invited one to step. He conformed in short to his necessity of absolute interest – interest, that is, in his own private facts, which were facts of numerical calculation altogether: how could it not be so when he had dispossessed himself, if there had even been the slightest selection in the matter, of every faculty except the calculating?

As for Daniel Touchett in *The Portrait of a Lady*, the focus of attention may be less on the American millionaire than on the New England patriarch. In *The Golden Bowl*, Adam Verver may appear to be saved from such a fate as Gaw's by his involvement with a Europe which provides an escape from the post-Civil War development of ruthless acquisitiveness in America. But his characterization provides its own insoluble ambiguities. His special mission in Europe is to ransack it of its spoils to

---

both to Nietzsche and to Marx. But precisely this notion, like all expostulation about lies, has a suspicious tendency to become itself ideology . . . With the logic of coherence and the pathos of truth, cultural criticism could therefore demand that relationships be entirely reduced to their material origin . . . But to act radically in accordance with this principle would be to extirpate, with the false, all that was true also, all that, however impotently, strives to escape the confines of universal practice . . . and so to bring about directly the barbarism that culture is reproached with furthering indirectly.'

fill a museum in 'American City'.[18] Having as a younger man discovered a genius for business which has made him fabulously (if antiseptically) wealthy, he has discovered later in life another genius for collecting and connoisseurship. It is in the spirit of the latter, and through the means of the former, that he 'collects' a husband for his daughter and a wife for himself. It is not clear in *which* spirit he takes greater pride for the quality and authenticity – the value – of these fine acquisitions. Although his taste is said to be as fine and as famous as that of the great traditional patrons of the European courts, it is curious that he appears not once to take up a living artist or to commission a single work. He insists rather on the marks and patents of respectability to be found in the already-established. So, too, the value of the Prince lies at least as much in the antiquity of his family and title as in any distinction in his own character or wit or taste. Charlotte Stant, it must be admitted, lacks great hallmarks, but this may explain the feeling that she has been picked up for convenience; she is a distinguished bargain. While James's novels heretofore may have helped us to see the important qualities which are common to art and to life, they have not prepared us to evaluate individual human beings as *objets d'art* in a buyer's market.[14]

Clearly, James's difficulties in dealing with the relationships between acquisition and art do not begin with *The Ivory Tower*, for they are central to the failure of *The Golden Bowl* as well. That the novel *is* a failure is amply testified to by a history of exegesis and criticism which proposes, with roughly equal eloquence, that Adam Verver and his daughter Maggie should be seen as God-the-Father and the Holy Spirit on the one hand, or, on the other, as vultures of American acquisitiveness, caught in the net of James's irony. If we accept James's intention as ironic, then certainly Adam and Maggie are the novel's

13 Curiously, in James's first novel, *Roderick Hudson*, Rowland Mallett's early ambition for a relationship to art is the same as Adam Verver's, but he decides that to support Roderick Hudson will be a better use of his money in the service of art. *The Outcry* (1911), a bad novel adapted from a play written in 1909, has as its central theme the despoiling of English art treasures by wealthy Americans.

14 Edward Rosier courts Pansy, and Gilbert Osmond 'shapes' her, in similar terms in *The Portrait of a Lady*; neither inspires James's admiration.

villains. If the novel is to be read straightforwardly, rather than as satire, then they become heroic figures. Crucial to our sense of these possibilities is the attitude we are expected to take toward the Ververs' extreme wealth – its source and its uses.

Both readings have much to recommend them; neither is conclusive. It is the mark of obscurity (as distinct from difficulty) that a text cannot be understood definitively, owing to the absence of the elements necessary for certainty. And *The Golden Bowl* is obscure. The relationships in the novel between art and money, culture and acquisition, are most ambiguous. It may be tempting for a variety of reasons to believe that James portrayed – or meant to portray – Adam and Maggie ironically; but I cannot persuade myself that the novel supports such a belief. If James's intention was to be ironic he failed in making the novel sustain that intention. If James meant instead for us to admire the Ververs (as the Assinghams both do, endlessly), the novel fails to sustain such a feeling. Whether we feel in the end that Adam and Maggie are most 'used' by Charlotte and the Prince, or that the Prince and Charlotte are most exploited by Maggie and Adam, may depend rather more on what we bring *to* the novel than on what the novel itself conclusively demonstrates.

I do think there is a provisional reading of the novel that glimmers through its obscurity. This reading may be seen as developing from the symbolic naming of Prince Amerigo, the descendant of the European who 'discovered' America. The conflict of the novel involves the question of which of two definitions of America will claim the European tradition or inheritance. Which America will Prince Amerigo discover and hence occupy? The claim to Europe may be seen as acts of aggression by both the Ververs and Charlotte Stant. Charlotte is a brilliant American beauty of impeccable style, whose initiations in Europe, like Madame Merle's, represent a complete mastery of form at the expense of moral integrity. Having surrendered the claims of her passion for Prince Amerigo earlier because of their poverty, as Mrs Verver she invites a resumption of their old relationship on the basis of the Ververs' preoccupation with each other, but, equally, on the basis of their great wealth. Maggie Verver, on the other hand, seems to represent a truly Europeanized American in her synthesis of culture and moral integrity. She discovers that she must fight to keep her rightful claim to Prince Amerigo, to the culture of Europe, the salvation of America. Parochial in her loyalties, she has clung too devotedly to her American father, and has taken the Prince too much for granted, almost as a handsome fixture on the property. Indeed, such a view might have been easy enough to acquire. The Prince all too rarely acts, but high symbol of Europe under American assault that he is, all too splendidly responds to the initiatives of others: of Fanny Assingham in arranging a handsome marriage, of Charlotte in arranging an attractive adultery, of Maggie in arranging tactfully to win him back on suitable terms.

Maggie, in any case, is willing in the end to *choose* between her father and the Prince in a way she has not done even when marrying, and to fight for her husband's love rather than to allow it to be simply purchased. She is prepared to fight, furthermore, without a rigid adherence to a nice scrupulousness so long as her deepest moral integrity, her true dedication to an honourable European marriage, sanctions the fight. Even the old strict 'American' demand for literal veracity at any price gives way to the deeper demand for spiritual loyalty. In these ways she marks a new strength of will in the Jamesian protagonist, unlike the passive readiness for defeat we have sometimes seen, or the mere stricken state of Ralph Touchett, or of Milly Theale.

Her intense loyalty to her father has paved the way for the Prince's infidelity, since it has been open to the Prince (and to the reader) to prefer genuine physical passion to absentee ownership, however luxurious. Maggie, once alerted to her danger, decides to fight for her husband, and also for their child, issue of this union of America and Europe. In the end she packs Adam Verver off to America with Charlotte, where she may become another high ornament to American City. Her father's 'cultured' acquisitiveness has proved to be dangerous to Maggie's true cause, which is to cling to the Europe her husband represents, and to claim his loyalty as rightfully belonging to her.

This reading has its own problems, besides the obviously dia-

grammatic effect of so brief an outline. But if the novel is
obscure, as I think it is, *no* reading can be argued with finality.
It is not the case, as has sometimes been suggested, that James's
highly wrought and mannered style in *The Golden Bowl*
obscures his meanings, but rather that the uncertainties and
ambiguities of his vision contribute to a consequent opacity of
treatment.[15]

Whether Adam Verver is regarded sympathetically or not,
the very *given* of his characterization raises problems. His
exceptional ability to achieve high eminence in two ways –
in acquisition and in culture – is difficult to believe in, even
when they are connected as the acquisition-of-culture. The
baronial wealth Verver has accumulated is scarcely credible
divorced from the intense concentration and specialization
James saw so clearly in Abner Gaw. The leisured cultivation of
the arts and of connoisseurship is classically the occupation of
the second or third generations in the great moneyed dynasties,
not of the first. That Verver is described, as though in mitigation,
as a singularly mild and contemplative gentleman simply com-
pounds the contradictions, rather than explaining them. His
relationships with the Prince and – even more – with his wife
Charlotte seem insufferable if they are not merely absurd, and
their presented sense is too ambiguous in tone as well as in
incident to support arguments about irony or special pleading.
On the other hand, those critics who think the Prince and
Charlotte, rather than the Ververs, are the admirable characters
of the novel are curiously blinded to the way this couple insists
on having the best of both possible worlds together. Without
the Verver loot where *is* their honest passion ?

In both *The Ivory Tower* and *The Golden Bowl* James failed
to achieve his desired 'synthesis of the future' – the marriage
of America and Europe in an ideal civilization. Although James
could be so intensely aware of the incompatibility of one
dominant mode of American life – the acquisitive society –

15 But some critics have liked James best at his most mannered. A reprint
of *The Golden Bowl* (Grove Press, undated) quotes R. P. Blackmur's claim
that of the three last novels, this 'is the most poetic in the sense of its
language as well as its structure'. I find this depressing as much for what it
implies about poetry as for what it suggests to be most valuable in James.

with one dominant mode of European life – the commitment to culture – he tried in both these novels to resolve these contraries, but without success.[16]

The most successful element in *The Ivory Tower* is the confrontation in symbolic form of what Abner Gaw and Graham Fielder respectively represent: the letter of damnation and the ivory tower. The most brilliant passages in *The Golden Bowl* are the dramatic confrontations of Charlotte Stant with Maggie Verver, where the same conflict is intended. In both cases the sharpness of vision and the brilliance of technique are found in this centring of conflict; in both cases the conflict fails to be convincing in its fictional development and in its various resolutions.[17]

In contrast, James's success in *The Ambassadors* is striking, and stems in part at least from the fact that he does not try to reconcile these disparate modes of American–European experience. Strether is not a millionaire-saint, and we may find it easier to accept his desire to make of necessity a virtue than James's desire to make of Verver's virtue a necessity. Chad Newsome's pledges to culture and to acquisitiveness are seen in unambiguous opposition to each other, and even Maria Gostrey's subtle relationships to these values present discriminations which James clearly recognizes and controls.

The successful American man of affairs in *The Ambassadors* is Waymarsh. He is in Europe for his health, which has forced him to leave his usual occupations. From the very early 'Travelling Companions' (1870) on, the most characteristic relationship of James's American millionaires to Europe is as the indulgently bored companions of wives or daughters whose pilgrimages they view as conferring status or as affordable amenities, like Parisian wardrobes. Alternatively, they stay at

16 It scarcely matters that Europeans can be acquisitive, or that Americans can make large commitments to culture: these are not the issues that vex these novels.

17 There are curious similarities, both in where they succeed and where they fail, in James's *The Golden Bowl* and *The Ivory Tower*, to Hawthorne's *The Marble Faun* and the unfinished *Dr Grimshawe's Secret*. The uneasy moral ambiguities, the excessive reliance on central controlling symbols, the failures of resolution in both the finished and unfinished works suggest interestingly similar problems.

H

home to work (as in 'Daisy Miller' or 'An International Episode', for instance), and send their women to Europe much as they send them to church on Sundays. Waymarsh may remind us of the older tradition of the Puritan-patriarch suggested in the admirable Daniel Touchett, or Mr Wentworth in *The Europeans*, but he has a familiar limitation in his dislike and suspicion of Europe. Meeting Strether in England, he is relieved to be able to tell an old friend, 'the fact is, such a country as this ain't my kind of country, any way. There ain't a country I've seen over here that *does* seem my kind. Oh, I don't say but what there are plenty of pretty places and remarkable old things; but the trouble is that I don't seem to feel anywhere in tune.'

His dislike of Europe is not merely passive. He achieves one heroi-comic act of protest against Europe, characteristically in an act of acquisition. This is an amusing and ironically reveal-ing episode in which James has Waymarsh rebel against the irritatingly cultured communications of Strether with his new and suspiciously Europeanized friend Maria Gostrey by sud-denly bolting from them toward a jeweller's shop. Miss Gostrey asks: 'What's the matter with him?'

'Well,' said Strether, 'he can't stand it.'
'But can't stand what?'
'Anything. Europe.'
'Then how will that jeweller help him?'

Maria fears that Waymarsh may buy something 'dreadful'. Strether – after he has 'studied the finer appearances' – replies, 'He may buy everything.' Waymarsh returns quite pleased with himself, but we are never told what has been the extent, or quality, of his purchase. Still, Strether has witnessed the protest and understands Waymarsh's intention: 'The thing is, you see, we "realize". He has struck for freedom.'

Waymarsh's gesture is not unlike that of the self-made millionaire who hates the higher education he has not had, and so buys a university. His fundamental resentment of Europe and of the demands its culture makes is expressed absolutely rightly by an act of acquisition or appropriation. James makes us see it with all its intended irony, as he does not make us see the similar acts which so ambiguously represent Christopher Newman or Adam Verver.

There is a further note in this episode which merits comment. Maria Gostrey thinks Waymarsh's gesture a high price to pay for 'freedom'. But Strether knows better. ' "No, no," Strether went on, frankly amused now; "don't call it that: the kind of freedom *you* deal in is dear." ' He means now the true freedom of Europe: the freedom to see, to judge, to appreciate, to enjoy. What makes it so dear is the 'remorseless analysis' of arbitrary assumptions and beliefs, of restrictive loyalties, all of which must be held up to the test of experience and the free intelligence.

This conversation of Maria Gostrey and Strether immediately precedes the discussion of Waymarsh's American success and Strether's failure, quoted earlier. It conditions our sense of these terms, alerts us to the possibilities of meanings more complex than the significations acceptable to Woollett, Massachusetts, possibilities which are suggested in Miss Gostrey's bold exclamation, 'Thank goodness you're a failure.'

What appears to be a rather innocent episode involving a rash purchase by Waymarsh, becomes in fact the first thematic statement of the novel's central idea. For it is the discovery of this freedom and its price which is Lambert Strether's adventure. Whatever synthesis of America and Europe which James, with 'the braver imagination' will attempt in this novel, it will not include the great American genius for money-making. His failure to reconcile this genius with the life of culture in the later novels is best understood in the infinitely more successful *The Ambassadors*, in which he shuns the attempt.

THE LIFE OF CULTURE

Chad Newsome is the dangerously unformed and susceptible young man whom Lambert Strether has been sent to rescue from the ensnarements of Europe generally, and of a wicked Parisienne particularly, and to bring back to the moral and economic respectabilities of Woollett, Massachusetts. But Strether discovers that the young man who was wild and rather worthless has undergone a remarkable metamorphosis in Europe. He appears now to be a highly civilized gentleman whose relationship with Mme de Vionnet has not corrupted him, but has apparently redeemed him. She has been, Strether says, the maker of 'his manners and morals, his character and life'.

Chad's situation in some ways resembles that of Roderick Hudson. Roderick is sent to Europe to improve his art; Chad, to improve his character. Europe succeeds to a surprising degree in both cases, but falls short of any final redemption when confronted with a radical moral weakness in each of the two men. In neither case is James's argument for the values of civilization invalidated. At the worst, the limitations of culture as compared with a more traditional view of religion are made manifest. Culture requires fairly good material to begin with, in contrast to some religious claims. Religious conversion may well make of a sow's ear a recognizable silk purse; culture is rarely seen to work so profoundly.

Strether is profoundly impressed with the transformation in Chad as he discovers him in Paris. It is only later that he will recognize its limitations. Then, Strether will see Mme de Vionnet, the 'wicked woman', as immeasurably better than Chad. The miraculous improvement he has been so impressed with in Chad has been his justification for acting against the counsels and convictions of Mrs Newsome, as it is for his great admiration for Mme de Vionnet and for the culture she represents. If Chad's history moves us to scepticism of James's argument in favour of culture, we must balance his history with the contrasting examples of Rowland Mallett and Mary Garland, of Little Bilham and Mme de Vionnet, and of course of Strether himself. His own development is marked by the process which takes him from urging Chad at first to return to Woollett, then to discouraging him from returning, and finally to making him *swear* that he will stay in Paris with Mme de Vionnet.

In the end, after Strether has failed Mrs Newsome, has disappointed Chad's family of their hope, and himself of his 'future', we learn that Chad will certainly abandon Mme de Vionnet. The brilliant reversal of plot goes hand in hand with a reversal of values: Strether comes to Paris to take Chad home in order to save him, but then – with the same motives – wants him to stay. Chad's more urbane motivations have led him to wish to stay, but then tempt him back to Woollett. It is in Chad's development that we approach the situations of *The American* and *The Golden Bowl*, but without their radical ambiguities. These novels all depict Americans, presumably admirable, who come to Europe to appreciate its treasures, and who mark their appreciation by acts of appropriation. It is only in *The Ambassadors* that James sees these acts for what they really are.

Chad will extract from Mme de Vionnet all that he can, and then abandon her. He will leave her for just that world of grab from which Strether wants to save him. By just so much as Chad has seemed truly civilized does his betrayal of civilized values disappoint Strether. For the reader, the stages of awareness of Chad's real nature match Strether's own; our disappointment coincides with his. Chad proves himself to be what Strether fearfully warns that he might become, a *brute*, 'guilty of the last infamy'. He joins that long line of Jamesian figures who care most, in embracing civilization, for its spoils. If along with Christopher Newman and Adam Verver he is not a deliberate 'villain', like them he is conditioned by warped values. He is unlike them, however, in the impact of his story : there is *no* ambiguity in James's vision of Chad's betrayal of essential values of culture.

James presents us with a hierarchy of Americans in Europe in *The Ambassadors*, and one fine aspect of the novel is in the discriminations James achieves in the scale of values represented by his Americans. If at one end stands the value of 'acquisition' and at the other, 'culture', we see quickly enough how many stages there can be, and how little each character duplicates any other as we move from Jim to Sarah Pocock, to the represented figure of Mrs Newsome, to Waymarsh, to Chad (whose place in the hierarchy is so painfully revealed), to Maria Gostrey, to Bilham and, finally, to Strether himself. One evidence of the increased complexity of vision in this novel is just this discrimination of subtly merging values.

Chad has before him an object lesson in the person of Jim

Pocock, the Woollett man of business (Maria Gostrey describes him as a 'warning'); but in the end Chad cannot resist the idea of money, or of the power he thinks he might possess with the money. To the degree that earlier in the novel Chad appears to be so much better than he really is, he has our sympathy and support. Yet we are given any number of warnings and foreshadowings which build up only gradually until almost the end, because of James's cleverness of control. Thus, in an early conversation with Bilham, Strether asks if he too has noticed Chad's fine transformation :

'The way he has improved? Oh yes – I think every one must see it. But I'm not sure,' said little Bilham, 'that I didn't like him about as well in his other state.'

Strether is not yet ready to appreciate whatever delicate warning Bilham may be giving him. Strether ought to be pleased when Bilham confirms our own impression that Chad is willing – almost too willing – to listen to Strether's arguments for returning to Woollett. Bilham says :

'He really wants, I believe, to go back and take up a career. He's capable of one, you know, that will improve and enlarge him still more . . . I ought, I dare say, to go home and go into business myself. Only I'd simply rather die – simply. And I've not the least difficulty in knowing why, and in defending my ground against all comers. All the same . . . I seem to see it as much the best thing for him.'

But why does not Chad, like Bilham, know exactly why *he* should stay out of business, and why he must defend *his* ground against Strether? His ground, obviously, is Mme de Vionnet. He defends her up to a point, but then is willing to sacrifice her. When Strether asks Bilham why he is so convinced that Chad should marry, Bilham answers that Chad isn't 'used to being so good'. The implications about Chad's fidelity are ominous enough in themselves, but even more is meant. The sympathetic acceptance which Bilham commands throughout the novel, Strether's admiration and respect for him, the 'certain moral ease' which Strether marks in him – all should make us take his warning seriously here. But the reader, like Strether, is still too dazzled by Chad's visible improvement to heed it.

Chad was packed off to Europe originally as a 'wild' young man. He is perhaps less wild than simply too impressionable, less reckless than rough. He needs the shaping which stronger hands will give. But Mme de Vionnet has impressed the lessons or advantages of culture *too* easily; they merely go along, in easy accommodation, with the weakness underneath. Strether impresses him too easily in the other direction when he tells him of the dollars waiting for him in Woollett. Poor Strether has to struggle painfully hard for his own transformation. But all through the novel one should be made suspicious by the very ease of accommodation in Chad, by a pliability too soft, too congenial. It pleases Strether at first, when he takes it simply as the sign of a cultured urbanity. It worries him later, when he sees how much it involves Chad's readiness to let others handle all his difficulties. Finally it disenchants Strether altogether. Chad simply cannot live up to the high standards imposed on him, neither those of Strether nor those of Mme de Vionnet. Bilham's observation that Chad isn't 'used to being so good' has thus its more profound applications.

Strether's own indifference to acquisition is made clear enough, in contrast. There is a telling scene in which Chad asks Strether what he has lost by antagonizing Mrs Newsome. Strether gives a half-wistful catalogue of her virtues, a catalogue which candidly includes her large fortune. Not to include it would be disingenuous or hypocritical. But he speaks also of her goodness and her kindness. Chad's response is portentous in the way it points to his own later choices :

'What it literally comes to for you, if you'll pardon my putting it so, is that you give up money. Possibly a good deal of money.'

Money alone then is 'literal'; goodness and kindness become nice but dispensable accessories. Strether reminds Chad that he too will give up money by staying in Paris, but Chad assures him, rather airily, that he has already 'a certain quantity'. Later, the quantity will prove to be insufficient.

Nothing will have prepared Strether adequately for the shock of learning that Chad, after he has sworn to hold fast to Mme de Vionnet, has again been investigating the field of advertising on his own. His enthusiasm persists, is renewed; he calls advertising an 'art' awaiting the hand of a 'master'. We may need to be reminded – for James does not make the connection explicitly for us – of the peculiarly 'vulgar' nature of the Woollett manufacture, the commodity which Strether is shy even of identifying to Maria Gostrey. For Chad to be lured back for the advertising side of the family business is a final confirmation, if any be needed, of his fatal acquisitiveness. Europe has become his apprenticeship for Madison Avenue, and James gives us a prophetic first portrait of the huckster in American literature.

At first, Chad's answer to Strether's protests is that his interest in business is 'purely platonic', but he dwells still on the *fact*: 'the fact of the possible. I mean the money in it.' His real ambition is allowed only those intermittent exposures that attend a large capacity for self-deception; rarely has a character struggled so little for a more steady illumination. James's characterization does him every justice.

'Oh, damn the money in it!' said Strether. And then, as the young man's fixed smile seemed to shine out more strange; 'Shall you give up your friend for the money in it?'
Chad preserved his handsome grimace . . . 'You're not altogether – in your so great "solemnity" – kind. Haven't I been drinking you in – showing you all I feel you're worth to me?'[18]

Chad does indeed 'drink in' Strether; so long as Strether talks, he listens. His inclination to virtue is as good-natured as a handshake, and as dependent on another's hand. Chad's further protest is beautifully disingenuous:

'What have I done, what am I doing, but cleave to her to the death? The only thing is,' he good-humouredly explained, 'that one can't but have it before one, in the cleaving – the point where the death comes in. Don't be afraid for *that*. It's pleasant to a fellow's feelings,' he developed, 'to "size-up" the bribe he applies his foot to.'

18 Later, James writes: 'Chad was always letting people have their way when he felt that it would somehow turn his wheel for him; it somehow always did turn his wheel.'

'He protests too much', Strether tells Maria later. In the same conversation, he points out the cruel irony for Mme de Vionnet: Chad has been 'formed to please', and it is she 'who has formed him'. Strether is not sure that Chad may not already be involved with another woman. But this kind of temptation for Chad is secondary to the temptation of Woollett. Chad allows himself to see this temptation not as a direct craven pursuit of money, so much as a curiously inviting way of life, preferable to everything he will leave behind in Paris. Strether's understanding and judgement of Chad, if late, is unmistakably *right*, and here too the novel is free of those unresolved ambiguities James allowed himself elsewhere in considering acquisition in relation to culture.

Strether comes to Europe as a willing ambassador for Woollett, but stays to become the most eloquent of all the defenders of civilization. Chad's betrayal of such values is of course his betrayal of Strether, and much of the book's pathos comes from Strether's intense, mistaken identification of his own lost youth with Chad, and especially with Chad's dedication to Mme de Vionnet:

'Though they're young enough, my pair, I don't say they're, in the freshest way, their *own* absolutely prime adolescence; for that has nothing to do with it. The point is that they're mine. Yes, they're my youth; since somehow, at the right time, nothing else ever was. What I meant just now therefore is that it would all go – go before doing its work – if they were to fail me.'

What is that work but the work of culture, which his own youth so vainly promised and which his commitment to Woollett so wastefully suppressed? Of course the pair will fail him; or rather, Chad alone fails him. Mme de Vionnet by the end of the novel is directly identified with Strether in her embodiment of high culture, and in what he recognizes as her 'high sense of duty'. As James has always insisted, duty is *part* of culture, when that culture is high enough.

CIVILIZATION AND FULFILMENT

Lambert Strether's culture is high enough to encompass all of James's ideals of character. This is what I mean by speaking of Strether as James's study of the Whole Man. From the moment he reaches Europe to feel its magic and – committed as he is to the New England mission – to fear it, the work of civilization has begun. It begins with the spell of Chester with its antique walls and its quiet crooked streets, where 'he had trod . . . in the far-off time, at twenty-five'. This spell includes his new acquaintanceship with Maria Gostrey, whom he recognizes as 'more subtly civilized – ' than the person at Woollett whose name he does not care to invoke for such invidious comparisons. It continues through his first excited re-introduction to Paris, with its reawakening memories of the broken pledges of his youth : 'this private pledge of his own to treat the occasion as a relation formed with the higher culture'. He remembers sadly the pledges particularly of the dozen lemon-coloured volumes confidently purchased as an 'invocation of the finer taste' :

They represented now the mere sallow paint on the door of the temple of taste that he had dreamed of raising up – a structure that he had practically never carried further.

'What had become', he wonders, 'of the sharp initiation they represented ?'

These rekindled memories of his own youth lead him to his rather shy identification with Bilham. We see how right James is in having Strether meet Bilham first, since at this point Chad represents simply the object of a duty to be performed. Prepared through this earlier initiation, when he does meet Chad he will see in his new European bloom the very incarnation of the Strether that might have been.

But all this while he has the Woollett burden, too; not merely the burden of present duty, but the psychological and moral conditioning of half a lifetime. It is this Woollett burden that explains the importance of 'initiation' which makes up so much of the novel's structure. Domestic and rural England confronts Strether before cosmopolitan Paris; Bilham before Chad; Maria Gostrey before Mme de Vionnet. Strether undertakes his ambassadorship determined on one line of action to which he is committed both by the trust of others and by his own convictions. But even the early pages of the novel 'give him away', as James might say, as a man burdened 'with the oddity of a double consciousness'. Thus, Strether thinks ruefully, and with an ambivalence that suggests difficulties ahead, of his 'odious ascetic suspicion of any form of beauty'. It is impossible to imagine Waymarsh complaining of *his* odious ascetic suspicion of any form of beauty; his certainties are undermined by no such divisions. Later, Strether will complain to Chad's young friends because he is fearful also of an opposite danger :

'You've all of you here so much visual sense that you've somehow all "run" to it. There are moments when it strikes one that you haven't any other.'

If Strether fears that among Chad's circle of friends the visual sense may too much replace the moral, it is not a danger which overtakes Strether himself. The central initiations of the novel brilliantly dramatize what is a conditioning and refinement of Strether's moral sense, but not its loss. Early in the novel, Bilham cautiously describes Chad's relationship with a woman as a 'virtuous attachment'. Throughout the novel, Strether's changing understanding of this crucial phrase marks the growth of just that wholeness I have claimed for him.

At first, given the limited frame of reference which Woollett affords, he interprets 'virtuous attachment' to mean that Chad must be in love with Mlle de Vionnet, the lovely young daughter of the great lady. He moves from that assumption to a deeper initiation when Chad confesses his allegiance to the mother :

'She's herself my hitch, hang it – if you must really have it all out. But in a sense,' he hastened in the most wonderful manner to add, 'that you'll quite make out for yourself.'

Strether, moving further away from the conventions of Woollett, does try to make it out for himself. Mme de Vionnet, then, is the 'virtuous attachment'; the relationship is all the more beautiful for its purity. There is, somewhere, an unsympathetic Comte de Vionnet with whom she finds it impossible to live; he is a brute. It has in the manner of this very different culture been a conventionally arranged marriage and there is no possibility of divorce. The very existence of Comte de Vionnet, however, must guarantee the innocence of his wife's relationship with Chad. It is an instance of the familiar European tradition in which a young man of promise forms a platonic relationship with an older married woman who will help to shape his manners, his presence, his general culture.

It is at this point in Strether's initiations that James, altering the plot as it had appeared in the synopsis for Harper's, arranges the descent of Mrs Newsome's new ambassadors, Sarah and Jim Pocock. Strether has courage enough to defy Sarah now, if he must, for though Chad's relationship with Mme de Vionnet may appear shocking to Sarah, it is not after all so disconcerting to him. He can accept it, and even defend it. He has already had to reprimand his own Woollett tendency to harbour suspicions:

Strether felt *his* character receive, for the instant, a smutch from all the wrong things he had suspected or believed. The person to whom Chad owed it that he could positively turn out such a comfort to other persons – such a person was sufficiently raised above any 'breath' by the very nature of her work and the young man's steady light.

When Mrs Newsome's formidable daughter, Sarah Pocock, is challenged by Strether to admire the great change in Chad, she disappoints his hopes for reconciliation by pronouncing the change '*hideous!*'[19] Strether finds that he must, however painfully, give up his loyalty not to Chad but to Sarah, and so of course to Mrs Newsome and to his Woollett past, as well as to any assured future.

19 There is an interesting but unanswered question here: does Sarah reject the cultivated image of Chad with the same understanding of his relationship with Mme de Vionnet that Strether has at this point, or does she with her own suspicious logic assume much more than he about the real intimacy of this relationship? It is clear that she would dislike the change in Chad in either case.

Strether has one more large fact to face, however, before coming to final terms with that innocuous-sounding definition, a 'virtuous attachment'. James prepares for it in one of his most careful and skilled passages. Strether has decided to take a day's holiday after his strenuous encounters with the Pococks, and has gone to the country. Reversing the traditional hierarchy in which Art imitates Nature, Strether finds in the lovely French countryside the fond memory of a painting by Lambinet which he had once coveted in the lean Boston years. What he sees is Nature imitating Art.

This reversal is not a new one in the novel, for *The Ambassadors* is filled with images in which some aspect of life is appreciated with the terms and standards of art. Chad, in his new and transfigured state, is compared to the work of an artist shaping the raw materials of his craft:

Chad was brown and thick and strong, and, of old, Chad had been rough. Was all the difference therefore that he was actually smooth? Possibly; for that he *was* smooth was as marked as in the taste of a sauce or in the rub of a hand. The effect of it was general – it had retouched his features, drawn them with a cleaner line. It had cleared his eyes and settled his colour and polished his fine square teeth – the main ornament of his face; and at the same time . . . it had given him a form and a surface, almost a design.

The sculptor Gloriani's face is 'medal-like', every line an 'artist's own in which time told only as tone and consecration'. The dim street noises of Paris include a 'voice calling, replying, some-where, and as full of tone as an actor's in a play'.

The appeal of the French countryside as it 'embodies' the painting by Lambinet receives a more extended treatment on the occasion of Strether's outing. The comparison stresses not only the sweetness and simplicity of Lambinet's version of landscape, but the composition, the design, the aesthetic satis-faction of the actual landscape's 'imitation' of Lambinet. Wait-ing for his dinner at a country inn, Strether sits at a little pavilion along the river where, after a while, he sees a boat approaching:

What he saw was exactly the right thing – a boat advancing round the bend and containing a man who held the paddles and a lady, at the stern, with a pink parasol. It was suddenly, as if these figures, or something like them, had been wanting in the picture, had been wanted, more or less, all day, and had now drifted into sight, with the slow current, on purpose to fill up the measure.

No landscape speaks of *value* so much as a landscape with figures, and this is just what Strether now has before him.[20] He notes that the figures are appropriately intimate: they are 'expert, familiar, frequent'. Only a moment later he recognizes the figures as Mme de Vionnet and Chad Newsome. The recognition scene which follows is both comic and pathetic in its humorously frantic explanations, its good manners, its embarrassments. Chad, as always, remains pleasantly amiable, leaving everything to her. It is clear, despite her brave and desperate inventions, that they have not been out just for the day. Neither of them is dressed for a day excursion from Paris; 'expert, familiar, frequent', they have been spending the last twenty-four hours together. Lambert Strether of Woollett, Massachusetts, is faced with his most violent accommodation yet in seeing their friendship as a 'virtuous attachment'.

The very setting of this discovery plays an important part in

20 The scene is a pastoral, and the figures who appear first suggest the shepherdess and swain. In 'Madame de Mauves', Bernard Littlemore encounters a similar pair in the French countryside; they make him envy their freedom from the complexities of the civilization which so besets him. Basil Ransom has an important rendezvous with Verena Tarrant in New York's Central Park in *The Bostonians*, and feels himself to be in a 'Pastoral'; Daisy Miller's 'affair' with Giovanelli has an innocence ironically placed by Mrs Costello: 'She goes on from day to day, from hour to hour, as they did in the Golden Age.' Hyacinth Robinson, in *The Princess Casamassima*, lounges under a great tree in Kensington Gardens and feels free for the time from his pressing conflicts, while he recognises in Millicent Henning the possibility of 'simple love'. In *The Tragic Muse*, Nick Dormer has his one love scene with Julia Dallow on a little island with a mock temple said to be dedicated to Vesta, and where life attains the simplicity, we are told, of the 'golden age'. In each case James seems to indulge in a brief nostalgia for a pastoral simplicity in human relations, a retreat from the problems and responsibilities of civilization. Perhaps it is a retreat to the dream of American innocence, the Garden with its Adams and its Newmans. The retreat in any case is always temporary; each such scene is replaced quickly enough by the harder light of the actual. These scenes seem simply to reveal, and to reject, the symbolic ideal of a simpler time, the '*ton* of the golden age', of primal American innocence. James's characters do not spend themselves in regret, however, for they always choose the world of civilization for what they take to be a fuller realization of human life.

determining Strether's responses. The landscape, so conducive to the idea of Art with its imposed order and its rigorous standards, has seemed to him to imply just such figures, even to require them. What values should then be applied in life, where standards are so much more mixed and diffused? In his all-night vigil – an episode which may recall Isabel Archer's discovery and her struggle to understand *her* experience – Strether faces just this implication:

That was what, in his vain vigil, he oftenest reverted to; intimacy, at such a point, was *like* that – and what in the world else would one have wished it to be like?

There is a reinforcing irony in this entire episode. Strether on several occasions has described his increasing identification with Mme de Vionnet as 'being in her boat'. In one scene particularly is this image stressed, when Mme de Vionnet calls on Sarah Pocock. Sarah appears to suspect Strether of being 'launched in a relation in which he really had never been launched at all' – a conspiracy, that is, with Mme de Vionnet. The truth, he feels, is rather that his 'sole license had been to cling, with intensity, to the brink, not to dip so much as a toe into the flood'. Nevertheless, as this critical encounter develops, he recognizes the need for some gesture of sympathy or loyalty to Mme de Vionnet:

To meet his fellow visitor's invocation and, with Sarah's brilliant eyes on him, answer, *was* quite sufficiently to step into her boat. During the rest of the time her visit lasted he felt himself proceed to each of the proper offices, successively, for helping to keep the adventurous skiff afloat. It rocked beneath him, but he settled himself in his place. He took up an oar, and since he was to have the credit of pulling he pulled.

Without the later encounter with Mme de Vionnet and Chad in their boat within the 'Lambinet' landscape, this rather extended figure would be merely ornamental; with it, the metaphor becomes part of the novel's meaning. Strether's identification with Mme de Vionnet, and his defence of her relationship with Chad, has then to withstand this new shock, that the 'boat' he has been helping to pull has taken him to a point of no return.

In the course of his all-night vigil, Strether discovers that his pain derives not, after all, from the real intimacy of this 'virtuous attachment', but from the deceptions it has generated, foremost among which has been his own :

It was the quantity of make-believe involved, and so vividly exemplified, that most disagreed with his spiritual stomach . . . It was all very well for him to feel the pity of its being so much like lying; he almost blushed, in the dark, for the way he had dressed the possibility in vagueness, as a little girl might have dressed her doll.

In accepting in life what by analogy he accepts in art, Strether pays tribute to the legitimate claims of both. To take art for life is a treacherous undertaking, and there were times, as we have seen, when James suffered its more insidious consequences. But the identification here functions rightly. Art for Strether means not an escape from character but its great exemplification; not an indifference to truth, but its essential property.[21]

The relationship has a sanctity for Strether more important than the fact, however lamentable, of its irregularity. He has seen in it his old dream of the union of Woollett and Paris, the same dream James himself called the 'brave personal drama of the future'. And for a time we are able to accept the relationship of Mme de Vionnet and Chad Newsome as the synthesis of discrete modes of life, 'the dauntless fusions to come', which was for James an ideal. But the synthesis, and the consequent wholeness, do not after all take place in this couple, but in Strether himself. It is he who is able to combine the best elements in American and European values. Not only does he remain immune to the great threat to culture embodied in the world of acquisition, he proves himself capable of that fullest expan-

21 Strether's applying to life a value he has found in art – as much in the *form* of art as in its substance – is of course the same as James's lifelong defence of art, and of culture, as necessary to the human condition. James's conviction, and his devotion to the writing of fiction, has an interesting re-affirmation in Thomas Mann's essay on Chekhov : 'And yet one goes on working, telling stories, and giving form to truth . . . in the dim hope, indeed the confidence, that truth and serene form can have a liberating effect, preparing the world for a better, fairer, more dignified form of life.'

sion of sensibility which accepts the moral, intellectual, and aesthetic attributes of civilization.

One important source of James's pride in *The Ambassadors* is his use of Strether as centre of consciousness. He limits completely the settings, the vision, the consciousness and qualities of all other characters to Strether's own view of these things:

Strether's sense of these things, and Strether's only, should avail me for showing them; I should know them but through his more or less groping knowledge of them, since his very gropings would figure among his most interesting notions . . . It would give me a large unity, and that in turn would crown me with the grace to which the enlightened story-teller will . . . sacrifice if need be all other graces whatsoever. I refer of course to the grace of intensity.[22]

At one point in the novel, it is said of Strether that

It was nothing new to him, however, as we know, that a man might have – at all events such a man as *he* was – an amount of experience out of any proportion to his adventures.

Experience – 'our apprehension and our measure of what happens to us as social creatures' – the quality which is determined by acuteness, is in turn the measure of intensity, the first requisite of representation in fiction, as it is of moral value in life. The characterization of Strether invites reading as a fine parable of the artist. One remembers James's description of the English woman novelist who, he tells us in 'The Art of Fiction', was able to write a convincing picture of French Protestant youth. Her experience of her subject consisted of her having

once, in Paris, as she ascended a staircase, passed an open door where, in the household of a *pasteur*, some of the young Protestants were seated at table around a finished meal. The glimpse made a picture; it lasted only a moment, but that moment was experience.

22 Preface to *The Ambassadors*, p. xv. Actually there are some five instances (discounting introductory foreshortenings) when James slips round his control to give us information or impressions which Strether's own point of view could not. But James handles them so cleverly that the reader is not likely to notice.

The anecdote leads to the formulation of this important truth :

The power to guess the unseen from the seen, to trace the implication of things, to judge the whole piece by the pattern, the condition
of feeling life in general so completely that you are well on your
way to knowing any particular corner of it – this cluster of gifts
may almost be said to constitute experience.

That James means far more by 'experience' than the amount
of objective adventure that befalls one is made clear in his well-
known definition :

Experience . . . is an immense sensibility, a kind of huge spider-web
of the finest silken threads suspended in the chamber of consciousness, and catching every air-borne particle in its tissue. It is the
very atmosphere of the mind; and when the mind is imaginative –
much more when it happens to be that of a man of genius – it takes
to itself the faintest hints of life, it converts the very pulses of the
air into revelations.[23]

How admirably does much of this describe Strether. He sees,
he reflects, he feels. With generous sympathy he senses much
in the inner lives of others so strongly that it becomes part of
his own experience. Alone among the characters in the novel
he not only learns, but changes as a consequence of the play
of his experience on his imagination. Above all, he reflects for
the reader everything there is to be known. His is both a receptive and a reflecting lucidity. In this sense, the technical device
of a single centre of consciousness is no mere aesthetic *tour de
force*; it is both a demonstration of and a tribute to Strether's
sensibility. One of James's 'proofs' of Strether's culture is just
this exhibition of his awareness and his responsibility. Technique merges into theme, form into content.

James's demonstrations are not always so clear-cut, however.
I should like to look briefly at one particular aspect of James's
civilization – his complex connoisseurship. It involves a certain
disparity between the sense he gives us of the cultured person's
interest in art and that of the dedicated artist or the serious

23 'The Art of Fiction', *Partial Portraits* (London, 1888), pp. 388–9.

student. James's interest in literature is serious and informed, but he has after all his own, writer's, commitment. His appreciation of the visual arts, while manifestly great, seems strangely to lack independence.[24] If there is at least a 'talking' familiarity with the pre-Raphaelites in his work, there seems to be none at all with the French post-impressionists, for instance, or with other contemporary art except that of a few painters known to him personally. His fictional descriptions of artists' studios and their work, despite what we know to be his first-hand experiences, seem usually either stereotyped or vague.[25] Virginia Woolf has described James's introduction to some of the new art in Roger Fry's basement studio:

Seated on a little hard chair Henry James would express 'in convoluted sentences the disturbed hesitations which Matisse and Picasso aroused in him, and Roger Fry, exquisitely, with something of the old-world courtesy which James carried about with him', would do his best to convey to the great novelist what he meant by saying that Cézanne and Flaubert were, in a manner of speaking, after the same thing.[26]

In contrast, James's supreme awakening to the ideal of 'style', which he described as having taken place in the Galerie d'Apollon of the Louvre (discussed in the preceding chapter) is a phenomenon interesting indeed when one remembers that the Galerie d'Apollon represented the gaudiest, most conspicuously ornate chapter in Western art, the gilt extravagances of Louis Quinze. It may be unfair to evaluate the responses of an eager young American of the later nineteenth century by the canons of a later taste; nevertheless the lack of reservation even in the mature James writing his account of this experience makes me uneasy.

Ford Madox Hueffer is made uneasy also, in his case by the

24 His familiarity with music, to judge from fictional allusions, was conventional and casual, in distinction from such great twentieth-century fictional stylists as Proust, Mann, Gide, or Joyce.

25 In non-fiction James could write interestingly on the work, itself elegantly conventional, of such artists as John Singer Sargent, as in *Picture and Text* (New York, 1893).

26 Virginia Woolf, *Roger Fry: A Biography* (London, 1940), p. 180.

photograph which James chose as the frontispiece to *The Spoils of Poynton* for the New York edition. Hueffer writes:

I must confess that I myself should be appalled at having to live before such a mantelpiece and such a *décor* – all this French gilding of the Louis Quinze period; all these cupids surmounting florid clocks; these vases with intaglios; these huge and floridly patterned walls; these tapestried fire-screens; these gilt chairs with backs and seats of Gobelins, of Aubusson, of *petit point*. But there is no denying the value, the rarity and the suggestion of these articles which are described as 'some of the spoils' – the suggestion of tranquillity, of an aged civilization, of wealth, of leisure, of opulent refinement.[27]

I question Hueffer's 'tranquillity', but read with interest this further comment:

No one else could have placed a marble mantelpiece (it is one of Mr. James's rare betrayals of himself, that photograph!) in a perfect specimen of a Jacobean manor house, and have invested the mantel-piece with such a veritable Jesuit's altar of gilding. They could not have done it and have called the results satisfactory to anyone but a collector.[28]

This may seem a bit harsh, for after all Mrs Gereth, the woman in *The Spoils of Poynton* responsible for the marble and the gilding, *is* a collector, and her spoils are branded 'Things'. But neither the sympathetic Fleda Vetch nor James himself ever suggest that they are not all quite magnificent specimens of art as well. James disapproves the uses to which 'Things' are put in his novel, but not of their intrinsic value as art.

Just as I sometimes have the feeling that James had not so much an actual 'sense of the past' as a sense of that sense, so do I suspect that he depends very much in his relation to art on an appreciation of appreciation. His taste is not that of the expert, or even of the serious student of art, but more often that of the 'collector', ready to accept the currency of his time, to assign 'value' in terms not always intrinsically aesthetic. His

27 F. M. Hueffer, *Henry James: A Critical Study* (London, 1913), p. 96.
28 *Ibid.*, pp. 103–4.

lapses in taste and authentic art history (more extensive than the 'anomaly' of Mrs Gereth's fireplace) are worth comment primarily because they suggest something about his sensibility. There is a weakness for the derivative and the over-mannered, sometimes surprising in a writer so committed to the cause of culture.[29] These confusions of connoisseurship rarely affected James's critical standards when he wrote of the art of the novel. Away from his own craft, he often allowed his conception of culture to become too much an abstraction.

On the other hand, his appreciation, even if sometimes specious, is always bound up inextricably with ideas of tradition, of age, of cultural continuity. If this is, strictly speaking, 'extra-aesthetic', it is a defensible, and honourable, extension of appreciation. The monuments and treasures of art for James are *part* of civilization as culture, and not detachable prizes. Removed from the atmosphere which generated them, they are always in danger of becoming either over-precious *objets d'art* or *spoils*. This is why the reader is likely to be suspicious of – or offended by – Adam Verver's systematic ransacking of Europe to fill his museum in American City. The work of art is steeped in its own cultural ambience, its own heritage; the tourist checking off the guide book's asterisked 'items of importance' loses something precious at the heart of culture.

I have spoken of the elements of acquisition in *The Ambassadors*, but have reserved one aspect of the subject for special consideration here, in the light of the brief discussion above. Lambert Strether's renunciation of Maria Gostrey at the end of the novel is conditioned by an important contrast between this expatriate American and Mme de Vionnet – a contrast expressed primarily in the imagery which is used in describing their homes. The impact of Mme de Vionnet's home, her very particular cultural setting, is great, and James's account of it is worth quoting at some length :

29 The 'Pateresque' is especially strong in early James, as in 'The Madonna of the Future'; but my other terms go beyond that, even to his use of Bronzino's elegant, Mannerist 'Lucrezia Panciatichi', and Veronese's aristocratic 'The Marriage Feast at Cana' in *The Wings of the Dove*. There is a good discussion of James's use of these two paintings in J. Meyers, *Painting and the Novel* (Manchester, 1975), pp. 19–30.

The court was large and open, full of revelations, for our friend, of the habit of privacy, the peace of intervals, the dignity of distances and approaches;[30] the house, to his restless sense, was in the high, homely style of an elder day, and the ancient Paris that he was always looking for – sometimes intensely felt, sometimes more acutely missed – was in the immemorial polish of the wide waxed staircase and in the fine *boiseries*, the medallions, mouldings, mirrors . . . He seemed to see her, at the outset, in the midst of possessions, not vulgarly numerous, but hereditary, cherished, charming . . . he found himself making out, as a background of the occupant, some glory, some prosperity of the first Empire, some Napoleonic glamour, some dim lustre of the great legend; elements clinging still to all the consular chairs and mythological brasses and sphinxes' heads and faded surfaces of satin striped with alternate silk . . . He had never before, to his knowledge, been in the presence of relics, of any special dignity, of a private order. . . They were among the matters that marked Mme de Vionnet's apartment as something quite different from *Miss Gostrey's little museum of bargains* and from Chad's lovely home; he recognized it as founded much more on old accumulations that had possibly from time to time shrunken than on any contemporary method of acquisition or form of curiosity. Chad and Miss Gostrey had rummaged, and purchased and picked up and exchanged, sifting, selecting, comparing; whereas the mistress of the scene before him, *beautifully passive under the spell of transmission* . . . had only received, accepted, and been quiet [my italics].

Strether's attempt to 'classify' his impressions of the place implies values, as I suggested earlier, which stem from a sense of tradition, of age, of cultural continuity. These values add immeasurably not only to the visual, but to the moral appeal of Mme de Vionnet's home. 'The general result', he concludes, is the 'air of supreme respectability . . . of private honour'.

There can be no doubt that James's strong contrast between Mme de Vionnet's and Maria Gostrey's relations to culture and to 'Things' was deliberate, since he so explicitly measures their differences in the passage just quoted. Furthermore, his first description of Maria Gostrey's house presents a marked contrast in the values which are evoked :

30 Was it some American privation that caused James to mark Isabel Archer's appreciation of Gardencourt with a keen awareness of its 'well-marked privacy', as Strether so many years later especially notes the 'habit of privacy' in Mme de Vionnet's home?

Her compact and crowded little chambers, almost dusky, as they at first struck him, with accumulations, represented a supreme general adjustment to opportunity and conditions. Wherever he looked he saw an old ivory or an old brocade, and he scarce knew where to sit for fear of a misappliance. The life of the occupant struck him, of a sudden, as more charged with possession even than Chad's or than Miss Barrace's; wide as his glimpse had lately become of *the empire of 'things'*, what was before him still enlarged it; the lust of the eyes and the pride of life had indeed thus their temple. It was the innermost nook of the shrine – *as brown as a pirate's cave* [my italics].

Maria Gostrey's culture is higher than the Pococks' or Way-marsh's by a long stretch – hers is an 'innermost nook' – but it is still heavy with the weight of acquisition. The nook is a 'pirate's cave' and the shrine dedicated to culture is overlaid with an atmosphere charged with possessions; she reigns in the 'empire of "things" '. Strether will be tempted to stop, at the end of the novel, in this innermost nook but for his renunciation of any personal advantage from his mission to Paris, the mission in which he has failed another lady reigning over another empire in Woollett, Massachusetts.

Late in the novel Strether pays his last call on Mme de Vionnet. His consciousness of the 'empire of things' even in his beloved Paris must loom large before him. When one by one almost all of the characters in the novel have been seen to be, in their various ways, after the loot of civilization – Waymarsh, the Pococks, Chad, even the 'wonderful' Maria Gostrey – it is not surprising that Strether should feel a deep foreboding about Mme de Vionnet, as a symbol of civilization itself :

The light in her beautiful, formal room was dim, though it would do, as everything would do, as everything would always do . . . The windows were all open . . . and he heard once more, from the empty court, the small plash of the fountain. From behind this, and as from a great distance . . . came, as if excited and exciting, the vague voice of Paris. Strether had all along been subject to sudden gusts of fancy in connection with such matters as these – odd starts of the historic sense, suppositions, and divinations with no warrant but their intensity. Thus and so, on the eve of the great recorded dates, the days and nights of revolution, the sounds had come in, the omens, the beginnings broken out. They were the smell of revolution, the smell of the public temper – or perhaps simply the smell of blood.

The feeling of dread for the future of civilization is borne out later in Strether's impressions of the great lady herself: 'it was almost appalling, that a creature so fine could be, by mysterious forces, a creature so exploited'. His simpler sense that 'what was at the bottom the matter with her was simply Chad himself' mounts, and grows to the sense of disaster:

He presently found himself taking a long look from her, and the next thing he knew he had uttered all his thought. 'You're afraid for your life!'[31]

The contrast established between Mme de Vionnet and Maria Gostrey in the imagery of their homes has an important bearing on Strether's decision at the end not to stay on with Maria. One may be reminded of the ending of *The Portrait of a Lady*. Just as the dying Ralph brings to Isabel a full consciousness of what real culture means, so that she is not willing to escape with Caspar Goodwood in denial of her deepest commitment, so too does the representation of Mme de Vionnet prevent Strether from accepting a surrogate happiness with Maria Gostrey. Both resolutions demonstrate nothing so much as that James's great renunciations (as opposed to the occasional merely theatrical ones) are moral decisions made in the light of a high ideal of civilization. The similarity in the two endings becomes stronger still when we consider the imagery of a dying epoch in relation to Mme de Vionnet, for it suggests that she, like Ralph Touchett, cannot survive. Lambert Strether loves Mme de Vionnet, as at the end of her story Isabel Archer loves Ralph. In both cases, though for somewhat different reasons, the Jamesian pursuers of civilization as culture are too late. The ending of *The Ambassadors*, however, gives us a stronger sense

31 James's sense of a collapse of Western civilization with the outbreak of the First World War ('to have to take it all now for what the treacherous years were all the while really making for and meaning is too tragic for any words': *Letters*, II, p. 398) seems to me to be anticipated by his portentous final look at Mme de Vionnet.

of moral victory in Strether, in contrast to the sense we have in Isabel Archer of victimized defeat.

Maria Gostrey may seem less stark as an alternative than Caspar Goodwood, by virtue of being more civilized, closer to the ideal which Strether pursues. The available best of European civilization has played richly on Strether's imagination and has transformed his values, even while to the Hebraic imagination of Waymarsh (to say nothing of that of Sarah Pocock) it all remains so alien. His conditioning elements have after all been much the same as theirs; the differences are exactly what constitute the 'story'. In this sense, *The Ambassadors* is like many of James's novels (from *The Europeans* to *The Princess Casamassima* and further) a novel of education.

There is an important scene in which we learn that Maria Gostrey has feared that Strether would suffer a strong revulsion of feeling with his discovery that the splendid Mme de Vionnet was involved in a sexual relationship with Chad, a discovery which must present moral perplexities – if not hostilities – to an American formed by such different traditions.[32] Her conversation with Strether when he justifies his remarkable loyalty to Mme de Vionnet is significant. Strether has returned, for a final time, to Bilham's early description of Chad's relationship to the woman who keeps him in Paris. He now says, 'It was but a technical lie – he classed the attachment as virtuous.'

'What I see, what I saw,' Maria returned, 'is that you dressed up even the virtue. You were wonderful – you were beautiful . . . but, if you wish really to know,' she sadly confessed, 'I never quite knew *where* you were. There were moments,' she explained, 'when you struck me as grandly cynical; there were others when you struck me as grandly vague.'

Her friend considered. 'I had phases. I had flights.'

'Yes, but things must have a basis.'

'A basis seemed to me just what her beauty supplied.'

'Her beauty of person?'

'Well, her beauty of everything. The impression she makes. She has such variety, and yet such harmony.'

32 Leon Edel sees a relaxing of James's more rigid attitudes toward European sexual mores from about the time of the writing of 'A London Life' (1887): see *Henry James: The Middle Years* (London, 1963), pp. 168–9.

She considered him with one of her deep returns of indulgence – returns out of all proportion to the irritations they flooded over. 'You're complete.'

Strether's sensibility *is* complete. James's use of the word 'taste' as the attribute that defines the quality of sensibility is largely replaced in *The Ambassadors* by the term 'imagination'. Thus, to Chad's repeated question, 'But what do you gain?' when it has become obvious that Strether's actions have lost him Mrs Newsome, Strether answers:

'. . . you have, I verily believe, no imagination. You've other qualities. But no imagination, don't you see? at all.'
'I dare say. I do see.' It was an idea in which Chad showed interest. 'But haven't you yourself rather too much?'
'Oh, *rather* – !'

Strether's imagination lies in having grasped an ideal quite beyond ideas of gain, and in having acted on it. But he has of course 'gained'. He has gained stature as a human being, for one thing; recognizing and, in one sense at least, achieving the moral and aesthetic integrity of ideal culture. He has lost Mrs Newsome and his assured future. He will refuse Maria Gostrey, determined that from the failure of his mission to Europe he should win nothing for himself – nothing, at least, short of the unachievable ideal. Mme de Vionnet represents that ideal for him as Maria Gostrey cannot. It does not follow that Maria does not exert a strong appeal for him; the reader indeed might wish it were stronger. But Strether too has a sacred moral identity which deprives him of the possibility of second-best rewards, of blinkered happiness. The wholeness he has found in Europe does not allow him the privilege of denying its moral imperatives. Maria Gostrey offers him sanctuary, but he rejects it, 'to be right':

'That you see, is my only logic. Not, out of the whole affair, to have got anything for myself.'

Maria knows how much Strether's European experience has meant for him, and she reminds him that he has got *that*. Strether admits that it is a good deal,

'But nothing like *you*. It's *you* who would make me wrong!'

Honest and fine, she couldn't pretend she didn't see it. Still, she could pretend a little. 'But why should you be so dreadfully right?'

'That's the way that – if I must go – you yourself would be the first to want me. And I can't do anything else.'

To marry Maria now, in the face of his larger disappointment, would be to repeat in a more complex way the lunge of Waymarsh into the jeweller's shop, at the beginning of the novel, when Waymarsh finds himself incapable of a larger involvement with Europe than that of acquisition.

In contrast to the 'Hebrew prophet' Waymarsh, with his 'sacred rage' of moral intensity which keeps him from seeing his limitations (even of morality); in contrast to Maria Gostrey, who wants at worst to add Strether to her 'pirate's cave', at best to shelter him from his own sense of right; in contrast particularly to Chad Newsome, whom Strether had looked to as his 'second chance', but who has exploited the personal advantages of civilization without accepting its commitments and responsibilities, Strether is unique, is complete. Tragic in his deprivations, his sense of wasted opportunities and of sacrificed life, he embodies for the perceptive reader one of James's great achievements in art, his justification of an abiding ideal. Poor perhaps in accomplishment, but rich in being, Strether emerges whole, James's persuasive tribute to the idea of civilization.

Index